
DEMCO

WILLIAM FAULKNER
The Journey to Self-Discovery

Suspended between the intolerable present and the unreachable past, he created a myth of his own.

WILLIAM FAULKNER

The Journey to Self-Discovery

By H. Edward RICHARDSON

UNIVERSITY OF MISSOURI PRESS
COLUMBIA

Copyright © 1969 by
The Curators of the
University of Missouri

SBN 8262-0078-8

Library of Congress Catalog
Card Number 76-80033

Printed and bound in
the United States of America

THIS BOOK IS FOR
BRUCE ROBERT MCELDERRY, JR.
AND
WILLIAM VAN O'CONNOR

Preface

The life in depth of William Faulkner has yet to be written. The biographical aspects of this book, although necessary for my purposes, are not intended to be exhaustive. The background material concerning the Faulkner family, from the writer's great-grandfather through the emergence of Faulkner as a mature artist, has been brought together mainly to depict the artist's regional, deeply personal, formulative heritage. Even as young Faulkner grew up "saturated with" the legends of his South, the active world of his present found him bereft of his own time. Caught in a kind of catalepsy between that fabled past and the stark barrenness of what he later referred to as "the sorry shabby world" around him, his search for identity became an imperative that drove him to create a world of his own, often with the past as prototype.

Within the context of this study, Faulkner's *juvenilia* are important mainly as they point to the development of the mature and distinguished novelist; but in order to understand his ascent from Romance to reality, from poetry to prose, and even from esthetics to local color, it has been necessary to work out a substantial body of critical and exegetical material in order to resolve the seemingly mysterious "How?" of this complex process. In so doing, the questions of balance and emphasis have been carefully considered. Although the thorough treatment of the early poems and prose pieces may appear to belie this intention, no attempt has been made to give them more intrinsic value than they actually have. Rather, they are a necessary part of the sequence and become important in understanding the subtle maturation of the artist. The major threads of his conscious literary development—the language, verbal patterns, influences, imagery (especially that of the French Symbolists), techniques, symbolism, content, and themes —are woven into the fabric of the text; but much of this material has been, more properly it seems, retained in the notes. Similarly, and most especially where it has been necessary to mediate between conflicting biographical data and several moot points, notes augment the textual substance.

Compelled as he was by the vaunted phantoms of the past and irresistibly drawn to identify with them, Faulkner also yearned to find his own niche in his own time. To deal with his enigma, the young man began to reach out, sometimes in *outré* ways, for the self that eluded him. Thus, he became a poseur, who did not know quite how to express himself. Fortunately, through a series of literary experiences, his talents began to find direction, but subtly, over the span of a decade. With consciously developed skills he was eventually able to transmute the materials of his regional past into a singular achievement of artistic purity and universal amplitude.

I have treated the published works of Faulkner through *Sartoris* (1929) in synchronal relationship with details of his life. Wherever they have shed light, I have brought the tools of psychology to bear on the subject—and although their use may appear to have led me far afield occasionally, I have nevertheless endeavored to use them with restraint and, I trust, responsibility. Sometimes the work and the life diverged in bizarre patterns, then moved in parallel currents; again, they crossed in strangely unexpected ways, and often they seemed to blend into a single stream, only to part again.

I began this study ten years ago in an effort to learn more about the work and the man who produced it—especially I wanted to know, as brash as it sounds, what made Faulkner "tick." As Faulkner scholars know, the Nobel laureate had an infinite capacity for keeping his life intensely private. Although his genius remains as elusive as ever, it is my hope that I have captured the pattern of his life and work so that each illuminates the other in ways not previously recognized. William Faulkner himself seems—it has been pleasant to discover—less of an oddity and more understandable as a human being. Finally, it is my fondest wish that this book will prove to be of value to students of American literature everywhere and of all ages; should I be granted a second wish, it would be that whatever original biographical and critical insights it contains will contribute significant material leading to a definitive biography of William Faulkner, which surely must some day be written.

In this effort to map Faulkner's journey to self-discovery as man-artist, I am happy to acknowledge foremost the immensely valuable aid of Professor Bruce R. McElderry, Jr., who read the manuscript in various stages of its development and gave freely of his wisdom and advice throughout its preparation. I am deeply indebted to Professor William Van O'Connor, who also read the manuscript, made suggestions for revisions, and left me the legacy of the title the book bears. Others who read the entire manuscript and offered me the benefit of their criticisms are Professors Aerol Arnold, Francis Bowman, Walter Crittenden, and E. R. Hagemann. Those who advised me concerning parts of the manuscript then in varied phases of preparation, and thereby encouraged me to continue the project, include Professors Harold Briggs and Carvel Collins. I am especially grateful to Professor Collins for permission to quote portions of his correspondence with me, so graciously shared from his mass of thorough and distinctive research on Faulkner, soon to culminate, I understand, in a two-volume biography to be published by Farrar, Straus & Giroux, Inc. Some portions drawn from my study had the benefit of readings and criticisms by Maurice Beebe, then editor of *Modern Fiction Studies;* Louis Bonnerot, editor of *Études*

Anglaises; Clarence Gohdes, editor of *American Literature;* and Albert Gegenheimer, editor of *Arizona Quarterly.* To William D. Templeman I am greatly indebted for the scholarly wisdom and incisive common sense that he brought to the earliest stages of the work and for the inspiration he gave me to continue it.

I owe thanks to those universities which provided me access to needed materials: the Doheney Library of the University of Southern California; the University of Mississippi Library, and especially to Miss Dorothy Zollicoffer Oldham, who granted me access to the valuable Faulkner Collection; the Research Library of the University of California at Los Angeles; the Los Angeles Public Library; the Huntington Library of San Marino, California; the John Grant Crabbe Library of Eastern Kentucky University; the Margaret I. King Library of the University of Kentucky; the University of Louisville Library; the New York Public Library; and the Princeton University Library, especially to Mr. Alexander Wainwright in helping to arrange my visit to Princeton, and to Mr. Alfred L. Bush, Associate Curator of Manuscripts, through whose courteous assistance I was granted expeditious use of the Faulkner Collection and related materials.

I wish to extend my profoundest gratitude to Phil Stone and William McNeil Reed, who kindly gave of their valuable time in sharing with me in interviews their special knowledge and rare insights into the life of William Faulkner. Without the help of these men most of the original biographical portions of the book simply would not have been possible. My special thanks are due also to attorneys T. H. Freeland, III, and G. A. Gafford, then partners with Phil Stone, for their assistance in arranging my first interview with Faulkner's closest friend. Among the many others in Oxford who granted me their time and hospitality was Mr. Kenneth Robertson, since an attorney but then the desk clerk at the Alumni House at Ole Miss, who helped to make my visit there delightful as well as informative.

I wish also to acknowledge the administrative faculties of California State College at Los Angeles and the University of Southern California for granting me successive visiting professorships for the summer of 1967 and 1968 respectively, thus allowing me the opportunity to review pertinent research materials in the area at propitious times. In this connection, I wish to express my special debts of gratitude to Professors Frederick Shroyer, Charles Beckwith, and John Palmer of California State College at Los Angeles as well as to Professors David Malone and Rosario Armato of the University of Southern California for their many personal kindnesses and help in arranging my visits.

No acknowledgment would be complete without recognition of the vast background of scholarship done in American literature and, especially, in the Faulkner canon, upon which I have drawn both directly and indirectly. Among those not previously named are Robert Cantwell, Malcolm Cowley, Robert Coughlan, Frederick J. Hoffman, Irving Howe, James B. Meriwether, Michael Millgate, Ward L. Miner, and Olga Vickery. To Cleanth Brooks, George Marion O'Donnell, and Robert Penn Warren, who have charted seminal critical approaches to Faulkner's work, I am indebted. Leslie Fiedler and A. O. Lovejoy have developed additional methods of critical approach, as has Richard Harter Fogle, whose *Imagery of Keats and Shelley* served as a model for my own imaginal analyses of Faulkner's poetry and lyrical experimentation. My debt to Freud and Jung is obvious enough, but I should mention also those who have more recently pointed the way to sensibly evolved relationships between psychology and literature: such scholars as Franz Alexander, Kenneth Burke, Henry Lowenfeld, Daniel M. Schneider, René Wellek, and Austin Warren. Special thanks are due Dr. Leo B. Froke, with whom I discussed various portions of the manuscript as it relates to the dominant themes of Faulkner's compulsive absorption with the past and his struggle to identity.

My students in American literature, and particularly in the seminars in Faulkner and Hemingway, have by their intellectual curiosity and atmosphere of excitement over ideas generated more incentive and stimulation leading to the production of this volume than they may have realized. I commend them for always wanting to know more, and thank them for helping me to learn with them.

To Maynard Smith, Sharon Spenik, and my wife Antonia, who typed the manuscript in its various stages of development, my earnest appreciation is extended. Graduate students Harold Blythe, Ann Giannini, and Victor Miller performed yeomanly service in proofreading; and Mr. Blythe's work on the index, carried out under last-minute pressures, was an invaluable aid to me. Of all these, I am most grateful to my wife for the many contributions she made to this project, for taking notes in shorthand in her capacity as stenographer during the various interviews, for typing the early drafts, for sharing the enthusiasm of new discoveries with me, for her good judgment, and for her constant faith and never-failing encouragement during the years of preparation that have gone into the making of this book.

H. E. R.

Louisville, Kentucky
December 31, 1968

Contents

I

Oxford and the Faulkners: Roots

Most of William Faulkner's books are interrelated with the northern Mississippi area. Some of their scenes are modeled after such hamlets as Dutch Bend in Lafayette County or such towns as Ripley, the county seat of Tippah County and the home of Faulkner's great-grandfather, Colonel William Cuthbert Falkner. Others are set as far north in the state as Holly Springs and in Memphis, Tennessee; or, southward again, along the Mississippi Delta and in Clarksdale. Oxford, however, long the home of the author and now his burial ground, is the principal source of his regional work.

For a person acquainted with Faulkner's books, visiting Oxford for the first time is a good deal like having the mythical town of Jefferson materialize before one's eyes. Actual details seem to be fictionally familiar: the courthouse and town square, the Confederate soldier on his narrow pedestal, the wooden galleries along the sides of business buildings, and the First National Bank on one corner—the same location as the bank Faulkner's grandfather, J. W. T. Falkner, known as the "Young Colonel," owned and operated when William was growing up in the town. For readers of William Faulkner's novels, the First National Bank of Oxford, Mississippi, may well be old Bayard Sartoris' bank in the first novel of the Yoknapatawpha series, *Sartoris* (1929).

The younger William Cuthbert Faulkner was born September 25, 1897, in New Albany, Mississippi, and although the family did not come to Oxford until 1902, the earliest Falkner forebear to settle in the area probably arrived there a few years before the Mexican War. Ripley, where Colonel Falkner settled, is approximately forty miles northeast of Oxford and twenty miles south of the Tennessee border. The Old Colonel, as he has come to be known, originally spelled the family name with the *u*, but dropped it in order to distinguish his family from others in the region; young William Faulkner simply restored the *u* to the family name, at first in an inconsistent manner, during the first World War. The *u* gradually persisted in his use, although most of the family retained *Falkner*.[1]

North-central Mississippi is sparsely settled in comparison to the rich Delta land to the west and the more productive grasslands to the east. Although there is some good land in the valleys, the soil is generally poor and the farms inefficiently cultivated. Oxford is bordered by red clay hills that, despite new conservational practices, are eroded and of little agricultural importance. In past years, many people who have come to the region for the first time have been shocked by the obvious poverty and lack of progress. But much of this is changing for the better. Agriculture is gradually giving way to minor inroads of small businesses and light industry. The population of Oxford was 3,967 in 1950, but by 1960 the municipal population had grown to 8,462; meanwhile, the population of its county, Lafayette, declined. The urbanization movement is evident in the new highways and subdivisions that have brought prosperity to construction businesses. Oxford now has its share of ready-mixed concrete companies, electrical contractors, and trucking firms, and general merchandising is brisk. In recent years, the Sardis Reservoir has stimulated a lively interest in the region in water sports, boating, and fishing. Oxford has put off some of its country ways, but its economy still depends chiefly upon the farmers of Lafayette County who transact their business in town.

In some areas of the county, however, progress seems to have been arrested or altogether avoided. Outside the environs of Oxford, the rolling hills and valleys extend into occasional stands of forests, and many of the narrow ravines and gullies are submerged in kudzu vines. Thus, the uncultivated regions retain a quality of primitive beauty.

Oxford's white stuccoed courthouse dominates the town square. Its most prominent features are its low arcades, tall columns, and its tower with a four-faced clock. Surrounding the square and facing the courthouse are commercial buildings of brick and stucco, in which a good portion of Lafayette County's business is transacted. A modern jewelry store contrasts markedly with tall, old-fashioned wooden galleries across the intersection of South Lamar Street. During my visits to the town, the farmers were displaying vegetables—"roasting ears," "half-runner" beans, ripe tomatoes, and "Kentucky Wonder" green beans—midweekly as well as on the usual Saturday market day. Cars parked casually and in some places two deep as buyers pulled up to the stands and chose their produce as leisurely as in a supermarket.

Among the townspeople were those a Faulkner reader would anticipate: shirt-sleeved merchants, the "rednecks," Negroes, housewives in starchy print dresses and broad hats— several ladies with umbrellas hoisted into the burning sunshine. But business seemed prosperous. People moved in and out of the stores, many of which glistened with modernized fronts and interiors. Not a few of the men were dressed in Palm Beach or seersucker suits and the women in modish summer garments. In contrast with these were the courthouse loungers, most of them senior citizens, who sat on benches under the shade trees and watched the activity about them. Present and past seemed to merge.

In the 1930's an iron fence, to which farmers tied their horses, still surrounded the courthouse grounds. Driving through the square one Saturday evening in 1938, Faulkner observed to a visitor, "There were no American flags here when I was a boy . . . . You never saw one except on the Federal building. But they came in during the [first World] war and now every store has a socket for a flag."[2]

Some older descriptions of this much-photographed heart of Oxford have been all too picturesque in their lack of toleration. The courtyard is a place where the pigeons have developed a remarkable degree of burliness, and where venerable denizens, "whose beards have become tobacco-tinctured to the required saffron," compete in a unique sort of legendary *bavardage.* The granite Civil War monument, depicting a Confederate soldier tranquilly holding his rifle in front of him, is "one of a multitude manufactured in equivocal Ohio and supplied to North and South alike." A grocery store once displayed the sign, "Don't go elsewhere to get skinned; come in here." And there is the "huge oak under which Grant wiped the perspiration from his brow on his way to Vicksburg," a march noted, incidentally, in Faulkner's *Sanctuary.*[3] Such individual impressions are not only varied, but sometimes contradictory. Some observers claim that as late as 1929 swine wallowed in the thoroughfare between the courthouse and the shops, while others remarked the neatly paved streets of the same era. *Mississippi: A Guide to the Magnolia State* states that Oxford was awarded a silver cup in 1928 for being "the cleanest and best kept town in the state" (p. 254).

Whatever the outlander's surface impressions of Oxford might be, the town's traditions remain old and deep. The title of City Founder will probably never be unanimously bestowed upon any individual, for a number of early settlers have been noted, each with his own claims for the privilege. Some details are recorded with annoying inconsistencies. John Chisholm, John J. Craig, and John D. Martin constructed a log store near what later became the town square, and on June 12, 1836, the three men purchased a large section of land from a Chickasaw Indian woman named Hokah and donated fifty acres for the purpose of establishing a county seat, which was incorporated on May 11, 1837. Robert Shegog and Thomas D. Isom arrived shortly thereafter and went into business, Isom being a clerk in a store built by Shegog. Other people maintain that Thomas Dudley Isom was the original founder, coming to the site of Oxford in 1835, when he was eighteen years old, and building the town's first store; but that about a year later he returned to his native Maury County, Tennessee, to become a doctor. Succeeding in changing his profession from storekeeper to physician, he then settled permanently in Oxford in 1839, finding it a young and growing town, having "two hotels, six stores, and two seminaries of education." However, courthouse records show the earliest deeds recorded to Craig, Chisholm, and Martin, and the weight of best evidence seems to favor them as cofounders.[4]

Many of the settlers were Jacksonian Democrats, pioneers who had come from Tennessee, Alabama, and the Carolinas. Although the town resulted from flush times, it grew strong enough during its infancy to survive the Panic of 1837, and by 1840 had recovered to the extent that its citizenry completed the courthouse. The best hostelry in town, noted in *The Observer* of September 16, 1843, was located on the present site of the Colonial Hotel and was operated by a Captain Butler, related to William Faulkner through Sallie Murry Falkner, his grandmother.

The establishment of the Federal Court for the District of Northern Mississippi in Oxford was one of the early incentives for bringing such men as Jacob Thompson and Lucius Quintus Cincinnatus Lamar to the town. The former, a congressman and Secretary of the Interior under President Buchanan, moved there from Pontotoc, Mississippi, about 1839. Lamar, Senator and later Secretary of the Interior in Grover Cleveland's Cabinet, was a man who, in his own words, "never made popularity the standard for my action"; and although his Mississippi neighbors could not quite understand his reasons for doing so, he eulogized Charles Sumner in a famous speech, which won the hearts of his Northern countrymen.[5] The early courts not only brought an influx of lawyers, but also contributed to a new community atmosphere. The frontier citizens were delighted with the wealth of legal talent exhibited on the days court was in session. Rhetorical wit proliferated. The whole atmosphere resulted in a unique emphasis being placed on florid language, highly entertaining for the local citizens.[6]

The town's name was chosen in expectation that a state university would be established there. Oxford was awarded the honor by the narrow majority of a single vote, and its Board of Trustees was named on February 24, 1844. Such a distinction was to ensure a further enrichment of Oxford culture, bringing to it such gifted men as Augustus Baldwin Longstreet, a graduate of Yale. When he became Chancellor of the University of Mississippi, he was already known as an educator and author, having served as President of Emory College and having published *Georgia Scenes* in 1840. Frederick Augustus Porter Barnard first came to the school as a professor of mathematics and astronomy, but served as Chancellor from 1858 until the beginning of the Civil War. His Union sympathies resulted in his resignation, but he later became President of Columbia University. Through both the interest of its citizens in procuring the university and its nearness, Oxford quickly came under the influence of the school's cultural and social life.

Although no major battles were fought in Oxford, the town was subjected to raids during the Civil War. The college was closed during the war, and many of its students fought heroically under the banner of the "University Grays." The wounded from the Battle of Shiloh were hospitalized in the university buildings. Grant himself occupied the town in December, 1862, but the town's worst experience of the war came on August 22, 1864, when the business section, courthouse, and some residences were set afire by the troops of General A. J. Smith.

Just how destructive the Civil War was to the area may be difficult to comprehend. From the standpoint of per capita wealth for the white population, Mississippi was richer than any other state in the country before the war. Specifically, the property of Lafayette County had been evaluated at $15,962,-200, but by the end of the war its value was only $3,339,716, and in 1880 it dropped further to a mere $2,303,405.[7] Under the sapping destitution of the Reconstruction period, it was natural that the waning aristocracy should look back to the days when its culture once flourished. In grandiose gestures, an opera house was built to bring entertainers to the town, and the young men actually organized tilting tournaments modeled after the romances of Scott. Students of the university practiced their oratory on the Saturday crowds around the courthouse square. But the gestures were vain. Prior to the war, the initial vitality of frontier Oxford, even as it grew and mellowed, was already in a process of decay. Physical courage was glorified and sentimentalized in high-sounding phrases. Trying to survive in a world of reality with impossibly romanticized ideals, the postwar Southerner was still haunted by his civilization's moral flaw of slavery. In retrospect, one can see that men the stature of Longstreet were subject to such attributes of decadence as provincialism and isolation. Even as Calvinistic New England was being liberalized under the influence of Emerson and other transcendentalists, the Jeffersonian liberalism which first characterized the ante-bellum South was gradually being displaced by the conservatism of wealthy self-serving interests and the emotionalism wrought by the fundamentalist circuit riders; ironically, A. B. Longstreet himself had once been a Methodist circuit rider.

Until 1890 Oxford continued to supply the state and the nation with such talented leaders as Lamar, Thompson, Isom, and Hill, but its citizens were no longer wealthy and powerful. From 1890, the state underwent a Populist revolt, and by 1904 James K. Vardaman became governor, and with him followed a succession of new political values and leaders— the "Jim Crow" law, issues of segregation, and the political demagoguery epitomized by Theodore G. Bilbo. Since then the state's power structure remained more or less static, changing very little during the first half of the present century.

Through its tragic flaw of slavery the ante-bellum South was fated from the beginning. Cursed with its legacy of moral guilt, derided by a North that never knew the institution of slavery or its sorry aftermath, yet still faced with the real social and economic problems of its Negroes and poor whites; defeated in war, its commerce irrevocably marred, its leaders

stripped of wealth and power, watching a way of life crumble
—the South could not conceivably turn to the future with hope
and faith in progress. Thus, Oxford's people, remembering
far-off things and battles long ago, may appear to the outlander to move in a world characterized neither by a reality
of the present nor an actuality of the past—but rather in
suspended and futureless time. Yet, upon closer examination,
the impression gives way to what may be termed "a reflective
sense of the present," a "now" so heavily grafted with the
lore of cultural memory that the active moment merely *appears*
to recede as the past advances. More than once the Nobel
laureate referred to time as "was," and, reflecting the cultural
context of his work, stated, "My ambition is to put everything
into one sentence—not only the present but the whole past
on which it depends and which keeps overtaking the present,
second by second."[8]

A mistaken impression one frequently receives of William
Faulkner's famous great-grandfather is that he was a typical,
native-born Mississippi aristocrat. One might make out a case
that he was "aristocratic," although not in the usual sense of
the word; actually, he was more of a pioneer of the vigorous,
enterprising sort. He was not a native Mississippian, and he
certainly was not "typical." Of Welsh descent, he was born in
Knox County, Tennessee, on July 6, probably in 1825.[9] The
family moved to Missouri shortly after the boy's birth, and
there he spent his boyhood in the old French Catholic town
of Sainte Genevieve. The real motivation for the boy's leaving
Missouri has been obscured by time and legend, but one prevailing story is that, at the age of fourteen, he engaged in a
bloody hoe fight with a younger brother and was so thoroughly
punished by his father that he ran away from home.[10] It is
uncertain how old the boy was at this time, or whether he
came directly to Mississippi from Missouri or by way of
Tennessee; but it is clear that he did walk to Ripley, only to
find that his uncle, a schoolteacher named William Thompson,
was in jail a few miles distant at Pontotoc, charged with
murder. The stories of the fatigue encountered during this trip
and his consequent discouragement upon arriving vary in

picturesque detail. One is that he sat down and cried, vowing he would some day construct a railroad over the very route of his arduous journey. Another specifies the place where he rested on the steps of a tavern, but fetchingly adds that a little girl, Elizabeth Vance, destined to be his second wife, upon seeing him in his wretched condition, went home to get him a glass of water, telling her mother about the "little old tramp boy." The Vance family took him in and saw that he caught the stagecoach to Pontotoc the next morning. His uncle was acquitted of the murder charge and took the boy to Ripley; and from that time until his death at sixty-four, W. C. Falkner's permanent home was Ripley. He never lived in Oxford.

Employed by the sheriff, young Falkner worked for several years in the jail at Ripley, while also attending school. He also helped his uncle—who in the meanwhile had become a lawyer —by working in his office, reading law, and performing clerical tasks. After the Mexican War began, Falkner was elected first lieutenant of his local company. He was wounded on April 14, 1847, seriously enough that he received a pension from the government until the outbreak of the Civil War. Back in Ripley once again, he began the practice of law with his uncle, and was married to Holland Pearce, a girl from Knoxville, Tennessee. They had but one son, John Wesley Thompson Falkner, before she died. He later married Elizabeth Vance.[11]

The serious trouble that was to mark him for the rest of his life began on May 8, 1849, when Robert Hindman, one of two brothers who were his comrades during the Mexican War, attacked him with a gun that failed to fire. Defending himself, Falkner killed the man with a knife. Although it turned out that the whole affair was the result of a misunderstanding, it was too late to rectify the damage. An additional irony of the affair was that the victim's brother, Thomas Hindman, prosecuted the case before his first jury. Pleading self-defense, Falkner was acquitted, but immediately after the trial Thomas Hindman assaulted him, and in the altercation one of Hindman's companions, a friend named Morris, was killed as

Falkner defended himself. He was acquitted once more, but the conflict went on in a strange and mysterious fashion. During the whole bloody episode, at least two men were killed and four murders were attempted. After the second trial, Hindman almost killed Falkner again. A duel was arranged, but a witness managed to prevent it, after which Hindman left Mississippi and went to Arkansas.[12]

By the time the Civil War broke out, Falkner had already made a fortune of $50,000. He organized a local company and was elected Colonel of the Second Mississippi Regiment. Although he saw service at Harpers Ferry, his first battle action took place at Bull Run, close to Manassas, Virginia, on July 21, 1861. His regiment was attached to the command of General Joseph E. Johnston, who had superseded Thomas J. (Stonewall) Jackson approximately two months before. Colonel Falkner was replaced in command by Colonel John W. Stone in April, 1862, as the result of a troop election. Outraged by the demotion and refusing to serve in such a situation, Falkner galloped away to Mississippi, where he formed the Seventh Cavalry, a band of irregulars attached to General Nathan B. Forrest. Again a Colonel, he became a hero of the Civil War by defending Ripley.[13]

During the Reconstruction period, his vigor did not wane, but grew in a less violent and more constructive way, at least until the end of his career. He became active in politics and began to realize the daydream that he had spun as a tired, sore-footed "little old tramp boy" so many years before. He organized his railroad, originally the Ripley, and known during most of the Old Colonel's life as the Ripley, Ship Island and Kentucky. It was completed in 1872 and reached over the distance of approximately twenty-two miles from Ripley to Middleton, Tennessee—the two points between which the boy had walked. Later it was named the Gulf and Chicago and extended through New Albany and Pontotoc. Originally begun as a narrow-gauge line, it was converted in 1905 to standard gauge, becoming part of the Gulf, Mobile and Northern; and in 1940 it was absorbed by the Gulf, Mobile and Ohio.[14]

Colonel Falkner did the first writing for which he received pay as a young man while he was working in the Ripley jail. He helped capture one McCannon, who was convicted of murdering an entire emigrant family. Falkner withstood a mob lynching party, protecting McCannon, and after the trial managed to write a story of the criminal's life. He published it on credit, and the day of McCannon's execution sold 2,500 copies, from which he supposedly cleared $1,250.[15] His most noteworthy literary success, however, was *The White Rose of Memphis,* originally published as a serial in the *Ripley Advertiser,* its first installment appearing in August, 1880, then in book form in 1881. Although originally considered a colorful, romantic, action-packed novel, to twentieth-century tastes it may seem contrived and artificial. Even as a product of the Old Colonel's imagination, the book is deserving of some attention; but as a tangible aspect of the patriarch's influence upon his most famous descendant—who as a boy stated that he wanted to be a writer "like my great-granddaddy"—the book may be significant in a number of ways.

The action begins as a Mississippi River steamer, from which the name of the novel is taken, is fitted out as an excursion boat and makes its maiden voyage from Memphis to New Orleans.[16] With characters taking the roles of such personages as Ingomar (taken from the then-popular comedy, "Ingomar, the Barbarian," by Friedrich Halm, first produced in 1842 in Vienna) ; Mary, Queen of Scots; Henry of Navarre; Napoleon; Ivanhoe; and Don Quixote—a "grand masquerade ball" is given the last evening of April, the beginning of a series of such lighthearted entertainments to be continued each evening of the round trip. Caught up in the spirit of revelry and inspired by the striking beauty of the Queen of Scots, the masquers decide to retain their disguises. They elect Mary their queen and agree upon a code that will furnish them with "innocent sport" during the voyage. The entertainment begins with Ingomar's narrative, which becomes the novel's major plot, and is interspersed with a mysterious sub-plot aboard ship, relieved by frequent dancing, dining, and promenading upon deck.

Ingomar, the protagonist, controls the action, never giving anyone else a chance to tell a story, for his is not concluded until the novel is nearly finished. It covers the childhood adventures of three orphans: Edward Demar, aged thirteen; Harry Wallingford, twelve; and Harry's sister, Lottie, who is ten. Edward's troubles begin when his mother dies and his father turns alcoholic. He enjoys a brief respite from the buffets of fate while in the care of his beloved stepmother, but she too passes away, leaving him alone with his little stepbrother and stepsister. After selling all their meager possessions to provide the deceased with "the finest rosewood coffin," the three start their two-hundred-mile journey from Nashville to Memphis *on foot,* where they hope to meet an uncle who will furnish them with a home. On the way some fantastic adventures occur, including these: Edward's saving of Lottie's life by sucking the poison from a rattlesnake bite, but nearly dying himself in the process; their encounter with a juvenile gang, led by one Ben Bowles, and a narrowly avoided travesty of justice; and Harry's heroism in saving Viola Bramlett's life by jumping from the front of an engine to push her out of the cowcatcher's swath. The boy is badly hurt in the incredible maneuver, but calmly ignores the entreaties of the old engineer:

"My brave little hero," he exclaimed as he pressed Harry's brow to his lips, "are you hurt?"

"Not much, sir, I believe, though my leg is broken," said Harry. (p. 70)

Little Viola's father, overwhelmed with gratitude, eventually provides for the support and education of the Wallingfords, while Edward is taken in by a friendly old druggist-physician. Harry grows up to be a lawyer, while Lottie receives a lady's education in Bards Town [*sic*], Kentucky, where she carries off all school honors. Edward prepares himself for medical school; but before he goes away to Philadelphia to study, he declares his love to Lottie, newly returned to Memphis as a refined and devastatingly beautiful young lady. Despite Edward's self-doubt, there is never any question that the two have been in love since their childhood, and, not surprisingly, the same romantic situation emerges between Harry and Viola.

These events set the tone for the romantic novel as tragedy enters. Viola's little brother is poisoned and she is blamed for the act. Lottie stands by her friend throughout the difficulty even though the boys are temporarily swayed from loyalty by circumstantial evidence provided by some Dickensian detectives. One difficulty is piled upon another, hearsay upon hearsay, misunderstanding upon misunderstanding, until Harry eventually challenges Edward, his best friend, to a duel. The fictional circumstances of the duel suggest, up to a point, the Thomas Hindman episode in Colonel Falkner's life, for the two men had once been strong friends; and the General Calloway of the novel, "a man whose opinions were respected by the community" (p. 289), is close enough to the actual witness, who was Colonel Galloway, editor of the *Memphis Appeal*. Edward is spirited away as a result of mistaken identity. Eventually, however, the mystery is solved, but not until the sub-plot develops and deepens aboard *The White Rose;* finally, Napoleon is exposed as none other than the escaped and dissolute culprit, Ben Bowles.

Some of the book's features which mark its genre clearly as that of the melodramatic, domestic-sentimental novel of the nineteenth century are its excessively knightly and all too grammatical dialogue; the extraordinary perfection of the hero and heroine; Lottie's three near-escapes from death; Edward's five-day coma and bout with brain fever; Harry's perpetual pallor, his hysterical pride, his fight to the death with Ben Bowles in the Mississippi River, and his near death from an ensuing wound; Mrs. Ragland's confession and suicide; Dr. Dodson's sentimental, didactic death scene; and the resolution of the murder mystery and ultimate poetic justice for all. Colonel Falkner's props included even the faithful dog, old Bob, and characters with such obvious names as Frazzlebrain, Colonel Confed and General Camphollower, Dr. Deediddle, Judge Flaxback, and Miss Clattermouth.

One gathers from internal evidence that the Bible, which is frequently alluded to and quoted, is Colonel Falkner's major literary influence in *The White Rose*. Aside from it, other influences upon his style and content seem to fall into the categories of general classics, the Romantics, and the American humorists.

The book has been generally ignored or roundly condemned as an incredible romance of the moonlight-and-magnolias school, and too excessively praised as a wonderful novel. Both views are extreme and misleading. The value of the novel, it seems to me, is not so much as a work of art, but rather as a literary curio. It not only depicts extravagantly an era of grace and chivalry that the South once deluded itself into believing actually existed, but also is a kind of fantastic masquerade of the Old Colonel himself—grotesque, exaggerated, drenched in tears, but still identifiable. The orphan status of Edward Demar suggests an autobiographical linkage with Colonel Falkner, and Lottie Wallingford's timely appearance certainly recalls Elizabeth Vance and the "little old tramp boy" episode upon his arrival in Ripley when he was fourteen. In this portion of the novel, Edward and Lottie converse as follows:

"Will you ever think of *the boyish tramp* who long ago claimed you as his little wife, after I am gone?"

"Yes, Edward, I never shall forget the halcyon days of old, for although we were poor, homeless wanderers, we were not unhappy." (p. 107, italics added)

As incredible as the book is, the unique quality of the author's imagination, his vitality, intensity, and incipient ability to interweave warring plot elements are all evident. Perhaps in some indirect, if not direct ways, one may be permitted to see the book's influence upon the author's great-grandson. Stylistically, Colonel Falkner seems to suggest his descendant's devices with the strange mixture of humor and grief revealed in Edward Demar's monologues as the duel scene develops, his surrealistic dreams stemming from fear, tension, and confusion, and the arrest scene with its mysteriously confounding subsequent action during which Edward is conducted from place to place until he seems to be secreted from all familiar life, adrift in helpless anger, and quite mad. The accurate recording of Negro dialogue and the use of polysyllabic names, some of them with Chickasaw overtones, seem to anticipate Faulkner's devices. But the driving intensity of the strongest scenes culminating in Lottie's return from the threshold of death seem to echo that fateful horror, haunting outrage, and perversely macabre absurdity which characterize such elements of Faulkner's work as Nancy's fear in "That Evening Sun," the convict's maddening efforts to free himself from the burden of the pregnant woman in *The Old Man,* and Jason Compson's chain of frustrations in *The Sound and the Fury.*

William Faulkner, however, said that *The White Rose of Memphis* was sheer escapism—"The men all brave and the women all pure." At the same time, he added some interesting observations of his great-grandfather, pointing out that he had written *The White Rose* simply because he wanted to excel all others in a literary effort, and that he never really desired to repeat his performance. He further related that he thought Sir Walter Scott was the Colonel's major inspiration and that he had honored that Romantic writer by naming his railroad stations after the man's characters: "The people could call the towns whatever they wanted, but, by God, he would name the depots."[17]

Mississippi: A Guide to the Magnolia State notes the violent death of the Old Colonel with the following statement:

. . . it is a family legend that when he made a bitter enemy of his old friend and railroad associate Col. R. J. Thurmond, by defeating him for the State Legislature in [1889], he refused to arm himself, saying that he already had killed too many men and did not want to kill any more. On the day of Falkner's [first] election to the legislature Thurmond shot him dead on the main street of Ripley. (p. 458)

Concerning the episode, William Faulkner consistently stated,

I don't believe Thurmond was a coward. But the old man probably drove him to desperation—insulted him, spread stories about him, laughed at him. Besides, he had killed two or three men. And I suppose when you've killed men something happens inside you— something happens to your character. He said he was tired of killing people. And he wasn't armed the day Thurmond shot him, although he always carried a pistol.[18]

All these points should make obvious the fact that the Old Colonel differed from the typical Southern planters. He was not an aristocrat, and although he became a planter, owning a 1,200-acre plantation outside Ripley, he also possessed the intelligence and flexibility to explore other commercial fields with extraordinary vigor and originality. He never completely accepted the Southern code of his neighbors, but he never completely rejected it either. In this connection it is interesting to contrast the hysterical Harry Wallingford and his impractical pride with the more rational, though yet idealistic, Edward Demar. The Colonel's gentlemanly associates were too often *esprits simplistes,* who oversimplified the complexities of human life, its social relationships, wars, politics, economics, and educational and religious institutions. He was never comprehended by his contemporaries, who tried to murder him. His practical achievements, overshadowed as they have been by his dashing and bloody exploits, indicate not so much an aristocrat hopelessly watching his power and wealth recede with the Reconstruction, but rather the new man of enterprising vision, who tried to bring an enlightened commerce to a way of life which was too rigid to accept it. He remained a paradox: caught up by and sharing in the current of a time which exaggerated its passions and existed by an outmoded chivalric code, he represented a bold pattern of progress for a hopelessly anachronistic age. Faulkner's own attitude toward his great-grandfather was a strange blend of the realistic and romantic:

People at Ripley talk of him as if he were still alive, up in the hills some place, and might come in at any time. It's a strange thing; there are lots of people who knew him well, and yet no two of them remember him alike or describe him the same way. One will say he was like me and another will swear he was six feet tall . . . There's nothing left in the old place, the house is gone and the plantation boundaries, nothing left of his work but a statue. But he rode through that country like a living force. I like it better that way.[19]

William Faulkner's grandfather was John Wesley Thompson Falkner, the only child of Holland Pearce, the Old Colonel's first wife. Grandfather John inherited his father's title, but the townspeople referred to him as the "Young Colonel," thus distinguishing him from his famous father. Although not the colorful figure of the Old Colonel, he did achieve distinction as an Assistant United States Attorney, a lawyer, banker, and politician. He at first improved the Old Colonel's railroad, but finally came upon hard times. He eventually lost control of the First National Bank to a country businessman named Joe Parks. The story is that he immediately withdrew his money and deposited it in a competitor's bank, having just carried it across the town square in a waterbucket. A heavy drinker, he made annual trips to a Keeley Institute, having his faithful Negro servant, Ned, drive him there in a fine carriage.[20] Like his father before him, he was interested in politics and did not hesitate to challenge the vague principles of aristocratic isolation and rigidity that characterized other once-prosperous planter families. Thus, he supported politically the rise of the "rednecks," the better side of which was favoring greater suffrage for tenant farmers. The Young Colonel established a law firm with Lee M. Russell and lived to see his associate become lieutenant governor of Mississippi during Bilbo's first term, 1916-1920, and governor from 1920-1924. One of the best first-hand descriptions of J. W. T. Falkner has been given by John B. Cullen, who recalls having seen and met him several times upon the streets of Oxford:

He carried a cane, and he would tap it along as he walked. His walk was peculiar, just like William's. The only other people I have known to walk like that were walking in their sleep. It is not a slow walk, but a kind of mincing step, an odd gait that I cannot describe . . . Like his grandson William, he would pass people by and not even notice them.[21]

The Young Colonel is also remembered as being deaf and temperamental. He was a man of rigid dignity, given to outbursts of temper. He once bawled out Governor Russell who had the temerity to get him out of bed too early in the morning. After tongue-lashing the Governor, he then refused to discuss business with him on the Falkners' front porch, saying he would meet him instead at his office. He died in 1922 and lies buried in St. Peter's Cemetery in Oxford.

The Young Colonel and his wife, Sallie Murry, had three children: Holland, a girl called "Antee" (pronounced Aun*tee*); John Wesley Thompson Falkner II, a lawyer known in Oxford as "Judge" Falkner; and Murry Falkner, the eldest child and William's father. Murry attended the University of Mississippi but never completed work for a degree. After quitting college he worked erratically at a number of jobs but, compared with his forebears, was a success in none. Eventually he became a railroad conductor, auditor, and depot agent at New Albany, Mississippi, the town where William was born in 1897. The circumstances under which the family left New Albany are associated with an action of reckless courage and chivalry strangely reminiscent of the Old Colonel. As the family story goes, the proprietor of a New Albany drug store named Walker insulted Murry's sister. Meeting Walker on the street, Murry slapped his face and told him that he would punish him that evening. Coolly entering the drug store and first endeavoring to make a purchase from the clerk, Murry turned to see Walker pointing a pistol at him. The druggist fired and the bullet struck Murry in the mouth, a wound similar to that inflicted on the Old Colonel by Thurmond. Murry dropped to the floor, where Walker then discharged both barrels of a shotgun into his back. The Young Colonel, hearing of the outrage, later caught Walker in another store and at point-blank range emptied a pistol at him, but the shots misfired, much as had Robert Hindman's before the Old Colonel managed to stab him to death. Walker then broke away and shot Murry's father. Incredible as it may seem, no one was killed. It was at this point that Murry Falkner's wife, the former Maud Butler, decided for the welfare of everyone concerned to move the family to Oxford.[22]

William Faulkner's father is remembered by Cullen as having operated a grocery store with his brother John—one of Murry's many jobs which did not last. The brothers were later in a draying business, after which Murry was proprietor of the old opera house when vaudeville was performed there. He then operated a hardware store, and Cullen recollects that "he was very lenient and would give me plenty of time to pay," and that he was "efficient, considerate and prompt" in dealing with others. Finally he became comptroller of the University of Mississippi, a position he held until his retirement.

The author's mother, who died in 1960, earned a local reputation for her painting, and it is generally believed by those who knew her well that much of William's talent came from "Miss Maud" and her mother, Lelia Dean Swift, who was an amateur sculptress—as well as from the Falkner side of the family.

Four children were born to Murry and Maud Falkner: William, Murry, John, and Dean. Next to that of William, John's reputation is the most notable. He wrote *Men Working, Dollar Cotton, Chooky,* and a biography entitled *My Brother Bill.* Known as "Johnsie," he made the spelling of the family name consistent with William's. He was a city engineer, draftsman, farmer, airplane pilot, and operator of a chicken broiler business. He also painted and exhibited his pictures. Cullen has commented favorably on his "rustic scenes," but has also made the judgment that John's abundance of talents prevented him from concentrating on any one of them long enough to achieve the success his older brother did. The only living brother, Murry C. Falkner, works with the Federal Bureau of Investigation, lives in Mobile, and is known by the nickname "Jack." Obscured until recently, his life has been a colorful and exciting one.[28] Dean, the youngest brother, was killed in 1935 during a barnstorming tour in an airplane owned by William.

One of the most revealing insights given into the Faulkners has been recorded by Cullen. As if he were speaking of the Sartoris family in Faulkner's fiction, he calls them "reckless" and maintains that they enjoy "thrills and dangers." Such a remark is not surprising to anyone who has the facts at hand and can trace them from the Old Colonel to the last years and weeks of William Faulkner's life. As recently as the summer of 1959, he broke a collarbone while fox-hunting in Virginia. A few weeks before his death, he was thrown from his horse again. On the morning of July 3, 1962, not quite three full days before his death, his old friend Mr. "Mack" Reed noted that he was still wearing his back brace.[24] "Twenty years ago," Cullen remembers, "Johnsie Falkner was talking with me about going in together and buying a cotton-dusting plane"; and he summarized his impression of the family in these words: "They are honorable, reckless, quiet, and kind."[25]

Other Oxonians—as the townspeople refer to themselves—are more critical of the Faulkners, describing them as "curious," "aloof," "cool," or "plain stuck-up." The day after Faulkner's death a Memphis reporter noted, under the headline "Storied Oxford Unruffled at 'Curious Bill's' Passing," that the natives of Oxford had "let him go his own (to them peculiar) way as he let them go theirs."[26] But the stereotyped impressions of Faulkner's quiet, often introverted, manner have probably been overdone. At the mention of this reputation for shyness, Phil Stone's black eyebrows raised and he said, laughing with good-natured overstatement, "Bill never had any *humility* about him at all." He talked on, referring to the family's ancient reputation for independence, headstrongness, and gall, then quoted Alexander Pope about fools rushing in where angels fear to tread. He neatly paraphrased, "The Faulkners rush in where *fools* fear to tread."

II

Boyhood:
Loomings

Life still moves at a slow pace in Oxford. Although the town is gradually changing, it lacks the booming new industrial growth that typifies the more progressive Southern communities. Today it remains substantially a small agricultural center, tending toward urbanization. Except for the cosmopolitan influence of the university, Oxford still has the substantial attributes of a provincial county seat in an isolated rural area. But if Oxford's growth since Reconstruction has been something less than progressive, the town has retained the advantages of its traditional character. The beauties of primitive nature lie just a walk away. It is a quiet, venerable Nature that has for generations endeared itself to the people of Lafayette County. For the outlander, the people's natural reticence may seem strangely kindred to the rough, muted beauty of this land, about which Phil Stone has written,

. . . sunlight spills dimly through the trees and there is no company but the birds. There are soft carpeted pine hills white with dogwood in the spring. There are rows on serried rows of far hills, blue and purple and lav[e]nder and lilac in the sun, hills upon which you can look day after day and year after year and never find light and shadow and color exactly the same.[1]

"In this country," William Faulkner once said, "I was born in 1826 of a Negro slave and an alligator."[2] The statement, with all its flavor of a tall tale, has a factual relevance that may point to ancestral identity: the date suggests the birth of the Old Colonel rather than that of his great-grandson. William Faulkner was born just south of Ripley, in New Albany, at a time when the Falkner ancestral home was still in Ripley, and the influence of the Old Colonel's legendary reputation upon the town, as well as upon the impressionable boy, was still profound. Born only eight years after the old man's violent death, Faulkner the boy knew firsthand the attitude of the people of nearby Ripley toward him and his family. He later spoke of it:

The feeling in Ripley did not die out with Colonel Falkner's death and Thurmond's leaving. I can remember myself, when I was a boy in Ripley, there were some people who would pass on the other side of the street to avoid speaking—that sort of thing.[3]

Shortly after the family moved to Oxford in 1902, William's father owned a cottonseed-oil mill and ice plant; later, he sold them and went into the livery stable business. The grandfather, J. W. T. Falkner, had built a three-story house on South Lamar two blocks from the courthouse square. William's family took up residence in the new home. Though now a converted apartment house, crowded in among several residences and fronted by a filling station, the old homeplace was once estate-sized and contained pasture fields reaching several hundred feet toward a wooded area. Beyond, the railroad bed separated Oxford from the campus of Ole Miss. At this time young "Billy" and "Jack" had ponies. Later, John Cullen remembered how he used to pass down the broad shady street by the Falkner home on his way to and from school. The Falkner children owned a "spotted pony and almost every kind of toy and gun that children could have in those days." In addition to the Falkner brothers, their cousin, Sallie Murry Wilkins, whom the Falkners reared, and Estelle Oldham, the future bride of William, were often part of the group. They played in the street for there was little danger from traffic at the time. In Cullen's words, the Falkner children "were friendly and pleasant even toward me, a country jake. Everyone liked them."[4] William's mother consistently reported that her son "was full of life and pep and played with the boys on his street in a perfectly normal way."[5]

Young Billy drew pictures of machines, built mechanical toys, and did some experiments in chemistry and flash photography that resulted in his brother John's temporary loss of both eyebrows. He and John also experimented with paint, and, just to see what would happen, they dipped twelve Wyandotte hens into a big can of it. By the time the paint dried, the hens had all died "with their boots on" so to speak. Such incidents bring to mind the comment his grandmother, the wife of Dr. Will Murry in Ripley, once made about the boy: "a child that for three weeks in the month . . . was an angel and the fourth week . . . a devil."[6] There seems to be a kind of poetic justice for the poor chickens in another of his childhood experiments. From the magazine *American Boy* William got the idea of building an aircraft. He supervised while his brother John and cousin Sally Murry did the work. The framework was formed of bean sticks, the covering of newspapers glued with flour-and-water paste. The test pilot, of course, was Billy. The memorable flight circumscribed an arc of about ten feet from a diminutive bluff to a sand ditch below, where young Daedalus landed, stunned but unhurt, in a flurry of kindling and newspaper.[7]

All available evidence indicates that William was nearly as precocious as Tom Sawyer. Like Tom, he was a great supervisor. Just as Tom escaped his responsibilities by Reynard-like subterfuges—particularly the psychological deception of having Aunt Polly's fence whitewashed—Billy also avoided his daily chores by bribing his playmates to do them for him, giving artful narrations of Indian stories and fairy tales of his own invention in return. He did not start to school until he was nearly eight years old, then made up four grades during his first two years. His third-grade classmate, Leo Calloway, a rural mail carrier in Oxford, remembered that, when questioned by the teacher concerning his future ambition, Billy would always stand up and say, "I want to be a writer like my great-granddaddy." Sally, William's cousin, recalled, "It got so that when Billy told you something, you never knew if it was the truth or just something he'd made up."[8] At the age of twelve, he produced a little hand-printed newspaper that "chronicled the happenings on South Street" and sold for a penny a copy.

William was formally educated until his sophomore year in high school. During these years there is little doubt that he exhibited some impatience with formal education, but statements that he was a poor student do not give all the information. Cullen recalls that Faulkner

was a little fellow when I went to school, about two grades behind me and small for his age. On the school ground he stood around a great deal, and I never saw him play many games with other children. He was more of a listener than a talker, yet everyone liked him and no one ever called him a sissy. (pp. 3-4)

Cullen's brother Hal, who was a classmate of William, said that the boy was "one of the two brightest" in the schoolroom and was outstanding for the skillful pictures he drew. Like John Cullen, Hal used to stop by the Falkner home after school and play when he was a boy; he told his brother that, as a child, William liked baseball, read a lot, but did not relish such pastimes as cowboy-and-Indian and wrestling. He took a strong interest in various school activities and showed an early tendency to write skits and poems and to draw sketches. From time to time he was wayward, and he was permitted to get by with his youthful impudence. Before he left school for a job in his grandfather's bank, however, he received a broken nose while playing quarterback on the Oxford football team against its traditional rival, Holly Springs.

Faulkner was an erratic student, by degrees successful, rebellious, creative, moody, cooperative, and withdrawn. What is generally overlooked is that he dropped out of school, not as a culmination of adolescent rebellion or through indifference, but rather by design, a plan arrived at partially through the influence of his older friend Phil Stone. William had been critical of the inadequacy of his formal education for a long time and had made ardent efforts to supplement it with innumerable books from both his grandfather's and Stone's libraries. It seems likely that he quit school not merely in order to work in his grandfather's bank, but also to avail himself of an education more unconstrained and better suited to his own tastes than the public school permitted or provided. As definite as this scheme of self-education may have been, he nevertheless wished to follow the example of Stone by tracing his friend's own paths of progress at the University. At this time a high school diploma was not an absolute prerequisite for entering college, and there was the possibility of attending classes as a special student. He could, therefore, prepare himself for university work through independent study.

The details of his position at the bank must be gathered by inference from Faulkner's own sketchy comment:

Quit school and went to work in Grandfather's bank. Learned the medicinal value of his liquor. Grandfather thought it was the janitor. Hard on the janitor.[9]

The job at the bank was one of the threads of experience the boy was gathering, which later would be woven into the fabric of his regional fiction. By his own account, he read little history but, rather, talked with people:

If I got it straight it's because I didn't worry with other people's ideas about it. When I was a boy there were a lot of people around who had lived through it [the Civil War], and I would pick it up— I was just saturated with it, but never read about it.[10]

Later, as a Nobel Prize winner, he was to elaborate upon these experiences in gathering local color through just listening:

I remember a lot of them [Civil War veterans]. I was five-six-seven years old around 1904-5-6 and 7, old enough to understand, to listen. They didn't talk so much about that war, I had got that from the maiden spinster aunts which had never surrendered. But I can remember the old men, and they would get out the old shabby grey uniforms and get out the old battle-flag on Decoration, Memorial Day. Yes, I remember any number of them. But it was the aunts, the women that had never given up. My aunt, she liked to go to the picture shows, they had *Gone with the Wind* in at the theatre at home and she went to see it, and as soon as Sherman came on the screen she got up and left. She had paid good money to go there, but she wasn't going to sit and look at Sherman.[11]

Faulkner said that he had grown up with a Negro boy like Ringo in *The Unvanquished,* with whom he played Civil War games. Contrary to Cullen's statement concerning the many toys the Falkner children had, Faulkner said, "There were no toys in this part of the country when I was a boy," indicating the statement as a partial explanation for adding, "We would fight over the battles and the old men would tell us what it was like."[12] The boy was imaginative and inventive. Working in his grandfather's bank, located just across the street from the courthouse, gave young William the opportunity to contemplate what was going on about him, to observe the ritual-like arrival or departure of his grandfather in his carriage, to converse with the Civil War veterans and "the old people" who did business at the bank, to mingle with them on the courthouse lawn during his idle hours—in short, to store up experiences which could later be drawn upon for writing.

Sometimes his wanderings took him to the Cullen home in the country and to old Thompson Lake, where the boys were fond of gathering. There he waded and swam and, like the other boys, occasionally shot bullfrogs and cottonmouths with a .22 rifle. He enjoyed listening to hunting stories told by older boys, and he often queried rural friends about the wildlife as they roamed the fields. Yet, he is remembered as one who did not ask too many questions, as town boys often did, and as one who took pleasure simply in strolling through the woods and observing things. His most distinctive personal trait at the time was an unusual pensiveness.

Of these years during which William was reading widely, his mother remarked that he possessed "an excellent memory for unusual and accurate words."[13] He was already using some of them in his adolescent poetry. "At the age of sixteen," Faulkner later wrote, "I discovered Swinburne":

Or rather, Swinburne discovered me, springing from some tortured undergrowth of my adolescence, like a highwayman, making me his slave. My mental life at that period was so completely and smoothly veneered with surface insincerity—obviously necessary to me at the time, to support intact my personal integrity—that I can not tell to this day exactly to what depth he stirred me, just how deeply the footprints of his passage are left in my mind. It seems to me now that I found him nothing but a flexible vessel into which I might put my own vague emotional shapes without breaking them. It was years later that I found him much more than bright and bitter sound, more than a satisfying tinsel of blood and death and gold and the inevitable sea.[14]

At this age he also "dipped into Shelley and Keats," but he was not moved by them because of "complacence and a youthful morbidity, which counteracted them and left me cold."

It was at this time, too, that he became a close friend of Phil Stone, the one person who was to have the most constructive influence upon his career as a writer. The Falkner and Stone families had been acquainted for many years, but William was four years younger than Phil, and the two as children had not been the close friends that they were to become after adolescence. Then in 1914, when Faulkner was seventeen years old, Stone—a graduate of Yale and at this time a law student at Ole Miss—went to the Falkner house one Sunday afternoon and read the boy's poems. Stone recalled that he was surprised and elated with the discovery he made that day: "Anyone could see that he had talent. It was as clear as that window there." Prior to their friendship, most of Faulkner's reading matter had come from the Young Colonel's library, whose "taste was for simple straightforward romantic excitement like Scott or Dumas. . . ." In addition, Faulkner later wrote, there was a "scattering of other volumes," including one by Henryk Sienkiewicz which made a deep impression upon him with the author's prefatory remark that the book had been written "to uplift men's hearts."[15] Even though the boy had read with little selectivity and seriousness of purpose, he was later to advise other young people that the best way to learn to write was to do the same:

Read, read, read! Read everything—trash, classics, good and bad; see how they do it. When a carpenter learns his trade, he does so by observing. Read! You'll absorb it. Write. If it is good you'll find out. If it's not, throw it out the window.[16]

Phil Stone lent young Faulkner many of his own books, some of them by Russian writers (Chekhov, Dostoevsky, Gogol); nineteenth-century French writers (especially Balzac); and, later, the French Symbolists (Mallarmé, Verlaine); the new American writers (Aiken, Anderson, Frost, Amy Lowell, Masters, Millay, Sandburg), and some works of the *avant-garde* (Eliot, Joyce, Pound). Faulkner's primary interests, however, were poetic rather than fictional. It was during these early years that some of the poems which later emerged in *The Marble Faun* (1924) and *A Green Bough* (1933) were first composed. In answer to a question concerning the period of development during which he wrote the latter book, Faulkner said:

That [*A Green Bough*] was written at the time when you write poetry, which is seventeen, eighteen, nineteen—when you write poetry just for the pleasure of writing poetry, and you don't think of printing it until later. (*University*, p. 4)

Taken at face value, this statement indicates that Faulkner was writing a good portion of his poetry between the years 1914-1917. But his declarations on the subject were inconsistent; in 1947, he said that the best age for writing poetry is from seventeen to twenty-six, explaining, "Poetry writing is more like a skyrocket with all your fire condensed into one rocket."[17] The date of publication for *A Green Bough*, 1933, is obviously misleading, for by early 1925 Faulkner had already prepared the basic volume under the title of *The Greening Bough*.[18] One could, then, logically assign the dates 1914-1925 as those during which he conceived and wrote most of his poetry, and that after early 1925 most of his verse consisted of revisions of old, rather than composition of new, poems.

During this early period and on through World War I, Faulkner was reading Hart Crane, Cummings, Housman, and Rossetti. As form the folk song and ballad were evident. The list can be expanded to include also Shakespeare, the Romantics (especially Keats and Shelley), the standard classics (Defoe, Dickens, Fielding, Thackeray), and the whole school of naturalists in America commencing with Norris and Dreiser. A further treatment of some of these influences, along with others, will be made as they relate to Faulkner's early literary production.[19]

Reading and writing poetry were not the only avenues which his self-expression sought. After he had left the tenth grade, he tried to do some painting also. Neither his mother, his Grandmother Murry, nor his brother John—had he been old enough at the time—would have been surprised, for the spatial arts were virtually a Falkner family trait. Drawings by Faulkner were good enough to appear in the yearbook of the University of Mississippi, *Ole Miss,* before his Royal Air Force training in Canada in 1917. As late as 1958 Faulkner stated that he painted, but

Not seriously. Occasionally when something comes to hand when they are painting barns and stables and things and I'll get a smooth piece of plank and knife or something to smear with and paint mules and people ploughing, things like that but never serious. Dogs in the woods, that sort of thing, horses. (*University,* p. 271)

With his strong literary inclinations and periods of taciturnity and moodiness, Faulkner the boy may appear delicate and physically inactive, but such an impression is erroneous. Perhaps too many critics, in writing of these years, for which reliable information is all too sketchy, tend to ignore such aspects of boyhood as his interest in sports, which he never lost even as an adult. When he was still a boy, he went on hunting trips to Colonel Stone's camp, where he stalked game with veteran hunters. The most venerable of these men, Uncle Bud Miller, remembered young William's killing a deer when the boy was only fifteen or sixteen years old. Another of Faulkner's hunting companions, John Cullen, has observed that many of the writer's stories are based on events of these days, although Faulkner wrote about many incidents which he never saw.

Faulkner's *The Bear* deals with the initiation of a teenage boy to the ritual of the hunt, beginning with the killing of his first buck and old Sam Father's marking of his face with the hot blood of the kill;[20] the hunt itself culminates with the heroic actions of Lion, the extraordinary mongrel dog, and the primitive Boon Hogganbeck in slaying Old Ben, the bear. Much of this story, as well as others, came from Faulkner's experiences in the camp of Colonel Stone, Phil Stone's father, who suggests the character Major de Spain. Of course, Faulkner amplified his own experiences and supplemented them with those of other hunters. He was once asked by a student if there was a dog, "a real Lion," and gave this reply:

Yes, there was. I can remember that dog—I was about the age of that little boy [Isaac McCaslin]—and he belonged to our pack of bear and deer dogs, and he was a complete individualist. He didn't love anybody. The other dogs were all afraid of him, he was a savage, but he did love to run the bear. Yes, I remember him quite well. He was mostly airedale, he had some hound and Lord only knows what else might have been in him. He was a tremendous big brute—stood about that high, must have weighed seventy-five or eighty pounds.

Faulkner then went on to explain that the dog did not, however, perform any

heroic action like the one in the story, not really. *There's a case of the sorry, shabby world that don't quite please you, so you create one of your own, so you make Lion a little braver than he was. . . . (University,* p. 59, italics added)

The great Lion, however, reminds John Cullen of another real dog which was observed on Stoval Bayou hunting all alone, a singular dog:

He must have stood thirty inches tall. He was of mixed breed and had the biggest, deepest chest I ever saw on a dog, tapering to the back like a prize English bulldog's, but he had the long nose and long ears and voice of a great hound. I hated to leave that dog out there alone baying that bear, but even more I hated to spend the night in the thicket. (p. 37)

Faulkner remembered the dog in one way, Cullen in another. Yet, the two views and the legendary nature of both animals are similar enough to suggest that only one such dog was the inspiration and that each man perhaps remembered the animal with different characteristics. Faulkner's motivations for his particular exaggerations are, of course, obvious enough, for he was, as he stated, trying to create a better world than his own "sorry, shabby" one by making Lion "a little braver than he was." The inconsistencies are explained then, in part at least, by his purpose.

One finds in dealing with Faulkner and his work that such clashes of apparent "facts" are not infrequent. In answer to the question about whether or not he had ever seen such an auction as that in "Spotted Horses" actually taking place, he replied,

Yes'm. *I bought one of these horses once.* They appeared in our country, every summer somebody would come in with another batch of them. They were Western range-bred ponies, pintos—had never had a bridle on them, had never seen shelled corn before, and they'd be brought into our town and auctioned off for prices from three or four dollars up to six or seven. And I bought this one for $4.75. I was, oh I reckon, ten years old. My father at the time, ran a livery stable, and there was a big man, he was six feet and a half tall, he weighed two hundred pounds, but mentally he was about ten years old, too. And I wanted one of those horses and my father said, Well, if you and Buster can buy one for what money you've saved, you can have it. And so we went to the auction and we bought one for $4.75. We got it home, we were going to gentle it, we had a two-wheeled cart made out of the front axle of a buggy, with shafts on it, and we fooled with that critter—*it was a wild animal, it was a wild beast, it wasn't a domestic animal at all.* And finally Buster said that it was about ready, so we had the cart in a shed—Estelle probably remembers this—we put a croker-sack over the horse's head and backed it into the cart with two Negroes to fasten it in, to buckle traces and toggles and things, and me and Buster got in the seat and Buster said, All right boys, let him go, and they snatched the sack off the horse's head. He went across the lot—there was a big gate, the lane, it turned it at a sharp angle—it hung the inside wheel on the gate-post as it turned, we were down on one hub then, and about that time Buster caught me by the back of the neck and threw me just like that and then he jumped out. And the cart was scattered up that lane, and we found the horse a mile away, run into a dead-end street. All he had left on him was just the hames—the harness gone. But that was a pleasant experience. But we kept that horse and gentled him to where I finally rode him. But I loved that horse because that was my own horse. I bought that with my own money.[21] (Italics added.)

Yet, John Cullen, who also observed Oxford during the same period that Faulkner recalled, relates the fictional episode to fact in these words:

He tells many stories just as they happen up to a certain point, then uses his imagination to change events and make them suit his purposes. *"Spotted Horses," for example, is mostly imagination.* When we were boys, however, a man from Texas did ship in a carload of mustangs and sell them in a lot near the old Jeff Cook boarding-house, which still stands. *So far as I know none of them got away or created any excitement.* (p. 62, italics added)

A third possible inconsistency is revealed in Faulkner's statement that the character Boon Hogganbeck was drawn from a man who worked for his father. Cullen claims that he never knew such a hunter, even though "I have known Faulkner's father and men who worked for him." Continuing, he gives this firsthand account of another possible source for the character:

An old fellow a little like Boon lived in the bottom, a great big bear-looking type of man, but he was not tall. He had eyes like a wild animal, and he let his hair grow all over his face. He went bare-footed, walking around among the rattlesnakes in the bottoms. We never killed anything but he was there to claim part of it. He was just a buzzard after the kill. He had little shoe-button eyes like Boon's and a great red beard. The bottom was a hide-out, a wild hide-out.[22]

In the first of the three previous illustrations of how Faulkner used the active experiences of his teens, an individualistic dog is made strikingly noble and heroic. In the second, an animal—possibly the same spotted pony that Cullen remembers young Billy and the other Falkner children playing with on South Street—becomes a wild, spotted beast, generating others of its kind that become epical. In the third, a human scavenger is changed into an elemental hunter, symbolical of primitivism and worthy of tribute.

Of course, Faulkner was writing fiction, and like any other writer, although he could use reality, he was not necessarily tied to it. But the high degrees of exaggeration suggest also the emotional necessity of the creator to seek a better world than the *"sorry, shabby"* one in which he had lived. Indeed, for Faulkner the boy the hunt was "a symbol of pursuit" of something finer than the life about him. It was not acquiescence, but rather movement, action:

. . . *the only alternative to life is immobility, which is death*. . . . I was simply telling something which was in this case the child—*the need, the compulsion of the child to adjust to the adult world.* (*University,* p. 271, italics added)

Beneath the obvious meaning of such comments, one can see reflections of Faulkner's attitudes toward his life as a boy. By further examining the reality of *"the adult world"* which surrounded him at that time, one can better understand why, as a child—when "I was about the age of that little boy" [Isaac McCaslin]—Faulkner felt the need and compulsion for gathering such experiences, remembering them, then later exaggerating them to make them heroic and grand, something like the Indian and fairy tales that got him out of doing dull chores and which once had made his Cousin Sally say, "You never knew if it was the truth or just something he'd made up." Faulkner later stated a basic reason for the renaissance in Southern writing with these words:

I myself am inclined to think it was because of the bareness of the Southerner's life, that he had to resort to his own imagination, to create his own Carcassonne. (*University,* p. 136)

What was the reality of that adult world which provided such an overwhelming motivation for creative aspirations? When as a boy Faulkner walked through the courthouse square, there were no American flags of a new industrialized nation, a country supposedly unified after the legendary battles of Americans against Americans. Those battles themselves, storied into glory, were yet part and parcel of the isolated Southern life. Before the first World War, Oxford's one American flag on the Federal building was looked upon as a kind of intrusive flaunting of an annoying present, less real than the living past. To vivify that past there were the old men who sometimes spoke of the battles, the maiden spinster aunts who "had never surrendered"; and on Memorial Day there was the heroic shabbiness of the gray uniforms and old battle flags.

For Billy Falkner specifically, the Old Colonel had become a formidable ghost. The epical facts of his life had been foreshortened by memory's glorification, and all that remained of that glory were such visible tokens as his decaying property in Ripley, the railroad—for a time controlled by the Old Colonel's son before it was lost—and the life-sized statue above a pillared pedestal, a monument that Colonel Falkner had posed for in Italy while on his European tour in 1883. The shaft of stone symbolized not only the looming sense of the past, but also a paling significance of the present. The boy grew up seeing the old man's work crumble. William's own father, the eldest child and most obvious heir of the family fortune, became a mere conductor and station agent on the line the Falkners had owned until 1902. By the time William was in his late teens, his great-grandfather's "dream" had been absorbed by the Gulf, Mobile and Northern. The adolescent boy was doubtless aware that his father had gone from business to business, drifting ever farther from the old grandeur. Even his distinguished grandfather had lost control of his bank to the clever financier from the back-country, Joe Parks. As venerable a figure as the Young Colonel was, he was only a dim outline of the Old Colonel. Phil Stone indicated to me that Faulkner's attitude toward Murry Falkner was respectful but unfamiliar, that he thought his father was dull and had once remarked, "Dad's square."

In the days of Jacksonian democracy, the Old Colonel had encountered a frontier, made a fortune, and fought bravely in two wars; but now there were no frontiers to conquer, no fortunes to be made in a land without promise, and no wars in which to find one's glory or destiny—at least, not yet, although there were rumblings over the Atlantic. At home the old plantation life was a fading mockery. The day of the great planter was gone. The land was eroding, and the Negroes, although they had been "freed" by the North, were as enslaved as ever to an economic overlord who was as nameless as he was niggardly, and who scarcely discriminated between white and black. Thus, for young Faulkner the South must have appeared as a kind of wasteland. The impression of dire economic and social conditions was further aggravated by the contrast with the past. The unscrupulous were rising; the principled falling. What new commercial activity there was seemed as destructive as it was helpful, the timber companies being a good example of this kind of "progress." They were ravaging the earth, depleting the old hunting grounds, and scarring the land. What was the difference between the old immoral system of slavery and the new amoral greed? To Faulkner the new must have appeared no better than the old—worse, if anything, for it was doing little to better the plight of the poor whites and Negroes. And it was inimical to the land's primitive beauty and destructive to the sustaining myth of the past.

Yet, the boy knew that his roots were in this land, and his loyalty, by turns fierce and bewildered, was still to the region, even though there was little logical promise to the future. Although he was not conscious of it, his mooring cables of identity had been cut, and he was adrift somewhere between the ports of the unattainable past and the unacceptable present. Before the dilemma was recognized—before it found externalization in rebellion and outrage—the boy evidently sought vaguely to identify with the past, in childhood games, romantic books, the substance of daydreams, and the ideals which he probably attributed to his great-grandfather. Then he began to write poems, first gathering his thoughts in the glossy film of nineteenth-century Romantic imitation. He later quite frankly admitted in his essay "Verse Old and Nascent" that he first wrote poetry "for the purpose of furthering various philanderings in which I was engaged," and second, "to complete a youthful gesture I was then making, of being 'different' in a small town." At this time poetry was not so much an unconscious attempt to discover himself and his problems, but rather escapism itself. At other times when his puzzlement had become too confining, he turned to the outlet of sports or sought release in hunting with the men of Colonel Stone's camp. Between these extremes of reaction, he went on long walks, sometimes to Thompson Lake, and sometimes to a hillside outside Oxford from where he watched the flights of birds. His childhood adventure with homemade wings had done little to discourage his interest in flying. By 1916, he had seen an "aeroplane" and his mind was enchanted with the names of heroic aviators: Ball, Immelmann, Boelcke, Guynemer, and Bishop. One of Faulkner's poems entitled "Boy and Eagle" lyrically recapitulates his mood at the time:

> Once upon an adolescent hill
> There lay a lad who watched amid the piled
> And silver shapes of aircarved cumulae
> A lone uncleaving eagle, and the still
> Serenely blue dissolving of desire.
>
> Easeful valleys of the earth had been:
>   he looked not back,
> Not down, he had not seen
> Lush lanes of vernal peace, and green
>
> Unebbing windless tides of trees; no wheeling gold
> Upon the lamplit wall where is no speed
> Save that which peaceful tongue 'twixt bed and supper wrought.
>
> Here still the blue, the headlands; here still he
> Who did not waken and was not awaked.
> The eagle sped its lonely course and tall;
> Was gone. Yet still upon his lonely hill the lad
> Winged on past changing headlands where was laked
> The constant blue

And saw the fleeing canyons of the sky
Tilt to banshee wire and slanted aileron,
And his own lonely shape on scudding walls
Where harp the ceaseless thunders of the sun.[23]

The vision of glory was upon him, and he was dreaming of becoming a beribboned hero in a remote war for which he could only yearn and wait.

III

Maecenas and Mars: Portrait in Marble

Both the famous Colonel Falkner and Phil Stone's grandfather, Major Philip Alston Stone, had served together in the Civil War and fought under General Nathan Bedford Forrest. The two families knew each other in the years that followed, so there was a wealth of background which young Billy Falkner and Phil Stone had in common. As they grew into manhood, they took walks together about Oxford and the surrounding countryside. Often they strolled westward on University Avenue, took their way around University Circle and the campus, and went northeastward through the woods along a ditch leading to the ancestral home of the Stones on College Hill Road. For a special treat, when freshly ground flour was available, the two young friends would take a pan full across the way to a neighbor, have a loaf baked, and return over a brick walk to sit upon the steps of a western sideporch and eat the hot bread. Sometimes they retired to Stone's upstairs room in the rear of the house where they discussed literature and perused Phil's library, particularly the first editions of the newly emerging American writers Stone collected. "If I thought the writer had *real* promise," Stone said, "I would sometimes get *two* first editions."[1]

By 1914, when Faulkner was seventeen, Stone had already completed a degree at Yale and was studying law at the University of Mississippi. His educational experiences, his additional four years of age, along with his natural precocity and literary interests, made him the teacher and Faulkner the student. In the summer of 1962 in his brick bungalow office on Jackson Avenue, Stone leaned back in his swivel chair and told me of these days. He spoke of having taught Faulkner grammar orally and demonstrated an example: "Listen to this sentence now. When you come to the pause, you put in a mark like this—" indicating a comma on his desk with an index finger. Stone laughed, then added quickly, "But he could use words fine. Anyone could see that he had talent."

They discussed the heydays of the past, the decline of the old way of life, and the rise of the new. Stone was more interested in the Civil War from a historical point of view, while Faulkner seemed satisfied to listen to local legends— heroic anecdotes, "smart-cracks," and tall tales. By blending his own ideas with Stone's, he apparently, without being conscious of it at the time, collected a mass of material from which many of his later stories and novels emerged. Specifically, the Sartoris episodes, and most certainly the Snopes materials, developed from the talks with Stone over these and following years. It was with an obvious sense of gratitude that Faulkner dedicated the Snopes trilogy to Stone: the dedicatory passages of *The Hamlet* and *The Mansion* read, "To Phil Stone"; *The Town* reads, "To Phil Stone/He *did half the laughing for thirty years*." Faulkner also gave a manuscript copy of *The Hamlet* to Stone's son, inscribed, "To My Godson, Philip Alston Stone/May he be faithful/fortunate, and brave/William Faulkner/Xmas 1945/Oxford, Miss[.]" Stone and Faulkner worked out between them in the form of tall tales many of the incidents which were to be chronicled in the Snopes trilogy. Stone told me that he had invented several of the characters himself, including Wall Street Panic and Montgomery Ward Snopes, and that the stories had begun as long ago as World

War I and had continued throughout the years, as recently as just before *The Reivers.*

Another fellow townsman of Stone, William McNeil ("Mack") Reed, remembers the closeness of Stone and Faulkner's friendship during these early years, first when he was a student himself at Ole Miss. "Bill Faulkner and Phil Stone were constantly together." A native of Houlka, Mississippi, in Chickasaw County, Mr. Reed moved to Oxford in 1923, where he went into partnership with a Dr. Gathright to form the Gathright-Reed Drug Store. "In their spare hours Bill Faulkner and Phil Stone roamed all over this countryside together." Reed spoke of Faulkner's deep affection for children and how, on one particular occasion as a boy, he spent many hours with a little girl who was "afflicted," drawing pictures and leaving them with her, telling her fairy tales and reading her his rhymes.[2] Of the days before World War I, Phil Stone remembered something of Faulkner's poetic fancifulness: "We were 'hep' on trees. One spring day we were out in the country about four miles from town, and the woods were just alive with dogwood—white, brilliant! I said something to Bill about the trees looking like girls, and he nodded and thought for a minute and said: 'If I were God, in the springtime every blonde girl would have an applegreen dress.' "

By 1918 Stone had returned to New Haven for a second law degree, a move consistent with his father's wish for him to gain the advantage of both a Southern and Northern education. In the meanwhile, Faulkner had failed to get into the Army Air Corps because he was too short and underweight. Stone feared that his friend might become romantically involved at home and felt that if he got married so soon "it would be the end of Bill as a writer." He opportunely learned that the Royal Air Force was in need of cadets and that Faulkner could probably meet the physical standards. Thus, he urged his friend to come to New Haven. From March through May of 1918, Faulkner shared Stone's quarters and was employed at the Winchester arms factory. A mutual friend attempted to teach them both to speak with a British accent, but they had difficulty, in Stone's words, "rolling our 'r's.' " These lessons turned out to be a lark for the young men, especially for Stone, who never joined the RAF. Faulkner was eventually accepted without having to resort to the ruse of pretending British citizenship.

One should first point out that no official war record of William Faulkner was ever released by him, nor has it been made public by any member of his family since his death. It is not surprising, therefore, that much inaccurate, contradictory information has been written about Faulkner's service record. The early reports vary in extravagant hues: he joined the Canadian Flying Corps and saw action overseas. He shot down several enemy planes, had several hairbreadth escapes from death, had two aircraft shot down under him, and was seriously wounded. Gradually, the dark places were illuminated, and critics disenthralled themselves from the Faulkner war legend.

But almost as interesting as the legendary "facts" themselves was Faulkner's own strange attitude toward his service experience. He lent credence to the extravagent statements. Laurence Stallings, in a talk to the Fullerton Junior College Literary Club, spoke blandly of the legend in these words:

He [Faulkner] sat down once and told me the damnedest story. All about how he'd been in the Canadian Air Force, and was flying in France, and crashed and got wounded—all in great detail . . . . Later on I found out he *hadn't ever* been overseas during the war, and the only time he ever was "wounded" was when he soloed up in Canada toward the end of the war. Now why did he want to sit down there and bother about telling me that damned lie?[3]

Faulkner often proved evasive when questioned on the subject. In answer to the question, "What effect did the RCAF have on you?" he replied,

I still like to believe I was tough enough that it didn't hurt me too much. It didn't help much. I hope I have lived down the harm it did me . . . . All we did was pray the plane didn't burn up. We didn't have parachutes. Not much choice. World War II must have been tougher.

But where Faulkner evaded or only suggested, others filled

in the appropriately colorful if inaccurate details; thus, the quotation above is followed by either the author's or an editor's resourceful note: "Mr. Faulkner had both legs broken in a plane crash in World War I."[4]

Whatever his training experiences in Canada in the fall of 1918, both he and Stone were back in Oxford by Christmas Eve. Concerning Faulkner's commission and "war wound," Stone said,

There was some talk about a silver plate in his head, but I never believed it. I was with him on the twenty-fourth of December when he got his pips in the mail. The reason I remember is that it was Christmas Eve. As far as I could see he wasn't injured at all.

If Faulkner was indeed injured in an Armistice Day crash, within six weeks he had recovered sufficiently that his best friend did not notice any injury at all. Moreover, Faulkner did not talk about it with Stone. One might summarize Faulkner's war experiences as definitely "stateside." He may or may not have been involved in a crash of some sort while in flight training in Canada. If he was hurt, it was an injury of a minor sort. One should be skeptical about the whole matter until the Faulkner family is willing to release his war record or to offer other evidence to clarify the confusion over this aspect of his life.[5]

The discrepancies between what Faulkner would have had others believe about his martial exploits, and the substance of the inaccurate reports themselves, reveal interesting personal attitudes during the period of World War I and its aftermath. Stallings' question, "Now why did he want to sit down there and bother about telling me that damned lie?" has in one form or another passed the minds of all Faulkner biographers.

One obvious answer which comes to mind reiterates this question: What is one to expect from a man about whom, even as a boy, his Cousin Sally Wilkins had commented, "It got so that when Billy told you something, you never knew if it was the truth or just something he'd made up"? In any statement of "fact," Faulkner's habit of mind as a creative artist must, of course, be considered. For him fact and fiction were always quick to mingle and often, apparently, too fascinating to separate. But were we to accept the war stories as mere colorful exaggerations, the question of motivation still prevails.

Not having seen action was doubtless a deep disappointment to Faulkner, for he had longed to achieve that glory in war that only youth can envision, and to find in that glory an individual significance which would link him to the legendary past. Faulkner expressed his own enchantment with the names of aerial heroes: of Albert Ball, who had shot down thirty-eight enemy planes by May, 1916; of Max Immelmann, the German pilot who had developed the famous maneuver known as the "Immelmann turn"; of Oswald Boelcke, the German pilot credited with forty victories; of Georges Guynemer, who was the leading French airman; and of William Avery Bishop, the young Canadian credited with shooting down seventy-two enemy aircraft. He had very likely read Bishop's colorful article, "Tales of the British Air Service," published in *National Geographic* in January, 1918, just six months before Faulkner enlisted in the Royal Canadian Flying Corps. He had watched the flights of birds from a hillside outside Oxford and dreamed of being decorated for valor.

Such a consummation would have impressed even the Old Colonel, the Falkner *paterfamilias*. More than that, it would have brought present-day distinction to the life of a Southern boy who had previously been able to find real meaning only in the past. The force of past, then—Southern tradition, especially of the extravagant Falkner variety—should never be underestimated in attempting to understand Faulkner's motivations and attitudes.

Anyone who has walked the streets of Oxford in the day, encompassed by its ancient homes, and at night picked his way over the weather-warped sidewalks, pondering the town's history, cannot but sense the weight of the past—indeed, almost feel its palpable presence. It is one indication of the force of past that even an outlander can sense. Faulkner, in his own words, "was saturated" with it—the places, stories, characters, and values of the old era. It was not only impossible, but must have been frustrating for him to identify with the glories of the past, especially those of his great-grandfather, of whom he was the namesake. As a boy he had tried to live in a normal relationship with other children in Oxford. Later, he had attempted to escape what might be termed "the obligation of past," but everything the sensitive boy saw—the courthouse and its Confederate monument, the venerable streets with old mnemonic houses, and the ritualistic hunts— were as so many arrows pointing backward in time. His escape was cut off, for in his blood ran

the blood of those who came before him. In his thoughts, his emotions, the very gestures of his body, whether he will or no, moves millions of unconscious reflections of the land which gave him birth. . . .[6]

If he could not escape his past then, perhaps he could compete with or recapture it in another form, possibly exceed it with a brand of derring-do all his own. He must have felt that the fortune of the Falkners had come full circle. The descendants of the Old Colonel seemed to be as so many ever-dimming copies. Faulkner's general attitude toward his father can be seen in the remark he once made to Phil Stone, "Dad's square." Now the focus of family leadership was upon him, the eldest son, the eponymous William Cuthbert Falkner. The obligation to past must have seemed keener than ever. If a Falkner were to recapture the grandeur of the Old Colonel's exploits, then the time had come. During his flight training in Canada the opportunity began to emerge, and he was ready to take the next step to heroism. Then, just as hope was highest, the Armistice came and the opportunity was never fulfilled.

To answer the "Why?" of Stallings' exasperated question, then, Faulkner simply improvised the romantic exploits which circumstances had denied him. He had probably felt cheated by fate. Imagination was his resource, and it supplied the vacuum of reality with the martial heroics about which he had dreamed so long and fervently. The almost desperate psychological need for this kind of recognition combined with imagination and circumstance to foist upon the public a tangled mass of part truths and inventions.

Faulkner's attitude toward his military experience in these early years seems to have been by turns moody, melodramatic, and fanciful. John Cullen reported an incident told to his friend, Walton Miller, known as "Uncle Bud," of Faulkner's return from the war. He changed trains at Holly Springs, twenty miles north of Oxford, and was

standing as still as a statue in the railroad depot. The engineer came by and stopped and looked at him. William was just standing there flat-footed, paying no attention to anybody or anything. He was thinking about something else besides his surroundings. After a while he moved a little, and the engineer remarked, "Damned if it ain't alive." When William heard that remark, he pretended he had not. He never said a word to the engineer, and the engineer never said a word to him. (p. 10)

Most imaginative extensions of his flight training that found their way into literary form are well known. The horribly scarred Donald Mahon of *Soldiers' Pay* (1926) returns with disillusioned friends to his hometown in the South. He is so badly wounded that he is hardly conscious of the weakening life in his body, and he dies remembering "the one trophy he had reft from Time and Space," firing the machine guns of his plane "into the bland morning marbled and imminent with March." In *Sartoris,* young Bayard, cursed with the memory of his brother's bailing out during a dogfight with the Germans, returns home to drive his car wildly over the Mississippi countryside. He meets an inevitable doom when he buckles the wings of an experimental plane. "All the Dead Pilots" (1931) and "Turnabout" (1932) are related pieces. "Landing in Luck," a less-known story printed in the campus newspaper on November 26, 1919,[7] about one year after Faulkner's training had ended in Canada, deals with the hero's nearly disastrous first solo. Cadet Thompson, risking his instructor's reputation, takes off. Without realizing it, he breaks his landing gear on a cable. When he begins to land he is warned off by people on the field "running and flapping their arms," and "another machine" rises to meet him, the pilot carrying a wheel in his hand with which he gestures. The British officers wait breathlessly." 'E's abaht out of petrol and . . . 'e'll be a coming down soon, sir," the C. O. is informed. Cadet Thompson begins to land, "watching the remorseless earth." His fate is "on the laps of the Gods," but he is also blind with fear. The plane hits on its tail: the plane "slewed around and stood on its nose." Later, Thompson brags to his fellow cadets, "tapping a boot with his stick," and is jeeringly told, "He's the 'f' out of flying." But Thompson has the last laugh as he goes through the room with his instructor ("his arm was through the officer's"), and gives his companions "a cheerfully condescending: 'Hello, you chaps.' " Although there are redeeming features of realism, as, for example, the cadet's actual fear in landing, the story strikes one as outrageously Quixotic.

During the winter of 1918-1919, both Stone and Faulkner were reading Balzac. Faulkner lived at his parents' home and wrote poetry at a rapid rate. After his father was appointed business manager of the University of Mississippi, the family occupied a campus home which originally stood on the present site of the Alumni House. By this time Faulkner and Stone were entering into a kind of literary partnership, which was to last through the publication of *Sanctuary* (1931). Faulkner wrote poems and, later on, short stories and novels which were edited by Stone, typed by his secretary, and sent off to publishers. It is not generally known that Stone also read proofs and made corrections on the galley sheets. Their first success was realized with the publication of Faulkner's poem "L'Apres-midi d'un Faune" [*sic*] in the *New Republic,* August 6, 1919. Although Stone subsidized Faulkner's early literary career, he consistently refused to take credit for it, saying, "It was a partnership. The idea was to use whatever money was realized from the sale of Bill's literature to keep things moving."[8] In the meanwhile, Faulkner helped support himself by working at odd jobs, among them carpentry, house painting, and sign painting.

Faulkner's first book, *The Marble Faun,* bears the dates of composition "April, May, June, 1919," although the volume was not published until 1924.[9] The book numbers 51 pages of 7½-x-5-inch size, contains a three-page preface by Phil Stone, a title page, and 19 poems including a Prologue and Epilogue. Stone's preface begins with the statement, "These are primarily the poems of youth and a simple heart." He mentions his friend's love of nature, a love "without evasion or self-consciousness." The book has "the defects of youth . . . impatience, unsophistication and immaturity," but "it shows promise," and the poems have "a hint of coming muscularity of wrist and eye." Stone refers to "one of our long walks through the hills" and concludes with an amusing anecdote indicating Faulkner's awareness of the fact that good writing is always competitive:

I remarked that I thought the main trouble with Amy Lowell and her gang of drum-beaters was their eternal damned self-consciousness, that they always had one eye on the ball and the other eye on the grandstand. To which the author of these poems replied that his personal trouble as a poet seemed to be that he had one eye on the ball and the other eye on Babe Ruth. (p. 8)

Because of the formative importance of *The Marble Faun* —the light which the language, imagery, and literal and symbolic content cast upon Faulkner's subsequent production —there seems to be some value in a condensed paraphrase of the nineteen poems and a sampling of their lines. The Prologue begins with a personification. Poplar trees move through a "gray old garden . . ./Like slender girls with nodding heads" (p. 11), whispering above the flowers and "the daisies dreaming gold." The comparison is extended into the second stanza. Roses are "candled flames" and "the days dream by." A fountain "shakes down its glistered hair" to a pool which mirrors its "fair,/Flecked face" (pp. 11-12). The marble faun then begins his monologue:

> *Why am I sad? I?*
> *Why am I not content? The sky*
> *Warms me and yet I cannot break*
> *My marble bonds. (p. 12)*

He sighs "For things I know, yet cannot know," and senses the rich world of nature calling to him.

If he were free, the faun reflects in the second poem, he "would go/Where the first chill spring winds blow" (p. 13). In copses where "Pan's sharp hoofed feet have pressed" as he has called the beasts to the rites of spring, "Follow where I lead,/For all the world springs to my reed . . . ."

In the two scenes that follow, the faun observes Pan in another mood,

> *Beside a hushed pool where lean*
> *His own face and the bending sky*
> *In shivering soundless amity. (p. 16)*

Now the music is pensive, moving like "shattered quicksilver on/The willow curtain" and wandering "Into silent meadows . . ." (pp. 16-17). The faun is not moved with life as are the living things about him, for

> *. . . I am dumb*
> *With sun-soaked age and lack of strength*
> *Of things that have lived out the length*
> *Of life . . . (p. 18)*

With the fifth and sixth poems the poplars return "through a valley white with may [*sic*]" (p. 20). Beeches, lilacs, aspens, and birches move with life. The faun follows the steps of Pan and sees pastoral scenes. A blackbird "knocks/At noon across the dusty downs." The imagery which follows is striking in anticipation of the Faulkner to come:

> *Now the blackbirds' gold wired throats*
> *Spill their long cool mellow notes;*
> *In solemn flocks slowly wheeling*
> *. . . as on blue space*
> *They thread and cross like folds of lace*
> *Woven black; then shrilling go*
> *Like shutters swinging to and fro. (p. 21)*

Pan's song follows in six quatrains. Then, in a kind of catalepsy, the world is still, except for the blackbirds that are "burned scraps of paper cast/On a lake . . ." (p. 24).

Summer is the season of the seventh poem. The poplars "turning in the breeze,/Flash their facets to the sun,/Swaying in slow unison" (p. 25). Then "nymphs troop down the glade" and "slip into the pool—/Warm gold in silver liquid cool" (p. 26). The pastoral mood is intensified, and as night approaches the faun sleeps. The eighth poem extends the description of twilight. Momentarily the viewpoint seems to shift: now it is "we" who "watch night fall . . ." (p. 29). The faun speaks in first person singular again in the ninth poem. His mood is one of sadness. The reference to "we" is clarified by the appositive, "marbles in the glade," who

> *. . . know that all*
> *Things save us must fade and fall. . . . (p. 31)*

The scene of the tenth poem is night. The moon is likened to "a mad woman in the sky," and the cries of the nightingales are "like scattered silver sails/Spread across the azure sea" (p. 33). The stillness of the hour is continued through the eleventh poem. Pan is asleep, and now the music which envelops him is "of all passing years" (p. 35). The world, likened to a "muted violin," is played upon by a descending "hand that grasps the bow," and the looming figure bends over the violin of earth with "dry stricken eyes" (p. 36), sighing with the knowledge of mutability. The faun is infected with the despondent mood. His feelings grow more intense, for he has known the earth intimately: "Her all-wise pain-softened breast," and his heart is hungry and filled with "aching bliss unbearable."

The faun's tension, wrought by his knowledge of life and death and their endless cycle, is broken in the twelfth poem. The hand which has played upon the violin of earth vanishes "down the skies" (p. 37). The early morning breeze blows across the sea. Pan dilutes the song of the nightingale, "Philomel"; the nightbirds hush and the lyric ends in alliteration:

> *. . . sound and silence soundless keep*
> *Their slumbrous noon. Sweet be their sleep. (p. 38)*

The thirteenth poem is shot through with the vivid life of nature.

Autumn comes with the fourteenth lyric, firing the trees "to slow flame . . ." (p. 41). Now the poplars run "Burnished by the waning sun," the "sculptured fronds" of "the pines are bronze," and in the ravine "waiting winter sleeps" (p. 41). The autumnal theme is pursued in the fifteenth poem with scenes of harvest time. The faun stands again in arrested motion, saddened with the knowledge of the dying year.

Winter is introduced with the sixteenth poem. The world stands motionless, "white silence gathered round/It like a hood" (p. 44). Now the faun's garden is "stark and white," its hedge "Ice-bound and ghostly. . . ." The flakes of snow "slide past/Like teardrops on a sheet of glass. . . ." An icy pool mirrors the skies. The faun finds grace in his "enthrallèd impotence" (p. 45), as the snow continues to fall. The winter night of the next poem is then disturbed by dancers, the sight of "paper lanterns," and the sound of "brass horns horrible and loud" (p. 46). The winter season suggests the Italian festival of the Faunalia, held on December 5, although there are suggestions of a more typical *soirée dansante*. To the faun, at any rate, man's intrusion is like a debauchery of spring. The poplars are frightened, and the night "Lifts hidden hands" to invoke the "flying stars" (pp. 46-47). Even though his heart is marble, the faun mourns the vanished peace

> *Until the east bleeds in the dawn*
> *And the clean face of the day*
> *Drives them slinkingly away. (p. 47)*

The eighteenth poem commences on a philosophical note: at first the faun feels that he has somehow been deceived by Time. Bringing the work full circle, the theme of puzzlement is repeated as the faun yearns "For things I know, yet cannot know . . ." (p. 48). As an immortal, the faun realizes that all living things, unlike him, "do not know, nor care to know" the answers to his questions: "They sorrow not that they are dumb. . . ." Then, strangely, desire seems to blend with fulfillment. The faun seems to be miraculously freed from his bondage and is one with the life about him. His gift is "sleep" or death:

> And in the earth I shall sleep
> To never wake, to never weep
> For things I know, yet cannot know. (p. 49)

Like the Prologue, the Epilogue begins with a personification. May is a girl with long hair, dressed in "green and gold," but still—the juxtaposition indicates the returning tension—the faun's "marble heart is cold . . ." (p. 50). For the first time the word "people" is used in the poem: they

> . . . pass
> Across the close-clipped emerald grass
> To stare at me with stupid eyes.

Once again distant scenes of nature call to him, but he knows that he is forever "marble-bound." The tension builds as desire is contrasted with a torturing impossibility:

> My heart is full, yet sheds no tears
> To cool my burning carven eyes. (p. 51)

The poem concludes with the rhyme which began it, "go/snow" and "fro/go" respectively, indicating Faulkner's awareness of the importance of structural as well as thematic unity.

Other than reviews, only two significant articles on Faulkner's poetry have, at the time of this writing, appeared.[10] Harry Runyan termed the *Marble Faun* pieces "immature romanticism," emphasizing the poetry's derivative aspects.[11] George Garrett took issue with Runyan, calling attention to the huge task which young Faulkner had set for himself in attempting "a pastoral cycle" of poems in the twentieth century. He considered the poet's success limited but hardly insignificant. Faulkner intended to write a mythological poem placed in the context of the English eclogue and employing the seasons of the year and hours of the day to relate separate parts of the poem. There is, of course, no doubt as to the poem's mythological basis. Faulkner's faun is close enough to the Italian divinity, the god of the fields and shepherds, represented by the statue of the Faun of Praxiteles in Rome. The prophetic talent of the deity ("things I know, yet cannot know") and his correspondence to the Greek Pan identify him consistently with the god of the Italian myth. However, the references to "we" who "watch night fall," and the appositive "marbles in the glade" suggest several fauns, and form a relationship to the Greek satyrs, creatures characterized by pointed tips of ears and goats' feet. The cover illustration of the volume, which also relates to the Pan figure, complete with pipes, bears out more closely the plural concept of the faun rather than the stricter one of the Italian deity represented by the Faun of Praxiteles in Rome, the only animal feature of which is its pointed ears. It is possible that Faulkner either merged the two concepts or alluded to them without distinction.

There are 810 lines, although eight of these are only half-lines, basically of iambic meter and almost uniformly octosyllabic. The poems average nearly 43 lines each but vary individually from 24 in the fourteenth poem to 74 in the seventh. The stanzaic organization is also fluid, guided by content rather than consistency of form: the total 55 stanzas, averaging 3 stanzas for each poem, vary from 1 stanza in the fourteenth poem to 8 in the sixth, although 8 of the poems have 3 stanzas each, 7 have 2 stanzas, and only 3 have 4 or more stanzas. The most obvious variation in stanzaic pattern occurs in the sixth poem with the song of Pan, which includes 6 quatrains, but the basic pattern is 12 and 14 lines. Within conventional limitations the form is varied, and flexible enough to give way to function. Although Faulkner relied heavily on the use of end-stopped lines, masculine rhymes, and monosyllabic words, several lines are more complex, as for example these from the second stanza of the sixteenth poem:

In its endless quiescence
For my enthrallèd impotence. . . . (p. 45)

Caesuras are not infrequent, nor are feminine rhymes, as in

The dying day gives those who sorrow
A boon no king can give: a morrow. (p. 28)

and slant rhymes, as in

> *With quiet depth and solitude*
> *And licks the caverned sky. The wood* .... *(p. 37)*

Conventional form is everywhere operative, but it is seldom rigid to the point of becoming artificial. Inverted lines, obsolete phrasings, old-fashioned idioms and syntax seem to have been not only controlled, but also consciously employed by Faulkner to contribute to an atmosphere of antiquity.

The Romantics and French Symbolists are the primary influences at work in *The Marble Faun*. Stone in his Preface mentions that the volume bears "traces of other poets" (p. 7), and he later acknowledged that Faulkner was reading, among others, Keats, Shelley, the French Symbolists, and Shakespeare during this period. Finally, the third—and most general—type of influence may be termed Elizabethan.

Many of Faulkner's images reflect the pastoral mode of such poems as Gray's "Elegy Written in a Country Churchyard." Some examples follow: "silent meadows" (p. 17), "the quiet browsing flocks" and "dusty downs" (p. 20), "the shepherds with thier flocks" (p 22), "A sheep bell tinkles faint and far" (p. 27), "the mellow sun-shot downs" (p. 39), and "hunchèd grain in shock/On shock in solemn rows" (p. 42). Faulkner's poetic techniques already referred to are, of course, more characteristic of the Romantics than, say, the neo-classical poets. The octosyllabic couplet, though frequently employed by the Augustans, was also used by Shelley in such poems as "Lines Written among the Euganean Hills," "Lines Written in the Bay of Leirici," and "The Masque of Anarchy." Interestingly, Shelley's stanzaic forms in these poems are much more regular than Faulkner's. The exaltation of wild nature, the subjects of myth and past, supernaturalism, an emphasis upon inner or subjective thoughts, and the profusion of sensuous images—all Romantic traits—are broadly reflected in *The Marble Faun*; but some portions of the poem are more specifically derivative. The theme of approaching spring, particularly Pan's message of "Follow where I lead" in the second poem, suggests Shelley's motif of spring in *Prometheus Un-*

bound (II, ii), specifically the repetitious "Follow, follow!" as Asia and Panthea musically progress toward a more universal spring upon earth; and the two fauns in the next scene anticipate Faulkner's method. It is revealing also to compare the iambic tetrameter couplets and images of music and seasonal change in Shelley's "To a Lady, with a Guitar" with those of Faulkner's poem: the hints of consistency are strong in Shelley's "summer winds in sylvan cells," "falling rills," "birds and bees," and "airs of evening." Keats' "The Human Seasons" and "To Sleep" suggest similarities of subject matter; but a more specific consistency is found in "Ode to a Nightingale" with its use of dream scenes and lush descriptions of nature—grass, copses, flowers, fruit trees, the moon and the nightingale itself.[12]

The French Symbolist movement can be traced back to such poems as Verlaine's *Romances sans paroles* (1874) and Mallarmé's *L'Après-midi d'un faune* (1876). These writers employed highly experimental language, particularly the frequent use of such devices as synesthesia, or the mingling of the senses. They juxtaposed in countless subtle ways a wide range of associated ideas, thus communicating their emotions in new castings of verbiage. They attempted to blend musical devices with language in strange and different ways, and, most of all, they labored to impart faint nuances of emotion and imagination through a deliberate indirection which, nevertheless, retained an oblique suggestivity which communicated to the reader, however transiently, the mood of the creative artist. Thus, concepts were often "symbolized" in original and subtle ways.

Admittedly there are characteristics which English Romanticism and French Symbolism have in common. The Romantics were often obscure; they presented images not always related by logic. Their language was shadowy, unreal, and imaginatively fluid while French lyrical style was still epigrammatic and precise, but then the Symbolists in the late nineteenth century made a much more dramatic cleavage with the rationalistic French poetry which preceded them than ever could the English after Coleridge, Shelley, and Keats.[13]

It is clear that Faulkner by 1918 had already gone beyond English Romantic influences, was studying the work of the French Symbolists, and had come under their influence. We have Phil Stone's declaration that Faulkner was reading the French Symbolists, some in the original and some in translation, and that he had loaned Faulkner copies of poems by Mallarmé and Verlaine. The titular association between Faulkner's "L'Apres-midi d'un Faune" and Mallarmé's poem of the same name is obvious enough; and *The Marble Faun* may be approached as a broadening of the original nucleus of Mallarmé's masterpiece, linked to the English eclogue. Finally, we know that of the poems published in the university newspaper, *The Mississippian,* commencing in the fall of 1919 and continuing during the next two years, approximately one-fourth are translations from Paul Verlaine,[14] and Symbolist techniques are echoed in several others.

A perusal of the text of *The Marble Faun* reveals a number of Symbolist devices. The activities of the faun are presented in such a way that the imaginary and the real are mingled and, as it were, purposely confused. In the eighteenth poem, the faun has apparently ended his bondage and earned the mortal reward of sleep in the earth, "To never wake, to never weep . . ." (p. 49), so real has his dream of freedom and mortality become; but in the Epilogue we see, as does the dejected faun, that the irrationality of illusion had simply displaced reality. His fantasies have tricked him, and the faun is returned to his eternal bondage.

More specifically, the profuse synesthesia is illustrated by the following: "living silence" (p. 15); "pipes weave magic on the sky" (p. 15); "shivering soundless amity" (p. 16), "the blackbirds' . . . long cool mellow notes" (p. 21); "the air/Is shimmering still" (p. 22); "cries like scattered silver sails/Spread across the azure sea" (p. 33); "Mists as soft and thick as hair" (p. 34); "dawns burn/Eastwardly" (p. 35); "water shivers black/With quiet depth and solitude/And licks the caverned sky" (p. 47); and "Stars that flare and freeze and burn" (p. 48). Beyond these are various complex associations of ideas expressed in what Wilson terms "a medley of metaphors," such as these figures: "fierce cold mountain tops" (p. 13); swallows are "arrows painted on the sky" (p. 14); Pan's pipes blow

> *Of fiery days that go*
> *Like wine across the world; (p. 15)*

Pan sits "garment-clad/In sadness with dry stricken eyes" (p. 17); blackbirds "Are burned scraps of paper cast . . ." (p. 24); "meadows stretching over me/Are humming stars as thick as bees" (p. 27); "silken-breasted skies" (p. 30); "a brooding moon-wet hill" (p. 34); "thin sun sifting from the sky" (p. 40); "her dreaming knees" (p. 41); desire is a "cry moonward in stiff pain" (p. 42); winter is "white silence gathered round" the earth "like a hood" (p. 44); a festival is "reft of grace" (p. 46); "The poplars shake and sway with fright" (p. 46); and "peace" is "calm handed" (p. 47).

In an age of industrialization and naturalism, reflected in the poetry of Carl Sandburg,[15] Faulkner was shunning a mechanistic view of life and emphasizing sensations and emotions in his poem in the most extremely individualistic manner, which I shall attempt to elaborate upon when I treat the theme and interpretation of *The Marble Faun*. Throughout the poem, suggestion replaces explicit statement; in the Symbolist tradition, Faulkner was intimating things rather than stating them plainly. For example, in the second poem the faun notes that Pan's music is "Thrilling all the sky and ground," and by implication, one perceives, all living creatures, including man; and thus the reader responds through connotative associations. Although the pure joy of a spring day and the inevitable interplay between male and female are not stated as such, along with associations of shock and passion, they are fleetingly and vaguely suggested by the faun's dreamed actions:

> *. . . I plunge in some deep vale*
> *Where first violets, shy and pale,*
> *Appear, and spring with tear-stained cheeks*
> *Peeps at me from neighboring brakes*
> *Gathering her torn draperies up*
> *For flight if I cast my eyes up. (p. 14)*

Finally, the Elizabethan influences, not necessarily disparate from those of the Romantics, of course, are of a general rather than specific nature. The pastoral mode itself, for example, suggests the monthly and seasonal devices of Spenser's *The Shepheardes Calendar* with its twelve eclogues. An interesting detail of Spenser's work is its dedication to Philip Sidney written in the form of octosyllabic couplets, the traditional form which Faulkner used throughout *The Marble Faun.* Some suggestions of traditional and, more particularly, Shakespearean imagery occur in the poem. The fairy scenes in the wood near Athens in *A Midsummer-Night's Dream* form an interesting image relationship with Faulkner's poem, Oberon's speech serving as an example:

> *I know a bank where the wild thyme blows,*
> *Where oxlips and nodding violet grows,*
> *Quite over-canopied with luscious woodbine,*
> *With sweet musk-roses and with eglantine:*
> *There sleeps Titania sometime of the night,*
> *Lull'd in these flowers with dances and delight;*
> *And there the snake throws her enamell'd skin. . . . (II, ii)*

Faulkner's arboreal images are broadly similar. His boughs also "lean/A canopy" (p. 26). The poplar trees have "slender graceful feet/Like poised dancers" (p. 11). As the faun listens in the forest, he hears a sound and glides "nearer like a snake" (p. 16). However, the images of flowers and trees (*e.g.,* pp. 11, 14, 18, 20, 39, 41), the fantastic scenes in moonlight (p. 30), and the intricate blendings of the real and mythical suggest a general similarity of image and tone rather than of any striking literal parallels.

To recapitulate, Faulkner's close friendship and literary association with Phil Stone, the "imaginative" as well as the substantive nature of his World War I experiences, the developmental aspects of his first volume of poetry considered in the context of various influences and literary traditions, and his continuing esthetic development may give us a more accurate, whole view of the young man-artist.

Similarly, the themes of *The Marble Faun*—mutability, isolation, the memory of past, and the struggle to identity—are particularly meaningful when considered alongside Faulkner's life and offer possible insights into his attitudes and values at the time. Taken together with his life, the themes suggest what may have been going on in his mind during the post-war months of April, May, and June, 1919, when he first wrote the poems, although he doubtless revised the book before its publication on December 15, 1924, as the differences between an early typescript and the published volume indicate. Even so, his life, when viewed in context with the poetry, may clarify and illuminate Faulkner's work.

Within the faun's world of forest and mirroring pools is man's world of nature. The cycle of time is telescoped into the passage of seasons, spring to spring again. The faun, as distinguished from the people and other creatures in the poem, is immortal—aware of a death which touches all but him. Time for him, then, is an endless cycle. His knowledge of birth and death—the cycle of all life—makes him prophetically conscious of the life about him, a life which he can share in only imaginatively: he cannot really know the animality of life because his knowledge ("things I know, yet cannot know") isolates him from the contentment of a pastoral or natural existence (those who "do not know, nor care to know").

Below the surface of pastoral and myth, the faun's world to some extent is the poet's world. To recapitulate briefly, Faulkner had been thoroughly steeped with a knowledge of regional past, "saturated with it" in his own phrase; but more than that, he had developed an unusual sense of obligation to that past, particularly to his own ancestral past, the best of which was symbolized by the Old Colonel, who in turn was a kind of intense allegory of all Southern Quixotes. In one sense Faulkner's war experience may have been one young man's desire for adventure—or again, regional escape—but I have tried to point out that it was also an attempt by young Faulkner to identify with the Old Colonel and his soldierly fame. When Faulkner's efforts were aborted, as we have seen, he simply lent credence to and, in some situations, improvised the martial heroics for which he had longed. Only by this fanciful means could he find a kinship with the past—the hope of measuring up to his sense of ancestral obligation.

His disappointment at not having been able to discover the Old South in the new war, or the Old Colonel in himself, seems to have been deepened by some new discoveries. The mirror images throughout *The Marble Faun* echo the poet's own introspection, and the faun's frequent sadness his own dejection. Faulkner appears to have been examining himself and finding that he was as different from his fellow townsmen as the faun from the living creatures that surrounded it. Faulkner was "saturated with" the past just as the faun was "sun steeped" with the memory of all things. For his people, it was as if the ante-bellum South, the Civil War, and even the Reconstruction had been forgotten; they moved in a pastoral existence as if they were unconscious of the South's old grandeur. Like the other creatures of the forest, in contrast to the faun, they did "not know, nor care to know."

Upon Faulkner's return to Oxford from his stay at New Haven and his training in Canada, he must have looked at his South with a new vision. Alfred Kazin maintained that Faulkner's reaction to the war was one of disenchantment evinced in "a vague and expansive moodiness." He felt a "bitterness with the South," which was only one part of "a generally self-complacent pessimism. . . ." His new awareness was "secret and violent."[16] At any rate, Faulkner was aware that the South was changing. He and Stone had discussed the subject on their long walks and over Stone's desk in the law office, as they would continue to do in the years to come. It is not surprising, then, that the theme of mutability is strong in *The Marble Faun*. The faun sees that all things change, save him. He, unlike the others about him, cannot forget his past; and though he desires to be one with the other creatures, his knowledge of past, along with his prophetic powers which enable him to see the endless cycle of life, isolates him from them. Like the faun who is his spokesman, Faulkner was caught between the two worlds of past and present, unable to be genuinely a part of either.

Faulkner had not solved the problem of his own identity, but he was attempting to work it out, as he would continue to do for several years to come. At this point in his career, he knew that he had failed to find the resolution he had sought, perhaps unconsciously, in the war experience. The incidents of the martial exaggerations and his assumption of the role of romantic poseur following his return to Oxford after World War I indicate just how far short of his expectations the war experiences had fallen. Disappointed as he was, however, he probably knew consciously or sensed unconsciously that if one could understand his failures, one could tolerate them. It was necessary, then, that he make an attempt to see himself in other terms. It was too soon to face his problems directly, and he had probably never consciously defined them anyway.[17] That he should resort to his own devices in exploring himself in relation to his surroundings was inevitable: in literature, he could probe his problems romantically, mythically, and symbolically.

All this is not to say that Faulkner was aware of what he wrote in just these terms; indeed, it seems to me that his creative compulsions were as much unconscious as cognitive—perhaps more unconscious during the early phases of his work. The faun is the disguise which holds the mirror through which the self-image can be contemplated and tolerated. The tortured ambiguity of the faun is also a self-portrait of the artist: his position between the life of nature and the knowledge of past, with the accompanying attraction of each, the impossibility of identifying with both, and the resulting tension between the two. Like the faun, an immortal, Faulkner in 1919 seems to have looked upon himself as a creator of lyrical experiences, hence immortal in the sense that poetry may be deathless. Like the faun, bound and isolated in his knowledge of past, Faulkner seems to have sensed that he, too, was inescapably "marble-bound" in the past of his own South.

IV

The Student "Count": University, Mississippi

When Murry Falkner was business manager of Ole Miss and the family was living on campus, it occurred to the young poet that course work in college would be convenient and might help him as a writer. Much later, he wrote of this period to Malcolm Cowley, "I didn't want to go to work; it was by my father's request that I entered the University, which I didn't want to do either." Some hesitation on the part of young Faulkner was natural. He had not finished high school and very likely felt that he would not be accepted as a college student. But his veteran's status, combined with Stark Young's intercession, made possible his enrollment as a special student on September 19, 1919. He took French, making "A's" both semesters, and Spanish, making "B's." Apparently, after receiving a "D" in English the first semester, he dropped the course the following semester with a failing grade. He withdrew officially from the University November 5, 1920.[1]

During this period of fifteen months he continued to write extensively. He had reason to hope for a successful future as a poet. Not only had he composed *The Marble Faun* poems in their early versions, but he had received $15.00 for "L'Apres-

Midi d'un Faune," published in the *New Republic* on August 6, 1919. This poem was reprinted in the college weekly newspaper, *The Mississippian,* in late October; and during the next seven months Faulkner published a total of thirteen poems, one short story, and two miscellaneous pieces. All of these except one poem appeared in *The Mississippian,* that exception being "To a Co-ed," which was published in the college yearbook, *Ole Miss.* The poems average twenty lines each, but vary a great deal in style and treatment. A list of the poems in chronological order will prove helpful for further references:

"L'Apres-Midi d'un Faune," [*sic*] October 29, 1919, p. 4, col. 3.
"Cathay," November 12, 1919, p. 8, col. 1.
"Sapphics," November 26, 1919, p. 3, col. 3.
"After Fifty Years," December 10, 1919, p. 4, col. 5.
"Une Balad Hedes [*sic*] Femmes Perdues," January 28, 1920, p. 3, col. 3.
"Naiads' Song," February 4, 1920, p. 3, col. 5.
"Fantouches" [*sic*], February 25, 1920, p. 3, col. 3.
"Clair de Lune," March 3, 1920, p. 6, col. 3.
"A Poplar," March 17, 1920, p. 7, col. 3.
"Streets," March 17, 1920, p. 2, col. 3.
"A Clymene" [*sic*], April 14, 1920, p. 3, col. 4.
"Study," April 21, 1920, p. 4, col. 3.
"Alma Mater," May 12, 1920, p. 3, col. 5.
"To a Co-ed," *Ole Miss* (the yearbook of the University of Mississippi), 1919-1920, XXIV, 174.

Faulkner's early poems, as schoolboyish as some of them are, nevertheless become important in demonstrating the generative elements of his work during this period—the influences, language, imagery, lyrical patterns, and thematic tendencies which were to be absorbed into his continuing production. For these reasons, and others, they should not be ignored. Six of the poems can be loosely classified as experiments in traditional verse forms. The first poem of this group, "Cathay," contains other features which relate it to the poems which appear to be extensions of *The Marble Faun,* and it will be treated later in more detail. "Sapphics" is a strong imitation of Swinburne's adaptation of the form in English.

The parallel of titles is obvious enough, but a comparison of Swinburne's first two stanzas with those of Faulkner indicates that Faulkner's work is really a close rephrasing of Swinburne's stanzas:

SWINBURNE	FAULKNER
All the night sleep came not upon my eyelids,	*So it is: sleep comes not on my eyelids*
Shed not dew, nor shook nor unclosed a feather,	*Nor in my eyes, with shaken hair and white*
Yet with lips shut close and with eyes of iron	*Aloof pale hands and lips and breasts of iron,*
Stood and beheld me.	*So she beholds me.*
Then to me so lying awake a vision	*And yet though sleep comes not to me, there comes*
Came without sleep over the seas and touched me,	*A vision from the full smooth brow of sleep,*
Softly touched mine eyelids and lips; and I too,	*The white Aphrodite moving unbounded*
Full of the vision. . . .[2]	*By her own hair. . . .*

Faulkner's six stanzas are drawn freely from Swinburne's twenty, but most specifically from the first, second, third, fifth, seventh, thirteenth, and eighteenth stanzas. Faulkner's lines follow the basic stanzaic pattern with its three verses of eleven syllables each and a fourth of five syllables, but only nine of the twenty-four lines are precise; he is more successful in meeting the demands of three spondees in each stanza, and occasionally achieves metrical units of triple accents. The other poems of the traditional group are "After Fifty Years," "Study," "Alma Mater," and "To a Co-ed." Of these all but "Study" are sonnets. "After Fifty Years" is an Italian sonnet, but within its form shows influences of both Romanticism ("Her house is empty and her heart is old . . .") and French Symbolism ("he feels her presence like shed scent. . . .").[3] Swinburne's musicality is echoed in such richly alliterative lines as "And with his bound heart and his young eyes bent/And blind. . . ." The rhyme scheme of the next poem of the group,

"Alma Mater," is an alternating duple rhyme in the octave, employing somewhat strained anapests and iambs. The poem is heavily Romantic and presents an awkward tension between a reliance upon frothy poetic devices ("voiceless dreams") and a reversion to hackneyed phrasings and archaisms ("Within thy portals" and "Success" draws "us infinitely/Upwardly" [sic]). An interesting combination of Italian and Shakespearean sonnet devices, "To a Co-ed" uses three rhymes in the octave rather than the customary two, and the sestet concludes with a couplet. The influence of Dante Gabriel Rossetti's Sonnet IV is evident in descriptions of the girl's throat and eyes. The poem is classically allusive with references to Venus, Helen, Beatrice, Thais, and Athens. The final poem of this traditional group, "Study," depicts a student torn between romantic and academic desires. It is an incomplete mood piece, in the first stanza relying heavily upon a linkage between nature and sex, in the second referring to a homey pastoral scene, and then in the third adding images that hint of *The Marble Faun* ("blackbird," "golden wired throat," and "mellow note"). But the poem fades away on an inharmonious tone with an introspective final stanza that is so poorly conceived as to create an ineptly comic effect:

> (. . . . *Exams are near*
> *And my thoughts uncontrollably*
> *Wander, and I cannot hear*
> *The voice telling me that work I must,*
> *For everything will be the same when I am dead*
> *A thousand years. I wish I were a bust—*
> *All head.)*

Five of the poems illustrate Faulkner's concurrent interest in the French language and his continuing interest in French Symbolism. The quotation at the beginning of "Une Balad Hedes Femmes Perdues" [sic], "Mais ou sont les nieges [sic] d'antan [?]" is from Villon's "Ballad of the Ladies of Bygone Times" ("des dames du temps jadis"). The poem begins,

I sing in the green dusk
Fatuously
Of ladies that I have loved
—Ca[sic]ne fait rien! Helas, vraiment, vraiment

The line of French is obvious enough, but "green dusk" hints strongly of the French Symbolists' synesthetic devices. Other lines indicate a Romantic tradition ("star dust from their wings"), but the Symbolist techniques dominate the piece (*e.g.,* "ethereal seduction"). The other poems of this group, "Fantouches" [*sic*], "Clair de Lune," "Streets," and "A Clymene" [*sic*] are all translations from Paul Verlaine. Faulkner's versions are interesting to compare with Verlaine's originals in French, for they reveal not only a sketchy knowledge of French, but also an early determination, if not perverseness, of the artist to go his own way with his own devices, even in the face of a rather strong demand for literality. Faulkner romanticizes the first stanza of "Fantouches" [*sic*], then distorts the second, especially the fifth line, rendering the stanza's original French,

Cependant l'excellent docteur
Bolonais cueille avec lenteur
Des simples parmi l'herbe brune.[4]

as

And the doctor of Bogona [sic]
In his skull cup [sic] *and kimono*
Seeks for simples with pale avid eyes.

He exaggerates the third stanza, a subtle "en quête," to read "to meet her lover," and in the last stanza refers the pirate-lover's passion back to the girl herself. Ignoring a metaphorical reference to a nightingale, he appropriates a final line in French, "La lune ne grade aucune rancune" [*sic*], an enigmatic understatement. The next poem, "Clair de Lune," begins with a stanza which generally parallels Verlaine's, except for a unique word "fanchise," which is not clear. The second stanza is fairly consistent, but the third adds an original adjective to "les arbres," which emerges as "slender trees" and produces an original personification. The fountains of Verlaine "sob with ecstasy" ("sangloter d'extase les jets d'eau"), but Faulkner's fountains "sob in silver ecstasies." The poem "Streets" consists of sixteen lines divided into four stanzas of triple rhymes and a refrain "Dansons la gigue!" Faulkner translates the refrain "Dance the Jig" in italics or bolder newspaper print than the other stanzaic lines, but without the exclamation mark. Other differences establish a pattern: Faulkner plays down where Verlaine plays up, or conversely, he plays up where Verlaine plays down. For example, there is no equivalent in Faulkner's poem of "surtout" in Verlaine's first line. On the other hand, Faulkner romanticizes where Verlaine is more subtle: he sees Verlaine's eyes "Plus clairs" as "Fairer than." Again, "malicieux" becomes in translation "malicious subtleties," although rhyme seems to be the controlling motive in this situation. Other illustrations of an over-particularization of images occur with "façons vraiment," which Faulkner treats as "dainty airs," and "désoler un pauvre amant," which becomes "fill poor hearts with tears." Where Verlaine is metaphorical, Faulkner becomes concrete, as in the third stanza in which "baiser de sa bouche en fleur" is transformed to "to kiss her mouth"; then, contrariwise, the simple phrase "elle est morte à mon coeur" is rendered "to her my heart . . . deaf and blind." The translation of the final stanza diverges completely from Verlaine's, although the tone and meaning are somewhat paralleled:

VERLAINE	FAULKNER
Je me souviens, je me souviens	*Her face will ever be*
Des heures et des entretiens,	*In my mind's infinity*
Et c'est le meilleur des mes biens.	*She broke the coin and*
	gave it half to me
Dansons la gigue! (p. 136)	Dance the Jig

The twenty-line poem "A Clymene" [*sic*], follows the form and metrics of Verlaine's "A Clymène," but the usual differences exist, Faulkner heightening and lowering his effects almost conversely to those of Verlaine. Thus "Chère" in the first stanza becomes "Dearest." Faulkner renders the third stanza image "l'arome insigne" as "your hidden slightness," and the original "odeur" becomes "perfume." Verlaine's expletive "Ah!" is ignored altogether by Faulkner, who later reverses "tout ton être" to "all *my* being" (italics added). In the last stanza Faulkner carries over a "Nimbes" reference from Verlaine's next-to-last stanza, blends it with "almes cadences," and gives us "A nimbus that dances." The word "correspondances" is personalized as "my heart," and the concluding lines

> *Induit mon coeur subtil,*
> *Ainsi soit-il! (p. 74)*

are loosely rendered

> *So shall it ever be*
> *Through infinity.*

The two poems "Naiads' Song" and "A Poplar" make up a third group closely related to *The Marble Faun*. "Cathay," which may be grouped as a traditional lyric, represents the most obvious thematic extension of the volume of poetry, while the other two poems reflect similarities and overlappings of its images. A piece of forty-eight lines in octosyllabic couplets, "Naiads' Song" features, like *The Marble Faun*, woodland nymphs, a garden, a twilight world of dreams and sleep, and a sighing Pan complete with pipes. Woodland images predominate, and some of them can be examined in paginal relation to the images of *The Marble Faun*: "glistered hair" (cf. p. 11); "garden level as a cup/With the sunlight that fills it up" (cf. p. 40); and "Come ye sorrowful and keep/Here in unmeasured dream and sleep" (cf. p. 49). Faulkner's free verse poem, "A Poplar," contains ten lines which vary in syllables from a minimum of five to a maximum of fourteen. The extended metaphor of a poplar as a young slender girl suggests a recurring metaphor of *The Marble Faun*.

It may now be helpful to examine in depth one of the most

representative and seminal poems which Faulkner published during his first year at the University of Mississippi. An explication of such a poem, when considered with a general review of the others, would give balance to breadth and perform a threefold service: it would help to place the work itself into a context of a literary tradition; it would tend to relate Faulkner to that tradition, clarifying his creative development at the time; and it would illuminate the poem itself, especially its theme, which may in turn suggest possible insights into Faulkner's thoughts, motivations, and behavior during a period when his ideas were beginning to find artistic expression.

To recapitulate briefly, Faulkner had written the nineteen pieces of *The Marble Faun* in April, May, and June, 1919. In August, "L'Apres-Midi d'un Faune" had appeared in the *New Republic;* and in October, after Faulkner had enrolled at Ole Miss, it was reprinted in *The Mississippian.* "Cathay" followed as the first of the poems originally published in the campus weekly. As such, it serves as a kind of bridge between the production of the spring and summer of 1919, and that which followed in the winter and spring of 1920. I have placed the poem in a traditional grouping, although it bears some close relationships to *The Marble Faun.* Finally, the fact that it also employs a number of French Symbolist devices makes it typical of all three groups which I have previously treated. I have chosen it for an examination in depth not only because of its representative character, however, but also because of certain qualities of naturalness, originality, and thematic vigor lacking in several of the other pieces. The text of "Cathay" follows:

LINE NO.

1 *Sharp sands, those blind desert horsemen[,] sweep*
2 *Where yesterday tall shining carvels*
3 *Swam in thy golden past. What Fate fortells* [sic]
4 *That now the winds go lightly, lest thy sleep*
5 *Be broken? Where once thy splendors rose,*
6 *And cast their banners bright against the sky;*
7 *Now go the empty years infinitely*
8 *Rich with thy ghosts. So is it: who sows*

9   *The seed of Fame makes the grain for Death to reap.*
10 *Wanderers, with faces sharp as spears,*
11 *And flock and herds on aimless muffled feet*
12 *Drift where glittering kings went through each street*
13 *Of thy white vanished cities[,] and the years*
14 *Have closed like walls behind them.*
     Still
15 *Through the span of lesser destinies,*
16 *We stare, where once thy stars burned, lest like*
     these,
17 *We lose faith. They know the[e] not,*
     Nor will
18 *To see thy magic empire when the*
     Hand
19 *Thrusts back the curtain of the shifting sand,*
20 *On singing stars and lifting golden hill.*[5]

Before any attempt is made to relate the poem to a literary tradition or to interpret it, both a paraphrase of the work on the level of information and some comment on its feeling and tone might lead us to a more accurate and complete understanding of what Faulkner was attempting. The term "Cathay," in addition to being more connotatively precise than, say "China," designates that China of the Middle Ages, referring specifically to the kingdom established in north China in the tenth century, and suggesting the adventures of Marco Polo, who introduced the word to the Occident in the late thirteenth century. Thus, the "sands" may well be those deserts which caravans spanned in trading expeditions to the Orient, perhaps the deserts of Persia or the Gobi Desert of Mongolia, moving all the way to Shangtu in farthest Cathay. It was such a journey which absorbed three and one-half years of young Marco Polo's life: he was a stripling of seventeen when he left Venice, but was twenty-one when he arrived in Kublai Khan's court. Eventually, the trade of overland expeditions gave way to that of more efficient merchant ships which traveled the new sea-ways to the Orient. The verb "sweep" is present tense and tells us primarily that today the sands, like nomadic "desert horsemen," blow unseeing across the remnants of Cathay; whereas, in the older times when Cathay was rich, "carvels" (or "caravels" as the word is generally spelled in English) sailed along the ocean routes to the great cities of Cathay. "Carvel" seems connotatively to be a happy choice, bringing to mind with greater imagistic precision the uniquely antique flavor of those small fast sailing ships with narrow, high poops and lateen sails, although the term is anachronistic and cannot be made to refer, except by poetic license, to the vessels which carried intra-Oriental merchandise up and down the China coast itself. What prophetic Power, the poet asks, can give the reason that today the winds, which propelled the merchant ships to the Far East, seem so light that traders no longer go to Cathay, almost as if they—and here the wind blends into a metonymous association with the merchants, or rather with those who manned their vessels—did not wish to awaken that sleeping Empire? Notice that Cathay is addressed directly, *"thy* sleep . . . *thy* splendors . . . *thy* ghosts" (italics added), the personification itself suggesting what may appear to be a paradox: on the one hand, a mystical union with the past is indicated; and on the other, a sense of *vis-à-vis* intimacy between the specific, fabled city and the poet himself. However, the use of direct address becomes more significant in the next stanza. Although Cathay was once a splendid nation, famed and colorful, now that glory has been relegated to the passing years which seem to go on endlessly, peopled by mysterious spirits. It is true that whoever builds his own fame actually causes the many fruits of that fame to be gathered eventually into the harvest of Death.

The second stanza continues: today the nomads, with their belligerently sharp features, quietly "drift" with their flocks of domesticated animals in seeming purposelessness, or in a jealously guarded, deeply introverted limbo. The "muffled feet" of the herds suggests a striking contrast with, say, the jingling war boots of Kublai Khan's soldiers, an implied comparison consistent with the martial aspects of the ancient civilization. Such concreteness in implied comparison is strengthened by the lines which follow, indicating that "wanderers," and by implication the peasants with their goat-herds, move over the gleaming alabaster ruins of great cities. The passing years since Cathay's zenith are as so many walls shutting her away in the past. Even so, we find ourselves at the present moment looking back to that antiquity, so brilliant then, it seems, that the very stars above the Empire appeared to be afire. We do not merely give a backward glance, but are momentarily entranced. Our vision exceeds delight, admonishing us not to become complacent as have the civilizations of "lesser destinies," whose people neither understand nor desire to gaze upon the mystical greatness of Cathay's past—even at those rare times when the "Hand" of imagination and aspiration unveils the concealing sands which have long ago buried Cathay, opening to view that city's greatness and fame. The magnitude of such moments is so overwhelming that it can be expressed only in wild imagination—in stars which seem to sing, and in the illusion of the city's lifting toward those singing stars, even as the moon rises to bathe the surrounding hills in a golden lustre consistent with the Empire's opulence.

The poet's subject, on the level of information alone, seems to be the greatness of Cathay's past, towards which he directs his imagination. Inspired and laudatory, he is also absorbed with interest and delight as he moves toward the resolution of a paradox: Cathay's one-time magnificence remains awesomely thrilling despite an insignificant and more immediate past which has tended to bury it. Faulkner's attitude toward his reader is both generous and discriminating. He desires to render the fleeting capture of Cathay's *l'âge d'or* in a lyrical *mystique,* and also to share it, but knows that only the rare "We" are capable of doing so. The pronoun obviously includes the poet himself, but what are its other components? That "We" could apply to "Cathay" (formerly "thy," later "thee") does not seem likely because of the obvious grammatical opposition. Nor do the earlier mentioned "Wanderers" seem directly to partake of "We," for they and the peasants are apparently as unaffected by the vision as the very animals they herd, although "Wanderers" are by general inference, perhaps, indirectly involved, as if they may be adrift *within* the dream, having become inured to it. It seems far more likely that "We" applies to both the acutely perceptive and sensitive, and the truly aware and concerned; for "They," logically the insensitive and unconcerned, do not really understand or even desire to see the visions of the past which carry the soul ecstatically skyward.

For the hasty reader, then, the poet's intention may seem to be a simple poetic tribute to the past fame of Cathay; but the careful reader becomes steadily aware that Faulkner is far more intent upon establishing a delicate, if not ethereal, mood, the appeal of which is to the imagination where mystery momentarily supplants rationality and becomes so real that the upper current of universal, rather than merely specific, applicability is rendered. With universality, of course, a wider range of personal identifications is implied. Thus, Cathay becomes a catalytic symbol of antiquity, giving rise to that mystical feeling which all too few are fortunate enough to experience, even when surrounded by the artifacts of a great civilization, much less when left to voyage alone upon strange seas of thought.

The heavy sense of the past, the struggle to identity—a vanished beauty recalled and held in transient suspension—as well as certain choices of imagery and phrasing suggest that Faulkner, perhaps unconsciously, was seeing in Cathay the vanished splendor of his own region, just as he was later to draw, through his remembered reading of Henryk Sienkiewicz's *Pan Michael,* a similar parallel between the fiercely proud, brave, but defeated people of Poland, and those of his own South to whom he was so deeply attached.[6]

That fabled ante-bellum South upon which, like Cathay, "the years/Have closed like walls" has found its way many times into Faulkner's conscious artistry. He often dramatized the conflicts and tensions between the ways of the old South and the new. That the poet's north-central Mississippi qualified as a representative of the Cotton Kingdom's highest achievement of civilization, and that its colorful way of life was obliterated by the Civil War and the Reconstruction are obvious enough; but even though the Falkner family was part and parcel of that celebrated antiquity, and suffered, particularly during the late Reconstruction, it would be difficult to support a thesis that the family, all the way down to its most notable scion, was deeply and collectively traumatized by the conflicts of the day. As has been pointed out, many of the stories with which Faulkner as a boy was "saturated" dealt with the Old Colonel, toward whom the poet's attitude was a curious blend of the realistic and romantic. All this is part of the social and historical backdrop of the young Faulkner's creativity and may suggest a better understanding of what he may have been trying to say in "Cathay," although at the same time one should hasten to admit other facets of interpretation which the poem offers.

Pursuing this hypothetical direction, however, we see the theme of past itself emerging more prominently with the distinction of a spiritual vitality implying the best features of the past; the poem indicates that the obligation to the past is essential to those sensitive few who understand and want to see the old grandeur in its finest sense—lest they "lose faith." The taciturn "Wanderers," then, suspended in a dreamlike existence, take on identifying features which no significant feat of the imagination is required to see, relating to the dirt farmers of the region, the "rednecks" who, sometimes in a very literal sense, tend their livestock among the ruins of a fallen civilization. Such an interpretation—not at all impossible, even if we are limited to internal evidence—clarifies the discriminative nature of "We" in the final stanza and gives added precision to the potentially tragic meaning of "lose faith." Men may be beaten, the poet seems to say, but not defeated as long as there remains close to the essence of things a people, the resourceful "We" who are *aware,* who "will" to see the eternal values that transcend time and place. Faulkner's "We" suggests such a force of strength and reliance, perhaps, as the Jewish nation's "very small remnant" referred to in Isaiah.[7] Thus "Cathay," when related to Faulkner's regional background and social and cultural milieu, takes on added significance and prophetic overtones. It seems to be the poem of a young Southerner looking out of the narrow confines of his own frustrations and conflicts, and finding, perhaps unconsciously, his own region's past in the past of Cathay and his own individuation in that pattern of an older rise and fall.[8]

A detailed treatment of the influences on Faulkner's work of this period will not only help to place the work into a literary tradition, but it should also clarify his literary development, demonstrating to us not only what he was reading but also what that reading meant to him. Faulkner was, of course, reading both the Romantic and French Symbolist writers before the composition of "Cathay." The evidence of the Romantic influences fairly leaps at one, and to do more than to summarize them would be to belabor the obvious; however, much remains to be worked out with the poetry itself in support of the validity of the French Symbolist influences, and they deserve a fuller treatment as developmental and philosophical techniques than has yet been afforded them.

A thorough study of "Cathay" reveals a profusion of images in this order: visual, motor, kinesthetic, organic, tactile, and auditory. In addition to the liberal employment of sensuous imagery, "Cathay" contains a number of evocative images of faint suggestion and time images, indicating French Symbolist devices.[9]

The combination of images of different senses, or synesthesia, another notable attribute of both Romantic and French Symbolist poetry,[10] is illustrated in Faulkner's "faces sharp as spears" (visual-tactual); "splendors rose and cast" (visual-motor-kinesthetic); "stars burned" (visual-tactual); "curtain of the shifting sand" (visual-motor-organic); "singing stars" (auditory-visual); and "lifting golden hill" (visual-motor-kinesthetic-organic). Thus, the rich employment of both sensuous and synesthetic imagery indicates a strong basis for supporting the poet's Romantic methodology in "Cathay."

Now let us examine "Cathay" for evidence of some of the generally accepted "Romantic characteristics" of a broader scope.[11] The most obvious is probably a choice of material from the past, specifically the Middle Ages. As Shelley's Adonais is "made one with Nature," Faulkner's implied pro-

tagonist—a component of the "We," perhaps the poet himself—is made one with the past, the Cathay of Marco Polo's
time and before. The Romantic parallel of the two examples
goes beyond the past as such and lies in the exaltation of
spirit, what may be termed the supernatural or extra-sensory.
The physical city of Cathay may perish, and Adonais may give
up his earthly body in a "dust to dust" sense; but

> *. . . the pure spirit shall flow*
> *Back to the burning fountain whence it came,*
> *A portion of the Eternal, which must glow*
> *Through time and change, unquenchably the same. . . .*

In a partially cognate sense, then, Cathay and all that it is
emblematical of have "outsoared the shadow of our night."

Though it would be ridiculous to compare the two poems
as anything approaching significant analogues, "Cathay" does
possess a thematic correspondence to Keats' "Ode on a Grecian
Urn" in that spiritual creations emerge from objects of the
past: specifically, Keats created a shimmering, eternal vision
of art and truth out of the image of an Attic urn; Faulkner,
the vision of hope out of a spiritually reconstructed and still
impalpable Cathay. Which height is the greater, of course, is
scarcely arguable and certainly not the point here. Rather, the
abstracting and examining of such relationships will serve, if
only in a minor way perhaps, to help us place the poem into
the literary tradition of Romanticism.

"Golden past" (1. 3) and "golden hill" (1. 20) may
faintly echo Keats' "realms of gold" in "On First Looking
into Chapman's Homer," but the circumstances of search and
discovery which produce the mood of awe-struck wonder with
which Faulkner's poem concludes is a much more substantive
consistency:

> *We stare . . . /*
> *. . . . .*
> *On singing stars and lifting golden hill.*

Faulkner's references to "Fate" and "Fame," undying "splendors," the "flocks," images of regality related to a decaying

past, and the "curtain" metaphor applied to time and death may all be verbal echoes of *Adonais* (see stanzas 1, 44, 9, 7, and 8 respectively). One could find these and many others in a host of representative Romantic poems, for taken out of context there is little unique about them—especially such figures as "bright against the sky," "stars burned," and "Rich with . . . ghosts."

"Cathay" tends toward iambic pentameter, although of the twenty lines only seven are characterized by strong mechanical repetition. Faulkner used nine lines in the first stanza, eleven in the second, and varied his meter frequently with a dactyl, trochees, spondees, and triple ictuses. Some reasons for metrical divergences seem grounded in an excellent union of form, sound, and sense, as for example in

> *Have closed like walls behind them.*
> *Still*
> *Through the span of lesser destinies. . . .*

in which "Still," ordinarily the final *arsis* in the foot of which "Them" is the *thesis,* is dropped into a new line, receiving in the process an auricular emphasis, visual distinction, and isolation which are highly consistent with more than one of the word's denotations, its transitional function, and its rhythmic purposes. Other lines, however, seem stilted by comparison, as if intention had gone awry. A repeated employment of *enjambement* is balanced by frequent caesuras, giving the poem fluidity of tone without monotony. Occasionally, however, the line is idiosyncratic, as in

> *Of thy white vanished cities[,] and the years*
> *Have closed like walls . . .*

where sense and emphasis would seem to demand a comma as indicated. Considering the other errors in the published poem, one may assume the possibility that the indentation of l. 14 is a printer's alignment error. Similarly, the spelling of "fortells" (l. 3) may be a proofreader's slip, like the missing comma in l. 13 above. But the unusual stanzaic division, metrical variations, shifts of line length, and exceptional indentations, apparently not of an unpurposeful nature, are unique enough to indicate that Faulkner at this stage of his literary career was experimenting with verse forms in the truly Romantic tradition.

We have thus far examined Faulkner's Romantic and French Symbolist imagery—its frequency rather than its quality—and considered in application to the poem "Cathay" his readiness to seek materials in the past, to deal with the spiritual or extrasensory dimension, and to experiment with metrical forms. In much Romantic and Symbolist poetry, too, there is an indirection that meaningfully eludes the merely concrete and prosaic—an indirection that symbolizes and faintly suggests. Faulkner experimented with such images of faint suggestion, the time images, and, in addition to these, the devices of synesthesia which tend to merge the amorphous with the concrete, the fluid with the solid, the intangible with the palpable. He attempted to organize and relate disparate imaginal elements.

Faulkner's achievement of universality in "Cathay" requires further examination. Just as Blake endeavored "to see the world in a grain of sand," Faulkner, it seems likely, tried to see something of all great past ages in Cathay's, including that of his own South. Such an interpretive vision takes us far beyond the merely sensory and allows us to perceive a kind of *Einfühlung* operative in the young poet.[12] Thus, Cathay, the place written of, becomes a type of complex symbol characterized by a more than mediocre, if not extraordinary, power of ramified suggestion.

Such an awareness calls forth the Romanticists' familiar trait of expressing their subjective thoughts. Faulkner may unconsciously have been doing just this, but his esthetic subtlety and methods of indirection—learned in large part from the Romantics and Symbolists—give evidence of what Keats called "negative capability," or the ability of the poet to obliterate his own ego long enough to absorb the impressions of reality from the world outside himself, to negate his own identity in order to perceive a greater external reality. Even at the period near the beginning of his literary development, Faulkner's conscious artistic control was such that his individual unconscious seldom intrudes awkwardly; rather, its substance undergirds his surface techniques, imparting to them an unusual power of ramified suggestion. In short, Faulkner was writing out of emotional depths, but his unconscious overflow was balanced by cognitive art.

Faulkner's surface techniques are evident in his Romantic and Symbolist methods in "Cathay." If we are to consider the poem representative of the *Mississippian* group and, to some extent, the *Marble Faun* poems written in the same year, we must conclude that the term "imitative" does not tell the whole truth about them, for it implies merely a kind of conscious manipulation. Despite the reaction of critics and scholars who, with few exceptions, have given little evidence that they have actually examined closely Faulkner's early poetry and its relationship to literary traditions, "Cathay" remains far from being either "derivative" in a pejorative sense or "gushingly romantic." Such glib summaries are too easy and do not take into account the poet's strong awareness of a traditional past and the struggle to identify with it as one of the very small remnants of the capable and sensitive few, the "We" of his poem.

This is not to say that "Cathay" has no faults, or that the young poet may not have been just as instrumental in producing some of the shortcomings as printers or student proofreaders were. Rather, whatever limited success the poem possesses lies close to both unconscious power and cognitive talent, corollaries of a mind that few could term superficial or unoriginal even early in its development. That "Cathay" is even partially successful indicates the presence of a lyrical technique capable of supporting an overbrimming unconscious power, and both together carry the poet beyond his developmental weaknesses. On the conscious level, then, Faulkner's artistic skill proved technically dominant over emotions growing restive under restraint.

During this period Faulkner's behavior mystified his elders and seemed bizarre to the townspeople who knew, of course, who the young poet was. Many of them remembered the Young Colonel, who had run the local bank, and a few oldsters dimly recalled the Old Colonel and his exploits. Bill Falkner's father was a respected townsman, now comptroller of the University. The young man came from an "old family" that had gained the reputation of being aristocratic, proud, headstrong, and sometimes cold and disdainful. Although the Falkners were far from wealthy when William attended the University, his mother felt it was only proper that he have a dress suit to wear, and bought him one. It was a typically proud gesture. He associated with Phil Stone, too, the bright young lawyer who had been to Yale, another local scion. Both of the young fellows had been away to the war and, although the details were a bit vague, it was pretty clear that Bill Falkner had been involved in some kind of action and was wounded. But now it seemed he wasn't going to let anyone forget it because he wore his "British uniform" about the town. It didn't seem quite right to "show off" that way, but then the Falkners never did seem to care much about what people thought. Sometimes, to make the talk worse, he even wore an overseas cap and monocle, and at other times he dressed up in his new suit with spats and carried a cane. It was natural that the town should resort to ridicule. Such outrageous behavior could not continue without retribution, so the townspeople and students alike retaliated by calling him "Count" or "Count No 'count." This was the brash and rebellious Bill Falkner, who externalized his inner conflicts. If he could not find his identity in the past, or in war heroics, perhaps he could create an identity all his own by being different in a small town.

But there were many other Bill Falkners. One was a moody young man, a dreamer, who, finding little in common with his own father, often visited Professor Calvin Brown, head of the Department of Romance Languages at the University. His wife remembers that

Billy seemed to be faltering and groping his way at that time. One day . . . he told my husband that he felt his thinking was fuzzy and wondered whether studying mathematics would help him. My husband said he certainly thought it would, and so Billy enrolled in a math course. He seemed quite interested the first few weeks, but then he began cutting classes more and more and finally just drifted away. He seemed to be the same way in most of the subjects he took. He was a gentle, nice boy, quite shy and sensitive, and always courteous. He was wonderful, too, with children. He's always liked children and known how to talk with them, tell them stories, and get along with them; they respond to him. That was an outstanding characteristic I remember from those times, and the other was his intellectual groping.[13]

During his walks about the town square, he would sometimes stand and stare raptly at the courthouse, perhaps for several minutes on end. In the early 1920's, "Mack" Reed recalls, he would enter the drug store with his friend, Phil Stone, where the two would sometimes discuss books and writing.

In November, 1919, his short story "Landing in Luck" appeared in the campus newspaper (see Ch. III), and his Canadian war experiences became known, if not already by his dress, then by the story. By the spring of 1920, Faulkner had gained the reputation at the University of being "a character." The following parody of his "Fantouches" [sic] appeared in the *Mississippian* on March 3, 1920 (p. 6):

WHOTOUCHES
Just a parody on Count's "Fantouches" [sic] by Count, Jr.

Hannabolus brings in the dish
Full of sausage and of fish
And sets them before the Spaniard

And the sausage of Bologna,
In its thin skin and kimono
Seeks alack! for foolish eaters.

While the wiener wurst unclad
Glides trembling from the plate
To meet a rapacious mouth.

A big mouth from the Spanish main,
Whose jaws crush it with a strain—
How long the old aucune raccoon!

—J.

In "The Ivory Tower,"[14] Faulkner replied to this parody and another, probably "A Pastoral Poem,"[15] scoffing at those who would deign to write an imitation of an imitation. Then in "The 'Mushroom' Poet,"[16] the parodist gave at least one student's reaction to the poet's appearance and the impression he made during his student days. The works refers to

a peculiar person who calls himself William Falkner and who from all accounts undoubtedly resides in *the remote village of Oxford,* Mississippi. He says that he "flatters" himself that he possesses a sense of humor. I say he flatters himself if he says he possesses anything . . . . I tried so hard to find what the Count was "driving at," and only that he himself, admits his work was "stupid." [Italics added.]

The article continues:

I have written the parodies to give Count's poems a meaning; and behold! how little he appreciates my humble efforts . . . . *wouldn't this be a fine University if all of us were to wear sailor collars, monkey hats, and brilliant pantaloons; if we would "mose" along the street by the aid of a walking prop; and, ye gods forbid, if we should while away our time singing of lascivious knees, smiling lute strings, and voluptuous toes? Wouldn't that be just too grand?*
Since Count used a quotation, allow me the same liberty. I use the words of Lord Byron, *"He brays, the Laureate of the long-eared kind."*

—J. [Italics added]

The author of this article and the parodies, possibly Louis M. Jiggitts,[17] could not see much "meaning" or significance in Faulkner's work, and thought it "just too grand," or too precious. Undoubtedly, he associated the poet's work with his antic appearance. Here was a rebel who made other students uncomfortable by going against the grain of collegiate good taste. The details of dress which the writer notes probably refer to his overseas cap and flaring military trousers. Like Whistler, Beardsley, and Joyce, he sported a cane. The nature of the parodies themselves, as well as the reference to "the remote village of Oxford" and the concluding quotation from Byron, indicate that the student thought Faulkner was a country boy putting on airs and could be likened to a braying ass trying to be a poet.

Faulkner's reply to "The Editor" follows:

DEAR SIR:—

An anonymous squib in the last issue of your paper was brought to my notice as having a personal bearing. I could, with your forbearance, fill som [*sic*] space in endeavoring to bite the author with his own dog; but I shall content myself by asking him, through the columns of your paper, where did he learn English construction?

Yours truly,

W. FALKNER.[18]

The letter indicates that he was proud, sensitive, and withdrawn. The tone of aloofness and the circumventing question (Jiggitts' "English construction," if indeed he was the writer of "The 'Mushroom' Poet," is not that bad) reveal that Faulkner preferred to back out of an argument, if he could do so gracefully. He had just published three poems in March and four more were to appear before the end of the semester. The content of the poem "Study" (April 21, 1920) indicates that Faulkner had some difficulty concentrating on his courses. Faulkner dropped English during the same semester after having made a failing grade. When the student criticism appeared, he was likely behind in his work. But the brevity of his claim that he could "fill som [*sic*] space in endeavoring to bite the author with his own dog" is almost too hesitantly snobbish to be believed. That the poet really did "content" himself with a single-question reply to "J." is doubtful. Faulkner most likely refused to exchange barbs with his antagonist because he was too sensitive to give further currency to his fellow students' criticisms. If he paused to think about and analyze his own eccentricities, he, too, might see the absurdity of them; and he was having too much fun playing his new role and shocking people. Underneath this surface insincerity, however, he remained sensitive and aloof. Stone notes that he was oversensitive about both his size and a receding upper lip. There was little he could do about the former, but he compensated for the latter by growing a mustache. The metamorphosis was slow to come. "Bill cultivated that mustache for years. It was a thin little old thing for a long time, but he finally made it."[19]

But Faulkner was not completely withdrawn and rebellious. Much of the time he dressed neatly, wearing open-collar shirts. He took an interest in school activities and attempted at least one drama, "Marionettes," which he hand-lettered and illustrated himself. During the years he had grown up in Oxford, he had been known not only as a child who liked to keep to himself, but also as a boy who wanted to write and draw pictures. "Mack" Reed recalls, in his words, "bits of his efforts—fairy tales, rhymes, drawings, and little stories." Professor Adwin Wigfall Green remembers that he "incessantly wrote jests, poetry, and short stories."[20] He did a number of ink sketches for the college yearbook, obviously influenced by John Held, Jr.'s style of "flappers and sheiks."[21] Jere R. Hoar includes one of these illustrations in his article on some of Faulkner's less known work. Labeled "Social Activities," it shows a black-and-white checkered pavillion, a dancing couple dressed in bell-like flaring garments, the girl's long lissom legs in black stockings, the boy's legs encased in tight clown's trousers with a diamond-shaped pattern. The girl wears a conical party hat miraculously adhering to her head although her head is thrown far back, her waist arched impossibly. The boy bends forward to this feminine creature with bobbed hair, his tight black scalp of pasted hair a parody of sophistication. A Negro in striped suit kneels with black head bowed out-of-sight, his left hand uplifted as if resisting the terpsichorean scene, his banjo hanging from his shoulder. In the background of this *bal masque,* above a rising cloud of balloons, two seven-pointed candelabra glow in white against the background of night or a black curtain.[22] The sketch is an interesting study in contrast and tension.

By the summer of 1920, Faulkner was doing odd jobs about the town and earning all of his living expenses except room and board. He was still living with his parents. He and his friend Stone often toured the countryside in the latter's car, dubbed "Suzy" according to Stone, sometimes taking extended trips to nearby cities such as Clarksdale and Memphis. O'Connor notes that Faulkner "was a witty and sardonic young man who was having difficulty in finding himself either as an artist or professionally."[23] But through Stone's benevolent influence an event occurred that same summer which was to be the first fortuitous link in a long chain of events resulting in the publication of his first novels. Stone's good friend, the novelist Stark Young, formerly of Oxford and then of New York, visited his father in Oxford for a short time every summer. Young had known of the Falkners, but it was through Stone, who brought Faulkner to the Youngs' home, that he came to know the poet personally. Young recounted the incident in an article for the *New Republic*:

. . . I used to see Bill Faulkner and read the manuscripts that his friend [Stone] had praised and pushed so. Finally in the summer of 1920, after the World War, I found him at Oxford in a rebellious mood. Despite the kindness of his parents, and so on, he wanted another sort of life, and I suggested that he come to New York and sleep on my sofa till Miss Prall, a friend of mine, manager of the bookshop in Lord and Taylor's corner, could find him a place there and he could find a room.[24]

It was through Miss Prall, who later became Mrs. Sherwood Anderson, that Faulkner was to meet the artist who used his influence to get him published.

Faulkner withdrew completely from the University in November, 1920, and made the trip to New York. Stone, feeling that his friend was not making much headway in Oxford, encouraged the move in the hope that New York would provide him an opportunity both to study the graphic arts and to avail himself of Stark Young's influence with publishers. Faulkner had managed to save $100 from various jobs, primarily painting roofs at the University, and so he spent $60 of it for railroad fare. The remaining sum managed to tide him over for a week until Young returned from a trip. Young did keep his promise of permitting Faulkner to sleep on his sofa and acquiring him a position of clerk at the bookstore, where he did become acquainted with Elizabeth Prall; but nothing came of his attempts to get his poems published.

Faulkner later mentioned that he "got fired" because he was "a little careless about making change or something. Then I came on home."[25]

Again it was Phil Stone who came to the rescue. When it became clear that Faulkner was not succeeding in New York, Stone wrote him some six months after Faulkner had first set out for New York, telling him that the postmastership of the University was now vacant, and he could have the position if he wanted it. Faulkner took the examination for the position on December 3, 1921. He was to hold the job until his resignation on October 31, 1924.

V

The "Tieless Casual": A Medley

Even though Faulkner was not taking classes at the University in the spring semester of 1921, he was a member of the *Ole Miss* yearbook staff and a contributing editor of the *Mississippian*. His name is listed as a property-man for the production "The Marionettes: A Play in One Act" in the *Ole Miss* yearbook for 1920-21. One of the six original manuscripts of this play contains fifty-five pages and nine pen-and-ink drawings. The first page presents a description of the stage setting for the first scene and is accompanied by a drawing of the protagonist, Pierrot, sitting alone at a table, on which stands a bottle. Clothed in a flowing robe and pointed shoes, he reclines his head upon the small table, pillowed by some object, perhaps a thick cushion. In the background, in front of a round white moon, the silhouettes of two poplar trees bend slightly toward the dark upsweep of a hillside. An abandoned high-heel slipper is delicately featured in the right foreground. As in the poem "Nocturne," also published in the 1920-21 edition of *Ole Miss*,[1] the "s's" are inverted, the hero is named Pierrot, and the drawing consistently depicts

86

such details as flowing garments and a romantic setting complete with prominent white moons.

On November 10, 1920—five days after his formal withdrawal from the University—Faulkner published his first piece of literary criticism in his column "Books and Things," a review of W. A. Percy's volume of poems *In April Once*.[2] He sets the tone of his review by the statement, "Mr. Percy—like alas! how many of us—suffered the misfortune of having been born out of his time," and continues to relate the poet's work to such writers as Swinburne and Browning. The criticism is at once his most shallow, condescending, and precious.

On February 16, 1921, Faulkner published his second piece of literary criticism in the *Mississippian* under the same column title, a review of Conrad Aiken's *Turns and Movies*. The article begins with a sardonically confident look at contemporary American poetry; Faulkner finds no difficulty in seeing through "a fog generated by the mental puberty" of these "versifiers." He condemns them for "writing inferior Keats or sobbing over the middle west," and points to Aiken as "One rift of heaven[-]sent blue." Aiken and perhaps a half dozen others have "a definite goal in mind," but all the other moderns are condemned for "Browningesque obscurity" and "mediocrity." He feels that art should not be treated mechanically according to formalized "scientific rules." Aiken, unlike the others, has made a real effort to discover true esthetic laws:

Nothing is ever accidental with him, he has most happily escaped our national curse of filling each and every space, religious, physical, mental and moral, and beside him the British nightingales, Mr. Vachel Lindsay with his tin pan and iron spoon, Mr. Kreymborg with his lithographic water coloring, and Mr. Carl Sandburg with his sentimental Chicago propaganda are so many puppets fumbling in windy darkness.

Later, he condemns Amy Lowell for her attempts at polyphonic verse, "in spite of the fact that she has created some delightful statuettes of perfectly blown glass. . . ."

The review indicates not only cleverly stated skepticisms

toward much modern poetry, but also an awareness of poetic techniques: "Mr. Aiken has a plastic mind, he uses variation, inversion, change of rhythm and such metrical tricks with skillful effect . . . ." Faulkner's consciousness of the importance of organizational skill and artistic unity can be inferred from his hesitancy to quote from Aiken's work because "he has written with certain musical forms in mind," and any division of a poem "is as a single chord to a fugue . . . ." He expresses an interest in Aiken's "abstract three[-]dimensional verse patterned on polyphonic music form" as exemplified in "The Jig of Forslin" and "The House of Dust," for "no one has made a successful attempt to synthesize musical reactions with abstract documentary reactions." Faulkner relates Aiken's steady development with "a cycle back to the Greeks," the "faint traces of the French symbolists," and the "soft sonority that Masefield might have formed." He concludes with the hope that "the tide of aesthetic sterility which is slowly engulfing us" will be withdrawn, leaving "our first great poet," perhaps Aiken himself.

The two poems which Faulkner published during this same spring are distinctly different pieces. "Co-Education at Ole Miss"[3] is light verse simply conceived and filled with youthful exuberance:

> *Ernest says, to Ernestine—*
> *Thou art my little queen—O,*
>   *Thou art the girl*
>   *Of all the world*
> *Who makes my heart beat mean—O;*
>   *For night and day*
>   *When thou art away,*
> *Thy fair face fills my bean—O,*
>   *And love'st thou me*
>   *As I love thee,*
> *Let's off to Gretna Green—O.*

"Nocturne," on the other hand, is more complex and finely wrought. Both the illustrated Columbine and Pierrot are presented, visually and lyrically, as white flames, flickering in human attitudes, each pedestaled above a candle:

Colombine [sic] *leans above the taper flame:*
Columbine flings a rose.
She flings a severed hand at Pierrot's feet.

. . . .

Listen! A violin
Freezes into a blade, so bright and thin
It pierces through his brain, into his heart,
And he is spitted by a pin of music on the dark.

. . . .

Black the taper, sharp their mouths in starlight
The sky with icy rootless flowers gauntly glows.
They are stiffly frozen, bright and stark.

The significance of Faulkner's publications during these months lies not so much in their quality as in their variety. He wrote two critical reviews, two poems, and a one-act drama; in addition to these, he made several pen-and-ink sketches. The drama appears to be fanciful and bizarre. Faulkner's treatment of Percy's poetry is shallow and precious; but the review of Aiken's *Turns and Movies,* despite its obvious attempts at critical ingenuity, indicates a surprising familiarity with much modern poetry, its techniques, and relationships to such literary traditions as classicism, French Symbolism, and Victorian poetry. "Co-Education at Ole Miss" is mere lyrical play.

But "Nocturne" is more deeply emotional and intensively condensed. The stark white and black contrast of the sketch is consistent with the more markedly idiosyncratic inversion of "s's" and "z's." Other contrasts are also significant: the heat of the flames and the chill of the dark; the sudden palpability of music as a pin, the dark as a substance on which a pin can be "spitted"; and the rose as paper, the paper rose then as a white moth. The dancing of the flame-figures in erratic whirls and at fantastic speeds starkly opposes their ultimate helplessness as flames against a backdrop of sky from which the stars do not burn with warmth, but rather glow as so many "icy rootless flowers." In this sky the moving brilliant stars are arrested and, as it were, held in catalepsy, "stiffly frozen, bright and stark." We have the oxymorons of shimmering motionlessness and burning coldness. Finally, as Pierrot whirls he tries to hide his head, but "the keen blue darkness/Cuts his arms away from his face."

Just as the device of contrast can be used to arouse emotional impressions of deep significance in the reader, it can also reveal profound emotions in the writer who uses it. It seems to me that such a profusion of oppositional images as Faulkner presents us in "Nocturne," along with the brutality of his resolution, suggests a powerful inner tension on the part of the poet-sketcher. To contrast "Co-Education" with "Nocturne" is, perhaps, to see in young Faulkner an externalization of a familiar subconscious conflict: on the one hand, he probably wished to live a normal, perhaps convivial college life; on the other, he still felt isolated from most of those companions who surrounded him, initiated as he was and as they seemingly were not, at least in the deepest personal, familial sense of loyalty, to a past heritage.[4] Thus, at the moment of fullest opportunity to surround himself with genuine life and the gaiety of college society, he consciously shaped his intuitional longings in a kind of pantomime: love emerged as fantasy, as puppets, as Harlequin and his sweetheart; and then the faint reality of these representational lovers was further diminished to the flames of candlesticks, sputtering and flickering against the inexorable freeze of night. "Nocturne" gives us the profile of a strained dichotomy. The cataleptic past still dominates the living present, and the conflict, though not consciously rendered, finds expression in this strange poem of juxtaposed oppositions. The tension evident in "Nocturne" is little less than that of *The Marble Faun*—though certainly not as sustained—in which the creature that yearns to gambol with nymphs of the glade when the world was young, paradoxically is marble-bound in the past. Thus, Faulkner in the spring of 1921 was still engaged in the unresolved struggle to identify with a past that was as yet irretrievable.

Faulkner's record of publication shows only one item for the fall semester of 1920 and nothing for the fall semester of 1921. His mind was filled with the vision of New York and the success that a life there might bring him. Some confusion has existed concerning the date of Faulkner's first New York trip,[5] although its important details are well known: he stayed with Stark Young and slept on a painfully short antique sofa; he worked in Lord and Taylor's book department; he met Elizabeth Prall; and, through Miss Prall, who became Sherwood Anderson's wife, he eventually became acquainted with the writer who was to help him publish his first novel. Faulkner set out for New York, probably during the summer of 1921. He stayed there six months without any notable immediate success, despite the sponsorship of Stark Young. He returned to Oxford at the urging of Phil Stone to take the examination for postmaster on December 3, 1921.[6] The local paper of December 9, 1921, observed the return: "William Faulkner, former Ole Miss student, who has been in New York City for some time studying art, has returned to the University to take the temporary postmastership at the University post office."

By 1922, then, Faulkner was launched on his career as postmaster of Ole Miss. A cartoon soon appeared, featuring the postal workers and their motto: . . . . "Mail never put up on time. Diversion: Read all the mail." The small brick building on University Avenue in which Faulkner served his famously dilatory term as postmaster still stood in 1962, serving as a speech clinic. Before 1922 he had driven a Ford runabout but soon after becoming postmaster, he purchased a red Buick roadster.[7] He continued his literary partnership with Stone, whose secretary typed Faulkner's manuscripts and mailed them to publishers. Their walks and drives about the Oxford area, and the longer trips to Memphis, Clarksdale, and other cities continued. In their conversations, Stone continued to encourage Faulkner by influencing his friend's reading and criticizing and editing his manuscripts. Stone said that Faulkner wrote the poems of *A Green Bough* while he was postmaster at Ole Miss. Before looking more closely at these poems, however, I believe it would be best to examine Faulkner's publications during 1922: four pieces of literary criticism, a prose sketch, and a poem.

The criticism shows that Faulkner was continuing his examination of a whole range of literary fields seriously begun, apparently, as early as November 10, 1920, with his review of Percy's *In April Once*. A chronological list of all six pieces of Faulkner's literary criticism published in the *Mississippian* under his column heading "Books and Things" will prove helpful for further references:

W. A. Percy's *In April Once* (rev.), November 10, 1920, p. 5.
Conrad Aiken's *Turns and Movies* (rev.), February 16, 1921, p. 5.
Edna St. Vincent Millay's *Aria da Capo* (rev.), January 13, 1922, p. 5.
"American Drama: Eugene O'Neill" (article), February 3, 1922, p. 5.
"American Drama Inhibitions" (article in 2 parts), March 17, 1922,
    p. 5; continued March 24, 1922, p. 5.
Joseph Hergesheimer's *Linda Condon, Cytherea, The Bright Shawl*
    (rev.), December 15, 1922, p. 5.

The beginning of Faulkner's review of Millay's *Aria da Capo* harks back to his review of Aiken's *Turns and Movies*: the former alludes to "this age of mental puberty," while the latter commences, "In the fog generated by the mental puberty of contemporary American versifiers." Both continue to denigrate much of modern poetry. Faulkner later admitted that it was about this time he "took seriously to reading verse":

With no background whatever I joined the pack yelling loudly after contemporary poets. I could not always tell what it was all about but "This is the stuff," I told myself, believing, like so many, that if one cried loudly enough to be heard above the din, and so convinced others that one was "in the know," one would be automatically accoladed. I joined an emotional B.P.O.E.[8]

Faulkner strongly censured the generally prevalent emotionalism of such contemporary poets as Amy Lowell and Carl Sandburg. But "Miss Millay," unlike the others, "might be said to have scored a 'beat'; truly so in . . . that she has done something 'different.' . . ." Her

idea of a pastoral tragedy enacted and concluded by interlopers against a conventional background of paper streamers and colored confetti in the midst of a thoroughly artificial Pierrot and Columbine suite alone makes it worth second glance.

Having been published in 1920, *Aria da Capo* features a Pierrot and Columbine who anticipate those of both Faulkner's one-act drama, "The Marionettes," and his poem "Nocturne." His technical aptness can be seen in his comments on Millay's choice of words (he finds fault with only one word, one "of inexcusable crudeness," but does not name it); rhyme ("Neither faltering through too close attention, nor careless from lack of it"); structure ("no padding, no mental soft pillows"); and the theme of "idea" (it "alone does not make or mar a piece of writing, but it is something"). In addition, Faulkner articulates his awareness of

those characteristics acquired without conscious effort by every young writer, from the reading done during the period of his mental development, either from choice or compulsion.

Finally, the Millay piece also bears some interesting relationships with Phil Stone's "Preface" to *The Marble Faun*, which was to be published almost two years later, first, in the general condemnation of much modern poetry, and, second, in some striking similarities of idea and phrasing:

STONE	FAULKNER
1. I thought the main trouble with *Amy Lowell and her gang of drum-beaters* was . . . that *they always had one eye on the ball and the other on the grandstand.* (p. 8) [Italics added.]	1. Something new enough . . . in . . . *this loud gesturing of the aesthetic messiahs* of our emotional Valhalla *who have one eye on the ball and the other on the grandstand.* [Italics added.]
2. They [these] poems have . . . *a hint of coming muscularity of wrist and eye.* (p. 7) [Italics added.]	2. *A lusty tenuous simplicity;* the gods have given Miss Millay *a strong wrist* . . . and this work . . . will live even though *Miss Amy Lowell* intricately festoons it with broken glass . . . [Italics added.]

Of this period of his life Faulkner later wrote, "I was subject to the usual proselyting of an older person, but the strings were pulled so casually as scarcely to influence my point of view."[9] If he had Phil Stone in mind—and the possibility is a strong one—then perhaps he did not realize just how closely Stone's choice of his reading, the man's literary preferences, and, perhaps, even his ideas and phrasing of them had influenced him.[10]

The article "American Drama: Eugene O'Neill" is significant for three general reasons. Faulkner mentions a number of possible literary influences on his own work: Balzac, Conrad, Flaubert (*Madame Bovary*), Hauptmann, Moeller, O'Neill (*The Emperor Jones, The Straw, Anna Christie, Gold, Diff'rent,* and of these the first three are "playing in New York this winter"), Shakespeare (*Lear, Hamlet, All's Well*), and Synge (*The Playboy of the Western World*). A second important point made is the importance of time and place in writing—local color. *Lear, Hamlet,* and *All's Well*

could never have been written anywhere save in England during Elizabeth's reign. Nor could *Madame Bovary* have been written in any place other than the Rhone valley in the 18th [*sic*] century . . .

Balzac found his materials in nineteenth-century Paris. "Synge is provincial, smacking of the soil from which he sprang as no other modern does . . . ." One great problem of American writing is that "America has . . . no tradition." Related to "the wealth of natural dramatic material in this country" is the "greatest source" of our language:

A national literature cannot spring from folk lore—though heaven knows, such a forcing has been tried often enough—for America is too big and there are too many folk lores: Southern negroes, Spanish and French strains, the old west, for these always will remain colloquial; nor will it come through our slang, which also is likewise indigenous to restricted portions of the country. It can, however, come from the strength of imaginative idiom which is understandable by all who read English. Nowhere today, saving in parts of Ireland, is the English language spoken with the same earthy strength as it is in the United States. . . .

Another important aspect of "American Drama: Eugene O'Neill" lies in the submerged focus upon O'Neill himself;

but even so, the playwright seems significant only in an ancillary way, his name serving as a convenient reference for the critic's observations. For example, O'Neill may be an exception to the idea of regional necessity in writing, and as such both he and Conrad are "anomalies." O'Neill, like Synge, has "gotten . . . force behind stage language . . . ." And, finally, O'Neill has developed

a changing attitude toward his characters, a change from detached observation of his people brought low by sheer circumstance, to a more personal regard for their joys and hopes, their sufferings and despairs.

This last critical remark reveals Faulkner's sensitivity toward the concept of an artist's having not merely sympathy for, but also empathy with, his characters.

In his fifth critical article, "American Drama Inhibitions," March, 1922, Faulkner resumed his censure of contemporary American artists for subjecting themselves to the shallow demands of a shallow reading public:

a frank pandering to the Frank Crane market—holding a spiritual spittoon, so to speak, for that strata [*sic*] which, unfortunately, has money in this country . . . .

Artistic aspirations are too low or, worse, lacking altogether. Writers are "so pathetically torn between a desire to make a figure in the world and a morbid interest in their personal egos . . . ." Because of the "paucity of mental balance" of American writers, "only the richness of our language saves them." They are motivated by an "instinctive quickness to realize our simpler needs, and to supply them from any source." Those who are most successful have too often found it necessary to escape the thin artistic atmosphere of America:

O'Neill has turned his back on America to write of the sea, Marsden Hartley explodes vindictive fire crackers in Montmartre, Alfred Kreymborg has gone to Italy, and Ezra Pound furiously toys with spurious bronze in London. All have found America aesthetically impossible; yet, being of America, will some day return, a few into dyspeptic exile, others to write joyously for the movies.

Faulkner also refers to Sigmund Freud, but with little sense of recognition: Freud's psychology is a "deadly fruit" grafted "upon the dynamic chaos of a hodge-podge of nationalities." Continuing, Faulkner writes of a New York drama critic who related to him the story of his friend Robert Edmund Jones, a stage designer, who repaired "to a certain practitioner of the new therapeutic psycho-analysis"; in short, the man "was 'siked' " and recovered. The whole episode has a sardonic tone. The designer, an illustration of a man with some talent, had succeeded simply in slaying the "dragon" which he himself had "raised." Finally, psychoanalysis is classed as a "tendency" to be combated, along with "socialism" and an "Aesthetic attitude" which are " profitable as well as popular."[11]

"American Drama Inhibition" is significant in at least three other ways. First, the young critic indicates an awareness of the importance of dramatic structure. In the first paragraph, he writes of "a fundamentally sound play—a structure solidly built," but believes that such a goal is hopeless as long as the judgment of imaginative people is "temporarily aberrant." A play should be "built according to sound rules—i.e., simplicity and strength of language, thorough knowledge of material, and clarity of plot." Second, Faulkner continues to express a keen interest in the possibilities of regionalism in literature, naming as "an inexhaustible fund of dramatic material" the American raw materials of local color, specifically "the old Mississippi river days" and the "romantic growth of railroads." In retrospect, the observation is an interesting one, for he eventually used the settings, not only in a traditional sense (*e.g., Sartoris* and *The Unvanquished*), but also in a modern sense (*The Old Man*). The literary artist "with real ability finds sufficient what he has to hand."[12]

Faulkner's review of *Linda Condon, Cytherea,* and *The Bright Shawl* is peculiarly interesting in that he takes Joseph Hergesheimer to task for his dream-like descriptions, cataleptic imagery, and other traits which detract from an otherwise tightly knit structure. To illustrate, Faulkner states that Hergesheimer has never written a novel—someone has yet to coin the word for each unit of his work—Linda Condon [sic], in which he reached his apex, is not a novel. It is more like a lovely Byzantine frieze: a few unforgettable figures in silent arrested motion, forever beyond the reach of time and troubling the heart like music.

Faulkner's work has been criticized for similar deficiencies and strengths.[13] The young critic continues his verbal foray upon modern writers and their "deliberate pandering to the emotions," upon a literature which has become mere "gestures in tinsel." Hergesheimer's *Cytherea* is dismissed first as "nothing," then as "A palpable and bootless attempt to ape the literary colors of the day." Faulkner indicates that good modern literature should be realistic, but that Hergesheimer with *Cytherea* and *The Bright Shawl* "has tried to enter life, with disastrous results":

Sinclair Lewis and the New York Times [sic] have corrupted him. He should never try to write about people at all; he should spend his time, if he must write, *describing trees or marble fountains,* houses or cities. Here his ability to write flawless prose would not be tortured by his unfortunate reactions to the apish imbecilities of the human race. As it is, he is like an emasculate priest surrounded *by the puppets he has carved and clothed and painted—a terrific world without motion* or meaning. [Italics added.]

The reference to Lewis and the *New York Times* is somewhat puzzling, unless Faulkner looked upon Hergesheimer's work as an artistic deferring to popular demands (and, if so, the criticism of Lewis seems deficient). Strangely enough, Faulkner seems to be writing as much of himself as of Hergesheimer. His *Marble Faun,* "Marionettes," and "Nocturne" are suggested by the emphasized portions of the quotation above. In addition, the part of the quotation referring "to the apish imbecilities of the human race" strikes one as an innuendo of misanthropy. Having returned from a six-month trip to New York, Faulkner was probably disappointed at having had no success with publishers. Some evidence of a discouragement tinged with bitterness can be sensed in this final critical piece published in the *Mississippian.*

In summary, these early critical works give a revealing picture of Faulkner's creative progress. At this time he was a young man much concerned with contemporary literary thought. An early quest for artistic integrity is indicated by his censure of writers who subject themselves to the shallow demands of shallow readers. He shuns the hollowness of much contemporary literature—"gestures in tinsel"—and the poor virtues of imitation. Instead, he commends technical originality and artistic individuality. These points are linked to specified technical demands of the American writer especially. His determination of Millay's *Aria da Capo* as a "pastoral tragedy" strengthened by symbolical devices can be related to an early perceptivity of literary techniques, at this point of his development most obviously respected in the Elizabethans and Romantics. The importance of dramatic structure, however, is to be undergirded by the multiple strength of imagination—of pure originality.

Already, he rejects "flat" writing and recognizes the more profound dimensions of reality and motion. Reality, in turn, should be rooted in native ground. The need of America to create a literary tradition of its own is obvious: the difficulty presented by the problem is that there are "too many folk lores." Yet, the necessity prevails, and the artist should face up to the challenge rather than run away from it. He suggests America's "imaginative idiom," the "earthy strength" of its "force of language" as places from which the earnest writer may begin.

There is much immaturity in this early Faulkner, too. His negation of Freudian illuminations seems today strikingly naïve, just as his dismissal of the efforts of such poets as Amy Lowell and Carl Sandburg smacks of the impatience of a tyro whose illusions of poetry are still so many figurative caravels harbored in the lagoons of tradition. But his condemnation of the *fin de siècle* externals—hence, precious "aesthetic attitudes" —seems remarkably good sense. His insight into the personal dichotomies of writers and their easy preoccupations with their own egos implies an early awareness of the need for a kind of artistic objectivity which is not always easily achieved.

Finally, concepts of artistic philosophy, influence, technique, and structure may be linked to an emerging awareness of the artist's need for compassion, indicated in his observation of O'Neill's changing attitude toward his characters—a change from detachment to "personal regard for their joys and hopes, their sufferings and despairs." The observation, even at this early date, anticipates the "old verities and truths of the heart" to which Faulkner eventually paid tribute in his Nobel Prize speech.

Faulkner's remaining publications in 1922 include a prose sketch, "The Hill," published in the *Mississippian* on March 10,[14] and the poem "Portrait," first published in *The Double Dealer* in June, 1922.[15] The theme of the poem, young love and innocent passion, is tempered with a kind of sad, all-seeing wisdom: the participating poet seems to stand aside in brooding omniscience while the girl's "talk of life, profound in youth . . . . is clear with frank surprise." The scene is a shadowed, familiar street, and the couple's passion emerges with power and beauty:

> *And we hear again a music both have heard.*
> *Singing blood to blood between our palms.*
> *Come, lift your eyes, your tiny scrap of mouth.*
> *So lightly mobile on your dim white face;*
> *Aloofly talk of life, profound in youth. (p. 45)*

Within the traditional verse form—there are six quatrains, the lines are generally decasyllabic, somewhat inconsistently iambic and trochaic—Faulkner succeeded in creating some original effects. For example, in these lines he avoids, though with some preciosity, the usual romantic commonplaces of noting that it is dark, that the girl is shy and, therefore, closes her eyes:

> *Raise your hand, then, to your scarce seen face*
> *And draw the opaque curtains on your eyes. . . . (p. 46)*

Even within the confines of traditional form, he blends old ideas with imaginative new expression.

For a number of important reasons "The Hill" strikes me

as a highly significant piece of Faulkner's early work. First, it serves as a kind of bridge between Faulkner the poet and Faulkner the novelist. The poetic devices are evident in the lyricism of the prose itself:

Before him and slightly above his head, the hill crest was clearly laid on the sky. Over it slid *a sibilant invisability* [*sic*] *of wind like a sheet of water*. . . . *Three poplars twinkled their leaves against a gray sunned wall* over which leaned peach and apple trees in an extravagance of fragile pink and white . . . bent narrowly to the quiet resistless compulsion of April in their branches. . . . the silver mist of *their never ceasing, never escaping leaves*. . . . *the heart-tightening grace of the poplars*. . . . The sun plunged silently into *the liquid green of the west*. . . . And *as the sun released him*. . . . Here, *in the dusk, nymphs and fauns might riot to a shrilling of thin pipes,* to a shivering and hissing of cymbals in a sharp volcanic abasement *beneath a tall icy star*. [Italics added.]

Here, I have emphasized the passages which pertain to *The Marble Faun* and Faulkner's other early poetry composed during the three years prior to the publication of "The Hill": both Romantic and French Symbolist devices are still obvious enough, but, more specifically, the recurring image of personified poplar trees, along with references to "a gray sunned wall," nymphs, fauns, and the music of "thin pipes," echoes his first volume of poetry; and "a tall icy star" harks back to "Nocturne," published nearly a year before the prose sketch. Various relationships between Faulkner's first novel, *Soldiers' Pay* (1926),[16] and not only "The Hill" but also Faulkner's other poetry, including *The Marble Faun,* can easily be traced.[17] Again as in "The Hill," the image of personified poplars is employed, this time in application to the heroine: "her crumpling body, like a stricken poplar" (p. 66). In the same novel one finds a prevailing Romantic treatment of landscapes at dusk, complete with nymph and faun (cf. p. 243). Early in the novel, the face of one character is described as "a round mirror before which fauns and nymphs might have wantoned when the world was young" (p. 41), a phrasing close enough to "The Hill's" similar "in the dusk nymphs and fauns might riot to a shrilling of thin pipes . . . ."

In addition to serving as a literary nexus between Faulkner's poetry and prose, "The Hill" is also the first work in which the lineaments of his mythical Jefferson appear:

> Here and there a thread of smoke balanced precariously upon a chimney. The hamlet slept, wrapped in peace and quiet beneath the evening sun, as it had slept for a century: waiting, invisibly honeycombed with joys and sorrows, hopes and despairs, for the end of time.
>
> From the hilltop . . . were to be seen no cluttered barren lots sodden with spring rain and churned and torn by hoof of horse and cattle, no piles of winter ashes and rustling tin cans . . . tattered insanities of posted salacities and advertisements. . . . no suggestion of striving, of whipped vanities, of ambition and lusts, of the drying spittle of religious controversy: he could not see the sonorous simplicity of the court house columns were discolored and stained with casual tobacco. . . .
>
> The slow featureless mediocrity of his face twisted to an internal impulse . . . before him lay the hamlet which was home to him, the Tieless casual. . . .

The general outline of Jefferson prefigures here as a sleeping "hamlet, wrapped in peace and quiet . . . as it had slept for a century"—even the town's age is generally accurate. The hamlet's life is clustered about the courthouse with its columns "stained with casual tobacco," this "hamlet which was home to him." The lives of its people are consumed in hard work, represented and acknowledged by the "Tieless casual," who has just spent a day at "harsh labor with his hands, a strife against the forces of nature to gain bread and clothing and a place to sleep." For the first time in any piece of Faulkner's work, conscious autobiographical substance—the stuff of regional realism—seems clearly to emerge and dominate other elements such as lyricism, which, though still strong, is here subordinate to content. At this time it seems clear that Faulkner was experimenting with realistic local color; yet, he seems to have been not quite aware of what he was doing, not quite aware of the rich possibilities of an experiment which seems to have been executed with unconsciously compulsive power. His indecisiveness can be partially illustrated with still another image, which may help us to understand his motivations more clearly. As the Tieless casual walks home from his hard day's labor and approaches the hamlet, he pauses upon the crest of a hill:

Behind him was the motionless conflagration of sunset; before him was the opposite valley rim upon the changing sky. For a while he stood on one horizon and stared across at the other, far above a world of endless toil and troubled slumber; untouched, untouchable; forgetting, for a space, that he must return.*** [*sic*]

The protagonist seems tautly suspended between two worlds. We recall the same sort of tension in such works as *The Marble Faun,* "Cathay," and "Nocturne"—a tension between past and present, related to Faulkner's problem of identity during these years. Specifically, his great-grandfather Colonel William Cuthbert Falkner seemed to represent for him the glory of the Southern past; yet, it sometimes appears that the primary emphasis on the Old Colonel gives way to a secondary emphasis on the Young Colonel, J. W. T. Falkner.[18] Psychologically, such tendencies in problems of identity are, by no means, unusual.[19] Concerning some images in the above quotation, certain associations with the past can be indicated. The setting sun may suggest, among other possibilities, past time; similarly, the "conflagration" of the sunset may suggest brilliance, fame, domination, and destruction. The world of home, this "hamlet" which is "wrapped in peace and quiet beneath the evening sun, as it had slept for a century . . . honey-combed with joys and sorrows, hopes and despairs . . . ." seems to bespeak the lethargic present which dreams under the bright dominion of the Southern past. The hamlet lies in a quiet valley.

There is another horizon, but it is far distant and remote, connoting, perhaps, an insubstantial future about which one can only speculate. Now the Tieless casual, whose features are commensurate with "mediocrity," knows that he must return to his world of the present, a world of "endless toil and troubled slumber." Yet, for a time, he stands "on one horizon" and stares "across at the other." The image at this moment suggests an isostatic condition of indecision and sustained tension. But the vignette's conclusion becomes meaningful in a new way: for the first time the condition of tension (externalized in prose, of course, but quite possibly still unconscious) is associated *not with indirect and impalpable symbols, but with a consciously recognized and recognizable place.* The place is intricately described with such details as "barren . . . torn by hoof of horse and cattle," "piles of winter ashes," "tin cans," "posted salacities," and "court house columns . . . stained with casual tobacco." It is true that the protagonist *cannot see* these details, even as he *cannot see* the suggestions of "striving, of whipped vanities, of ambition and lusts, of the drying spittle of religious controversy," but he *knows* they are there; and as far as the reader is concerned, the presentation of these realistic and unpleasant details significantly lacks such Romantic disguises as those evident in *The Marble Faun,* "Cathay," and "Nocturne." It seems clear that at this time Faulkner was beginning to move in the direction of regional realism, although he had as yet made no conscious decision to direct his writing primarily toward that goal—one which proved to anticipate his major literary achievement.

IV

Intermezzo:
A Green Bough

Faulkner once said that he wrote *A Green Bough* when he was seventeen, eighteen, and nineteen years old. At another time, he said that the best age for writing poetry was from seventeen to twenty-six. The date of publication for *A Green Bough,* 1933, may therefore be misleading in regard to the time of its actual composition; for we also know that by 1925 Faulkner had already prepared the basic volume under the title of *The Greening Bough.* One could, then, logically assign the dates 1914-1925 as those during which he wrote most of the poetry, at least in its initial form.[1]

To recapitulate, Faulkner had composed a substantial number of the early versions of *The Marble Faun* poems in the spring of 1919, and he was working on other poems, essays, and prose works from the summer of 1919 to the end of 1922, with time out for wide reading, odd jobs, and a trip to New York. By 1922 he was postmaster of the University of Mississippi station, where he was employed until his resignation on October 31, 1924. If we are to take Phil Stone's word on the dating of the composition of the *Green Bough* poems, Faulkner wrote most of them while he was postmaster. Thus, it appears that Faulkner was working on the poems from early 1922 to early 1925.[2] Faulkner's record of publication shows only one poem from spring of 1922 until *The Marble Faun* was published in December, 1924, and the record is entirely blank from December, 1922, to December, 1924. No doubt he spent some of this time revising the poems of *The Marble Faun* for publication; but the greater portion of these months was very likely spent on the composition of the *Green Bough* poems.

It would be unreasonable to assume that the forty-four poems of *A Green Bough* were written by 1925 in just the way that they appeared in 1933. Evidence drawn from poems which first appeared in periodicals and then were reprinted in *A Green Bough* at a later date indicates that Faulkner revised his work to some extent. To explore the poems with complete thoroughness would be to anticipate Faulkner's development as an artist after 1929,[3] which, though interesting, would be beyond the proper limits of this book.

The poems of *A Green Bough* have already been treated with general accuracy in several scholarly articles. My remarks on the poems are limited to three general areas: first, a summary of the chief scholarship and most significant reviews of the volume; second, an outline of the poems themselves as they pertain to literary traditions, various influences, and Faulkner's previous work, such as *The Marble Faun* and the *Mississippian* and *Ole Miss* pieces, which will demonstrate the writer's continuing development; and third, a tracing of the various themes of the volume, especially those of the artist's traditional past and his struggle for identity, which will continue to reveal the evolution of Faulkner's literary and personal motivations.

Runyan's and Garrett's articles on Faulkner's poetry are the most significant treatments.[4] Runyan relates some interesting information concerning the dating of *A Green Bough,* prior publications of twelve of the forty-four poems, and some general opinions about Faulkner's imagery and influences. Runyan views Faulkner's effort as " 'Waste Land' poetry, presented in a *fin de siècle* manner." Cummings, Eliot, Housman,

Rossetti, and Swinburne dominate as influences. His criticisms of *The Marble Faun* and *A Green Bough* seem undifferentiated; both are apparently lumped together in his concluding sentence: "The final effect is one of immature romanticism."[5] Garrett's article is over half again as long as Runyan's, exclusive of the latter's two-page bibliography of Faulkner's poetry, and his inquiry is more exegetical in nature. He has examined the interrelationships of Faulkner's poetry, distinguishing between his early and later, revised efforts; has seen in the poetry as a whole a "restless experimentation," "new variations on the oldest themes"; and has evaluated Faulkner's poetry much more tolerantly than Runyan. The ultimate effect of the poetry, he says, writing three years after Runyan, "is not one of 'immature romanticism' " (pp. 132-134). Runyan, on the other hand, appears to have based his judgments on a more restricted reading, made in the first place for bibliographical rather than explicatory purposes.

Several reviews of *A Green Bough* are worthy of note. William Rose Benét in the *Saturday Review* rated the work as that of a "mere gifted amateur," who seems "precocious, peculiarly enough, rather than accomplished," but admits that "There are gleams."[6] Eda Lou Walton, writing for the *New York Herald Tribune Books,* noted the breadth of the poems and praised the volume in these words:

If William Faulkner had not been interested in becoming an important novelist and short story writer, it seems most probable that he would hold rank as one of the better of the minor poets of this period.[7]

Peter Monro Jack in the *New York Times Book Review* expressed pleasant surprise with the work and referred to it as "a book of most exciting poetry," despite its "lack of originality."[8] The reviewer writing in the *Nation,* however, felt that Faulkner, although he had debts of technique to various writers, had developed a style of his own. Elaborating on the concept of the poet's originality, the *Nation* reviewer observed that the poems are both Romantic and modern, and that they are "never commonplace" although "They sing of love, of beauty, of loss, of the rather typical poetic subjects."[9] Finally, Morris U. Schappes, reviewing the volume for *Poetry,* indicated a strong social bias in stating that Faulkner did not go behind "the dramatic forces at work" in the South. The poems "are not the lyric definition of the relation of an integrated personality with the world about him but mere emotional poses." Even so, "there are good (but often borrowed) rhythms, some felicitous images, a well-turned sonnet or two, and a number of resonant lines. . . ."[10]

Faulkner relied upon a variety of literary traditions in composing the poems of *A Green Bough.* To classify the poems into mutually exclusive categories would be both inaccurate and excessively rigid, for some of the individual poems reflect a variety of literary traditions. Romantic influences dominate, however, being reflected in eighteen of the poems. The French Symbolist elements are nearly as prevalent, indicated in seventeen. Elizabethan forms are evident in twelve poems, Housmanesque forms in seven, the folk ballad in one, and a variety of conventional forms in three others. Finally, the modern poets, such as Cummings, Eliot, Joyce, Robinson, and Yeats, are suggested by ten of the poems.[11]

Faulkner often finds originality of device, imagery, and effect within conventional forms, as the many examples of overlapping classifications indicate. Moreover, the volume contains obviously experimental passages throughout its pages. To illustrate, a ghostly woman walks "musicfleshed" (III, p. 17) ; a sentinel is "moonwashed" (p. 19). Poem IV contains a number of run-together words, *e.g.,* "neufcentvingtsome-thingorother" (p. 20), and such odd juxtapositions as "white unsubtle thighs" (p. 21). Out of the bosky nature of poem VIII, "a spurting yellow/Rabbit bursts, its flashing scut/ Muscled in erratic lines/Of fright from furrow hill to rut" (p. 27). The "day lay stark with labor" (p. 30) is a nature description of poem X. "Young breasts" are "hollowed out with fire" (p. 31) in poem XI. The evening is described "with a silver star like a rose in a bowl of lacquer" (p. 38) in poem XVI. The coined negatives of "unprobes," "unblend," and "undrown" (p. 48) appear in poem XXVI. Spring is "southflown" (XXX, p. 53); "abelard evaporates" while "paris/tastes his bitter thumbs" (XXXII, p. 55); and Mary has "soft doveslippered eyes" (XXXIV, p. 57).

In answer to Runyan's disapproval of Faulkner's poetry as "almost wholly derivative" and as "immature romanticism" (pp. 24, 27), Garrett points out that only eight of the forty-four poems serve as a basis for such complaints: these are I (Eliot); II (Eliot's "Portrait of a Lady"); XXVII (Eliot's "Sweeney among the Nightingales"); XV (Housman); and four poems which suggest Cummings "in the absence of capitals at least." However, Garrett further qualifies this observation with the statement that Faulkner made "no attempt to disguise allusions to the work of other poets," and that distinct imitation is evident only in "superficial aspects" (p. 133). One finds evidences of Browning in two poems, Cummings in four; de la Mare in one; Eliot in six, Housman in seven, Joyce in one; Keats in one; Mallarmé in one; Robinson in one; Swinburne in two, Verlaine in one, and Yeats in one.[12] These writers appear to be the major identifiable influences operative in *A Green Bough,* although there are doubtless others. Even so, it seems clear that Faulkner had, by and large, absorbed his influences and dominated them with his own individual style and images. The poems show that Faulkner continued to use Romantic and French Symbolist devices in his work, and added to them various methods of the emerging contemporary poets, especially those of Eliot and Cummings. However, these sources are, for the most part, submerged within Faulkner's own methods. Less than half of the forty-four poems contain significant passages or other attributes which could be said to bear identifiable influences; and many of these are merely superficial or suggestive.

Faulkner's own devices can be seen in some of the poems which illustrate a strong continuity between *A Green Bough* and his earlier work, especially *The Marble Faun* and *Mississippian* poems. Certain phrases reappear, *e.g.,* "silent amity" (I, p. 8) can be traced back to *The Marble Faun's* "soundless amity" (p. 16). Such images as "a white wanton near a break" (I, p. 8) echo previous, similar ones in *The Marble Faun*

(p. 26) and the *Mississippian* poem "Naiads' Song." A locale amid water, glade, and moonlight (II, p. 14) reiterates the dominant one of *The Marble Faun* (cf. p. 26). The image of poplar trees (IV, p. 20) with its familiar personification of girls harks back to the earlier volume (p. 25) and to such *Mississippian* poems as "A Poplar." The "inky shadows" of *A Green Bough* (V, p. 22) recall the "inky trees" of *The Marble Faun* (p. 31), as do the similar conceptions of Death as a boon for man: "man in amnesty may sleep" (VII, p. 35) and in the earlier volume, the "gift of sleep to be my morrow" (p. 49). Both works present similar images of blackbirds: "A blackbird whistles, cool and mellow" (VIII, p. 27) and in *The Marble Faun* "the blackbirds' . . . throats/Spill their long cool mellow notes" (p. 21). The pastoral images of *A Green Bough* seem more natural and less remote than those of *The Marble Faun:* "he a farmer can/Furrow the brown earth . . . bread him with his hands and feet" (VIII, p. 28), while the earlier volume contains only generalities of the same idea, expressed in such forced inversions as "Go the shepherds with their flocks" (p. 22). The mirror images of *A Green Bough,* though similar to those of *The Marble Faun,* indicate a merciless self-recognition, for example:

> *"Ho . . . One grows weary, posturing and grinning,*
> *aping a dream to a house of peopled shadows!*
> *Ah, 'twas you who stripped me bare and set me*
> *gibbering at mine own face in a mirror." (XVI, p. 37)*

Poem XXX begins, as does *The Marble Faun,* with an image of gray. The spring is "southflown" with "April and May and June," and November approaches; the effect is that of an extremely condensed eclogue similar to the manner of *The Marble Faun,* although the purpose of the device in poem XXX is to establish a kind of prologue for the return of a soldier. The image of the reaper in "Cathay" ("who sows/ The seed of Fame makes the grain for Death to reap") reappears in *A Green Bough* as "The sower who fears to sow and reaps no grain" (XXXIX, p. 62). There are thirteen poems in *A Green Bough*—perhaps more—which illustrate obvious relationships between the volume and Faulkner's earlier poetic work.[13]

At least eight of the poems in *A Green Bough* form a nexus with Faulkner's earlier poetry through the repetition of the familiar themes of the past and the artist's struggle to identity.[14] Poem V emphasizes the past with such images as "inky shadows," "grave," "headstone," and "memories that swim between the walls/And dim the peopled stillness of a room." Here, "no light breaks," "the shadows crowd within the door/And whisper in the dead leaves as they pass," and here,

> . . . *there is no breast to still in strife*
> *Of joy or sadness, nor does any life*
> *Flame these hills and vales grown sharp and cold*
> *And bare of sound.*

The final stanza relates the images of the past to what may suggest Faulkner's local region: "these hills and vales. . . ." Similarly, poem XXVIII expresses an awareness of a past which tends to dominate the present:

> . . . *the moons of cold*
> *What do their lonely voices wake to remember*
> *In this dust ere 'twas flesh? What restless old*
> *Dream a thousand years was safely sleeping*
> *Wakes my blood to sharp unease. . . .*
> . . . .
>
> *The hand that shaped my body*
> *Made me a slave to clay for a fee of breath.*

Past glory finds fulfillment in the present:

> *Over the world's rim, out of some splendid noon,*
> *Seeking some high desire, and not in vain,*
> *They fill and empty the red and dying moon*
> *And, crying, cross the rim of the world again.*

The "restless old / Dream" that has been "sleeping" has been reawakened; the poet's recognition of these things of antiquity is accomplished with "sharp unease." Yet, the forces of the past, perhaps his Southern tradition and forebears ("The hand that shaped my body"), seem, paradoxically, to have granted him life in order to sing of the past, to be "a slave to clay." This being his *raison d'être,* he as poet can—indeed, must— envision the past and, more specifically, that which is most worthy of the past ("some splendid noon") which, through him as a kind of amanuensis, will inevitably find expression once more ("crying, cross the rim of the world again"). One can sense in the stated inevitability of the return of the past and in the choice of such words as "crying" a kind of ir- resistible poetic feeling toward Faulkner's subject, as if he were at once resigned and compelled.

In poem X one finds a close adaptation of a line from Faulkner's prose sketch "The Hill," which a comparison will clearly show:

THE HILL	POEM X
Here in the dusk, nymphs and fauns might riot to a shrilling of thin pipes, to *a shivering and* hissing of cymbals *in a sharp volcanic abasement* beneath a tall icy star. [Emphases added.]	Nymph and faun in this dusk might riot *Beyond all oceaned Time's cold greenish bar* To shrilling pipes, to cymbals' hissing Beneath a single icy star [Emphases added.]

The themes, too, coincide.[15] Just as the protagonist of "The Hill" is caught between two horizons ("For a while he stood on one horizon and stared across at the other . . . ."), so is the protagonist of this poem:

> *Where he, to his own compulsion*
> *—A terrific figure on an urn—*
> *Is caught between his two horizons,*
> *Forgetting that he cant* [sic] *return.*

Other aspects of the two works also coincide, strongly sug- gesting that the poem may be a kind of lyrical paraphrase of the earlier prose sketch.[16] The stanza above indicates the same sort of tendency on Faulkner's part to identify with the past, while at the same time struggling to find his own identity in the present. One should recall the details of these technical and thematic tendencies not only in "The Hill," but also in the earlier "Nocturne," "Cathay," and *The Marble Faun.* The imagery in poem X is also characterized by the same sense of tension between past and present as exists in the earlier pieces. In a familiar way, the potency of the antipodal forces is such as to render the central figure static, as fixed as a "figure on an urn."[17]

Similarly, other poems repeat this by now familiar image of cataleptic tension in different terms: poem XX places the protagonist "Between two walls of gray and topless stone,/ Between two walls with silence on them grown" (p. 42); and poem XXVI describes a loved one, perhaps, as being "withdrawn" and "sundered by a tense/Like this: Is: Was: and Not. Nor caught between/Spent beaches and the annealed insatiate sea . . ." (p. 48).

Finally, three other poems are revealing commentaries on Faulkner's continuing struggle to identity. Poem XVIII, the familiar "Boy and Eagle"—dealing with an adolescent's dreams of flying and probably inspired by Faulkner's youthful habit of watching flights of birds from a hill outside Oxford— bespeaks the misty "loomings" of the boy-man who in heroic quest was to seek "the fleeing canyons of the sky," but who as yet was still a boy earth-bound and yearning beyond the rural Oxford of his day. Poem XVI is a work which appears to reveal Faulkner's dissatisfaction with his own present condition in the world of Oxford, and, more specifically, with himself as a poseur. The poem is a dialogue between a first-person centrality and an "old spectre," perhaps Death or Fate. The protagonist speaks first:

> ["]*Behold me, in my feathered cap and doublet,*
> *strutting across this stage that men call living:*
> *the mirror of all youth and hope and striving.*
> *Even you, in me, become a grimace."* (p. 37)

The "old spectre" replies that the first speaker's position is one of helpless mortality; but even so, the protagonist continues to speak to his antagonist with laughter, scoffing, and braggadocio. The spectre is unperturbed and always has an answer: "darkness," he says paradoxically, outlives all. The human hero attempts to scoff once again, but the laughter fades on his lips:

> *"Ho. . . . One grows weary, posturing and grinning,*
> *aping a dream to a house of peopled shadows!*
> *Ah, 'twas you who stripped me bare and set me*
> *gibbering at mine own face in a mirror." (p. 37)*

The spectre then answers again, saying that he will be waiting "with sleep" after "you have played your play and at last are quiet . . ." (p. 38).

If one may assume for a moment that the speaker of the poem relates closely to Faulkner himself, then it seems to be clear that Faulkner was tiring of his "posturing" in Oxford. He later acknowledged that he was a poseur, admitting that he read and wrote verse "to complete a youthful gesture I was then making, of being 'different' in a small town."[18] Other familiar aspects of his rebellion as "Count No'count" of rural Oxford may be looked upon as externalizations of his struggle to identity. In this poem Faulkner was possibly making a lyrical acknowledgment of his ostentation, of his "aping a dream" to his fellow townsmen, the dream, perhaps, of being a poet. The creation of poem XVI may have involved not only the conscious critical faculty, but also, on the unconscious level, a psychological transference which produced curative effects. The phenomenon of transference can be seen in Faulkner the poseur, in the immaturity of the very "posturing" over which "One grows weary," and in the working out of that anxiety through the artistic expression itself—the transmuting of the unconscious incentives into cognitive communication. Faulkner as an emerging adult saw the futility of his pretense in Oxford, and verbalized his transference. As artist, the verbalization took the unique form of poetry. The poem itself, then, may possibly be said to represent his dissatisfaction with his unfruitful—indeed, his deceptive—position in Oxford.

Poem XLIV, originally published under the title "My

Epitaph" and then as "This Earth" and "If There Be Grief,"[19] is the closing piece of *A Green Bough:*

> *If there be grief, then let it be but rain,*
> *And this but silver grief for grieving's sake,*
> *If these green woods be dreaming here to wake*
> *Within my heart, if I should rouse again.*
>
> *But I shall sleep, for where is any death*
> *While in these blue hills slumbrous overhead*
> *I'm rooted like a tree? Though I be dead,*
> *This earth that holds me fast will find me breath.*
>
> *(p. 67)*

The poem relates to the poet's search for identity and offers a projected resolution which is strikingly prophetic: he will make his home in "these green woods" and "these blue hills" of Mississippi, where he is "rooted like a tree"; the union of man and place seems, by implications of deep devotion, to encompass life as well as to transcend death. But without the retrospection which comes from a knowledge of Faulkner's life pattern, the thematic nexus between poem XVI ("Behold me, in my feathered cap and doublet") and this concluding piece may seem at first difficult to establish: in poem XVI the poet seems bitterly dissatisfied with his position in northern Mississippi, whereas in poem XLIV he appears to be deeply satisfied with it. The difference of feeling and tone in the two poems lies not so much in the poet's emotional attitude toward his home, I believe, for he always loved it,[20] as in a developing artistic conception toward Oxford, northern Mississippi, and, in a larger sense, the whole tradition of the South and the various complex relationships of that tradition to the universal levels of human existence. That is to say, in poem XVI such an artistic scope or *Weltanschauung* is altogether lacking, as though yet undiscovered; but in poem XLIV that artistic conception is either consciously or unconsciously present.[21]

At any rate, it was to be a few more years before Faulkner could find the kind of rest in this earth of his Southern homeland which resulted from unconscious, emotional affinity on the one hand, and cognitive artistic conception on the other. In early 1925, he had yet to learn that he could find artistic fulfillment in the very midst of the South he had tried to escape in various ways: through the war experience, his outlandish dress and *outré* behavior,[22] the trip to New York, and the ostentatious cleverness of his reviews and articles in his *Mississippian* column, "Books and Things." True, he had expressed a critical recognition of the importance of local color in several of these pieces, and he had used some of its elements in "The Hill," such as descriptions of the hill country, its tobacco-chewing rednecks, and their argumentative religious fundamentalism. Such points indicate during this stage of his literary development an incipient move away from such Romantic devices as those found in *The Marble Faun* and toward an emerging awareness of the fictional possibilities of his own geographical region. Still, he had made no conscious decision to direct the whole of his literary effort toward regional realism, and by 1925 he had yet to make that decision.

There was still time for another effort at escape, an escape, oddly enough, which Faulkner had already condemned in Eugene O'Neill, Marsden Hartley, Alfred Kreymborg, and Ezra Pound in his article "American Drama: Eugene O'Neill," published February 3, 1922 (*Mississippian,* p. 5). He would go to Europe by way of New Orleans. On October 31, 1924, Faulkner resigned the University postmastership. He later gave as a reason that he desired to be free to do what he wanted most, "to take pipe and paper, and to dream and write."[23] He did not know then that after his experience in the Vieux Carré of New Orleans, a trip to Europe, and a sojourn in Pascagoula, his dream would bring him home again.

VII

The Vieux Carré:
Anderson's Influence

The major literary influence on William Faulkner's early fiction was Sherwood Anderson. Up to the period of their friendship in New Orleans Faulkner had almost exclusively written poetry; then he turned to prose and, within a few months, wrote his first novel, *Soldiers' Pay* (1926). It was a memorable friendship for both men. Anderson described his meeting with Faulkner in these words:

I first saw Bill Faulkner when he came to my apartment in New Orleans. You will remember the story of Abraham Lincoln's meeting with the Southern commissioners, on the boat, on the Potomac in 1864. The Southern commissioners had come to try to negotiate some sort of peace and among them was the Vice-President of the confederacy, Alexander Stephens. He was such a small man and wore a huge overcoat.

"Did you ever see so much shuck for so little nubbin?" Lincoln said to a friend.

I thought of the story when I first saw Faulkner. He also had on a big overcoat, it being winter, and it bulged strangely, so much, that at first glance, I thought he must be in some queer way deformed. He told me that he intended to stay for some time in New Orleans and asked if in the meantime, while he was looking for a place, he could leave some of his things with me. His "things" consisted of some six or eight half gallon jars of moon liquor he had brought with him from the country and that were stowed in the pockets of the big coat.[1]

Anderson's "A Meeting South" was first published in *The Dial* in April, 1925; in this first-person sketch he produced a character named David, who is probably modeled on Faulkner:

Evening was coming, the abrupt waning of the day and the quick smoky soft-footed coming of night characteristic of our semi-tropic city, when he produced a bottle from his hip pocket. It was so large that I was amazed. How had it happened that the carrying of so large a bottle had not made him look deformed? His body was very small and delicately built. "Perhaps, like the kangaroo, his body has developed some kind of natural pouch for taking care of supplies," I thought. Really he walked as one might fancy a kangaroo would walk when out for a quiet evening stroll.[2]

The setting of this scene is New Orleans. The narrator— undisguisedly Anderson himself—first describes David as telling "me the story of his ill fortune with a very gentlemanly little smile on his very sensitive lips . . . . I liked his tone, liked him" (p. 269); then later as "the little Southern poet" (p. 276) who says, "If I could write like Shelley I would be happy. I wouldn't care what happened to me" (p. 279). As they go down the stairs Anderson observes,

I noticed that he was a cripple. The slight limp, the look of pain that occasionally drifted across his face, the little laugh that was intended to be jolly, but did not quite achieve its purpose, all these things began at once to tell me the story I have now set myself down to write. (p. 269)

Anderson desires to take the poet to see Aunt Sally, a motherly woman in her sixties who has successfully operated a house of gambling, bootlegging, and prostitution. "One does not take every chance caller to Aunt Sally" (p. 269), Anderson observes, but he likes this person: the pseudonymity of Anderson's persona is further suggested by the narrator's statement ". . . I shall call him David" (p. 269).

Aside from the fact that David's home is in Alabama and Faulkner's in Mississippi, the two have many remarkable similarities. As Anderson observes, David is "not affected" by "drink" (p. 269). His moon liquor "was made by a nigger on his father's plantation somewhere over in Alabama" (p. 27). Again,

David is a poet and so in the darkness by the river we spoke of Keats and Shelley, the two English poets all good Southern men love. (p. 271)

David eventually relates "The story of how he chanced to be a cripple . . ." (p. 272); even as exaggerations the details form a striking congruity with aspects of Faulkner's war "legend":

When the World War broke out he went over to England and managed to get himself enrolled as an aviator, very much I gathered in the spirit in which a countryman, in a city for a night, might take in a show.

The English had been glad enough to take him on. He was one more man. They were glad enough to take any one on just then. He was small and delicately built, but after he got in he turned out to be a first rate flyer, serving all through the war with a British flying squadron, but at the last got into a crash and fell.

Both legs were broken, one of them in three places, the scalp was badly torn and some of the bones of the face had been splintered.

They put him into a field hospital and had patched him up. "It was my fault if the job was rather bungled," he said. "You see it was a field hospital, a hell of a place. Men were torn all to pieces, groaning and dying. Then they moved me back to a base hospital and it wasn't much better." (p. 272)

David continues his story, pointing out how he deceived the hospital authorities by claiming that the nerves of his face and leg did not hurt. "It was a lie of course. The nerves of my leg and of my face have never quit hurting" (p. 273).

If David was indeed modeled on Faulkner, then the following reaction of Anderson may partially explain his admiration for the young poet:

I got it. No wonder he carried his drinks so well. When I understood

I wanted to keep on drinking with him, wanted to stay with him until he had got tired of me as he had of the man who lay beside him in the base hospital over there somewhere in France. (p. 273)

David, as Faulkner did, suffers from insomnia. Drinking promotes his ability to sleep by dulling the pain of his nerves. When the two men finally arrive at Aunt Sally's, David relates several stories about his father's plantation and how, on certain nights when he has difficulty sleeping, "I take the bottle in my hand and go into the fields, unseen by the niggers" (p. 277). Another biographical element concerning Faulkner is Anderson's summary of the Southern poet's ancestry and, perhaps, the family's condition at home:

The Southerner's great[-]grandfather was English, a young son, and he came over here to make his fortune as a planter and did it. Once he and his sons owned several great plantations with slaves, but now his father had but a few hundred acres left, about one of the old houses—somewhere over in Alabama. The land is heavily mortgaged and most of it has not been under cultivation for years. Negro labour is growing more and more expensive and unsatisfactory since so many negroes have run off to Chicago, and the poet's father and the one brother at home are not much good at working the land. "We aren't strong enough and we don't know how," the poet said . . . . "In a few years now I reckon our family won't have any land. The banks could take it now if they wanted it. They don't want it. It would be too much trouble for them to manage I reckon." (pp. 277-278)

Just before the sketch ends, David goes to sleep on the bricks of the patio. The narrator observes, "What a small huddled figure of a man he looked, lying there on the brick, under the night sky, in the deep shadows of the banana plants" (p. 279).

Many circumstances involving Anderson's persona David are remarkably similar to the facts of Faulkner's life: the locale of New Orleans itself, the time, and the friendship with Anderson, along with certain paralleling details between the recorded facts of their meeting and the incidents of the sketch; David's small size and general appearance; his being an aristocratic Southern poet; his admiration for Keats and

Shelley;[3] the particularized aspects of insomnia; both the
facts and the guises of the war experience; the imbibing of
homemade spirits;[4] and the tracing of the poet's family background, especially the amplified comment on the "great[-]
grandfather" and his notable individualism. Indeed, these traits
of Faulkner presented in the persona of David tempt one to
consider the piece in the light of biographical reporting as
well as fiction. If Anderson was writing from what he thought
were the facts of Faulkner's war experience, then various
aspects of the portrait he created may suggest that Faulkner
himself was continuing to play the role of the tragically injured aviator, at the time perhaps as necessary to his sense of
identity as the veneer of his "Count No'count" days at the
University of Mississippi.

Faulkner certainly made a trip to New Orleans late in
1924 and met Anderson then.[5] Anderson, who was in the city
during the winter of 1923-24, took up residence there by
August, 1924, with his new wife, Elizabeth Prall. In the fall
of 1924, Horace Liveright, who was anxious to become
Anderson's publisher, also made the trip to New Orleans to
meet him. During January and February of 1925 Anderson
was making a lecture tour of various colleges and universities.
He returned to New Orleans by March 20 and finished the
first draft of his *Mid-American Childhood;* and on April 10
he signed a five-year agreement with Liveright. Faulkner had
known Elizabeth Prall during his months in New York as
a bookstore clerk at Lord and Taylor, probably in 1921, and
he thus had an opportunity through her to meet Anderson.
When a student later asked Faulkner, "Was there something
in New Orleans that pulled you down there, or were you just
making the trip?" Faulkner replied,

Well, yes, I had heard of *The Double Dealer* and the people there
for years. At that time I went to New Orleans to get a job in a ship
and go to Europe, that was why I happened to be in New Orleans
at the time. That I hadn't—it was no pull to be a part of a literary
group, no. That I had felt the pull—I think that any young writer
does feel that pull to be with people that have the same problems
and the same interests as him, that won't laugh at what he says

no matter how foolish it might sound to the Philistine, but that was
the reason I was in New Orleans, was to get a job with a ship.[6]

Faulkner, no doubt, had planned to go to Europe at about the
time of his resignation of the postmastership: the town paper
had reported his intention to do so, and so had John McClure
soon after Faulkner's arrival in New Orleans in January, 1925.
After Faulkner's *Marble Faun* had been published in December,
1924, Phil Stone wrote letters to such people as Harriet
Monroe, editor of *Poetry*, and possibly to Sherwood Anderson,
hoping to get additional support for his protégé's new career
as a published poet. Harriet Monroe was in agreement with
Stone concerning Faulkner's promising future as a poet—or,
at least, so stated to Stone—but Anderson apparently felt that
Faulkner needed more experience as a writer. Stone himself
felt that a trip abroad might help Faulkner to gain a reputation as a writer, which the publication of *The Marble Faun*
obviously was not accomplishing. So, following the example of
other expatriates such as Eliot, Pound, and Hemingway,
Faulkner was to go to Europe, too, by his own way of New
Orleans. Stone went along as far as New Orleans for a short
vacation.

Anderson was away on his lecture tour until late March,
but by February, Faulkner was publishing in both *The Double
Dealer* and the *Times-Picayune*. He had already made himself
known to the staff of *The Double Dealer* with the publication
of his poem "Portrait" in June, 1922. It is also possible that
Anderson, if he had been communicating with Stone about
Faulkner, had used his influence on Faulkner's behalf with
such members of the magazine staff as Julius Friend and
James Feibleman, with whom Anderson had previously become
acquainted. John McClure's review of Faulkner's newly published *Marble Faun* in January of 1925 indicates that his work
was well known by still another staff member. McClure, who
also wrote a regular column for the *Times-Picayune*, became
"an active sponsor and close friend" of Faulkner.[7] The following list of Faulkner's publications during 1925 will prove
helpful for future reference:

PUBLICATIONS IN THE DOUBLE DEALER
(prose)

"On Criticism," 7:83-84, January-February, 1925.

"New Orleans," 7:102-107, January-February, 1925.

  These comprise eleven short sketches, some of which reflect those published in the *Times-Picayune* from February to September, 1925.

"Verse Old and Nascent: A Pilgrimage," 7:129-131, April, 1925.

(poetry)

"Dying Gladiator," 7:85, January-February, 1925.

"The Faun," 7:148, April, 1925.

"The Lilacs," 7:185-187, June, 1925. Slightly revised as Poem I in *A Green Bough.*

PUBLICATIONS IN THE TIMES-PICAYUNE
(Sunday magazine section)

"Mirrors of Chartres Street," February 8, pp. 1, 6.

"Damon and Pythias Unlimited," February 15, p. 7.

"Home," February 22, p. 3.

"Jealousy," March 1, p. 2.

"Cheest," April 5, p. 4.

"Out of Nazareth," April 12, p. 4.

"The Kingdom of God," April 26, p. 4.

"The Rosary," May 3, p. 2.

"The Cobbler," May 10, p. 7.

"Chance," May 17, p. 7.

"Sunset," May 24, pp. 4, 7.

"The Kid Learns," May 31, p. 2.

"The Liar," July 26, pp. 3, 6.

"Episode," August 16, p. 2.

"Country Mice," September 20, p. 7.

"Yo Ho and Two Bottles of Rum," September 27, pp. 1, 2.

By the time Faulkner and Anderson met, Anderson had already published the works on which his fame chiefly rests, *Winesburg, Ohio* (1919), *The Triumph of the Egg* (1921), and *Horses and Men* (1923). He was the lion of the literary-art group in the Vieux Carré, and it was natural that the aspiring young Faulkner would seek him out. Faulkner later gave this summary of their meeting in New Orleans:

Later I had heard that she [Elizabeth Prall] had married Anderson, was living in New Orleans, I happened to be in New Orleans and I had gone to call on her, because I wasn't going to bust in on Mr. Anderson without an invitation from him, I didn't think that I would see him at all, that he would probably be in his study working, but it happened that he was in the room at the time, and we talked and we liked one another from the start, and it was just the chance that I had gone to call on Miss Prall that I had known who had been kind to me when I was a clerk in a book store [in New York] that I came to meet him.[8]

It was possibly through Anderson's favor that Faulkner received such understanding support from the staffs of *The Double Dealer* and the *Times-Picayune*; but Anderson's influence went deeper than mere patronage. Doing some collaboration on the traditional kind of southwest humorous tales, the two men exchanged a series of letters. Several times Anderson criticized Faulkner's writing, and once required him to revise his work or stop the arrangement altogether.[9] He finally urged Faulkner to write a novel and inspired him to a fever of creation: the young writer's first novel, *Soldiers' Pay* (1926), was completed in about two months. Anderson apparently then went to his new publisher, Horace Liveright, and argued successfully for its publication.[10]

When Faulkner read Anderson's books, lent to him by Phil Stone, he was encouraged at the possibilities which prose fiction offered. Anderson's "I'm a Fool," he thought, was "the best short story in America."[11] Thus, it seems clear that Faulkner was thoroughly impressed by Anderson's work; and it is all the more likely that their ensuing friendship first altered Faulkner's intention to go on to Europe—although one must also suspect such deterrents as economic necessity and the lack of opportunity in finding a job on an available ship. Whether through desire or necessity—or both—he temporarily accepted the bohemians of the Vieux Carré in place of the Parisian rebels of the Left Bank. Through Anderson's example and advice, he became increasingly aware of the possibilities of art at home. Later, he was to recall the fact that Anderson's example gave birth to his decision to be a novelist.

By April 26, 1925, Faulkner knew Anderson's work well

enough to write a thorough review of it.[12] He gave *Winesburg* and *Horses* fulsome praise, disparaging such epithets of his friend as the "Phallic Chekhov" and the "American Tolstoi," insisting that Anderson was "American, and more than that, a middle westerner, of the soil: he is as typical of Ohio in his way as Harding was in his."[13] The article reveals a close friendship between the two men; Faulkner refers to a yacht trip they took together, then to a most peculiar dream which Anderson had related to him:

> We were spending a week-end on a river boat, Anderson and I. I had not slept much and so I was out and watching the sun rise, turning the muddy reaches of the Mississippi even, temporarily to magic, when he joined me, laughing.
> "I had a funny dream last night. Let me tell you about it," was his opening remark—not even a good morning.
> "I dreamed that I couldn't sleep, that I was riding around the country on a horse—had ridden for days. At last I met a man, and I swapped him the horse for a night's sleep. This was in the morning and he told me where to bring the horse, and so when dark came I was right on time, standing in front of his house, holding the horse, ready to rush off to bed. But the fellow never showed up—left me standing there all night, holding the horse." (p. 93)

Twenty-eight years later Faulkner wrote in a tribute to Anderson of the greatness of *Winesburg, Triumph,* and *Horses;* and he mentioned this same peculiar dream in a somewhat different focus. The dream itself is essentially the same, but the setting varies; in the early piece, Anderson relates the dream on a ship's deck, while in the later piece he is sitting on a bench in Jackson Square.[14] It is interesting that Faulkner's retrospection of 1953 admitted the obvious part of the Anderson influence: the man's example as a writer, his admirable sense of métier, his instruction in the tall tale, the fostering of *Soldiers' Pay,* the favor with Horace Liveright—but Faulkner, although he mentioned it, failed to emphasize the part Anderson played in steering his early work in the direction of regionalistic impressionism and away from the futility of his post-war disillusionment. But perhaps, just as time had confused the details of the dream Faulkner retold in 1953, time had also limned over the extent and depth of Anderson's influence on not only his early work, but also on his more mature, subsequent novels, which extend the substance of the regional myth.

The Anderson overtones in Faulkner's *New Orleans Sketches*[15] and *Soldiers' Pay* tend to be general rather than specific. The emphasis on local color and naturalistic devices, rather than the exotic and Romantic, is certainly observable. Whereas Faulkner had been largely interested in poetry before his six-month stay in New Orleans, his interests turned to prose—and, more particularly, to the substance of local color. It is this very general kind of emphasis on subject and treatment, clearly emerging in the sketches, which is important to see; for the long-range effect of the sketches on Faulkner's later literary production cannot be overrated. Carvel Collins in his introduction to the seventeen New Orleans sketches points out their many geneses of characterizations, technical devices, and themes, then traces them to Faulkner's later, more mature work, including *Sartoris, The Sound and the Fury, As I Lay Dying, Light in August, Pylon, The Hamlet,* and *A Fable.*[16] In one of these vignettes, "The Liar," published July 26, 1925, Faulkner used the local color of Lafayette County, replete with men talking on the porch of a general store (one of them named "Ek" suggests *The Hamlet*), a tall tale (the action of a horse running through a house anticipates "Spotted Horses"), and "poor-white" dialogue. Most of the other sketches, however, deal with New Orleans settings.

Although purposely gleaning the *Picayune* pieces for specific parallels between them and Anderson's pre-1925 work reveals nothing as clearly apparent as, say, Hemingway's influence on Faulkner's *The Wild Palms,*[17] there nevertheless are some interesting coincidences of a specific nature. The first lies in the personification of death as a close relative. In Anderson's "Out of Nowhere into Nothing" from *Triumph* (1921), Rosalind Westcott's city lover, Walter Sayers, in the company of the now-dead love of his wife in name, thinks mysteriously as a vision of Rosalind obtrudes itself upon his consciousness in the evening, "Night is the sweet little brother of Death."[18]

Faulkner's sketch "The Kid Learns" concludes with the protagonist's envisioning a girl as he actually dies, she taking his
hand and identifying herself as "Little sister Death" (p. 167).

A second parallel involves the stylistic use of classical
metaphorical materials. In "The Egg," from *Triumph,* to
which Faulkner paid homage, Anderson described his father—
whose attempts at success, he felt, were arrested by Fate's
caprice—as a working man with a bald head, which reminds
Anderson of "a broad road, such as Caesar might have made
on which to lead his legions out of Rome and into the wonders
of an unknown world" (p. 50). Faulkner in his sketch "Mirrors of Chartres Street" wrote of the frustrations of an arrested
working man. After the man vanishes in a police wagon, the
author philosophizes,

And one thought of Caesar mounting his chariot . . . and driving
along the Via Appia . . . and centurions clashed their shields in the
light of golden pennons flapping across the dawn. (p. 57)

Aside from allusive similarities, both metaphors are related
to the frustrations of unsettled working men and are conjoined
in the common man's attitude of inviolable hope even in the
midst of defeat.

Other parallels can be drawn between the two writers' uses
of archaisms and prose lyricism, the latter often related to
man's mysterious communion with nature. But the writers
deal also with themes common to them both: life's impressions
which are deeply felt; life's corruption; death; decay; youth's
disillusionment; faith in life and a persistent hope of its
betterment; work with the hands; man's dignity, especially
the common man's dignity; and the beauty of earth, specifically
scenes of auroral splendor, the sky, clouds, and the river at
night. The quality of Anderson's writing, which involves a
poignant mingling of regional realism, lyricism, and psychological insight, did not go unobserved by the twenty-seven-year-old
Faulkner: rather, the Romantic influences which had been
evident in such poems as "Cathay"—those influences which
can be attributed to Keats and Shelley and further attested to
by Anderson in his telling characterization of David in "A
Meeting South"—gradually gave way to a manner more

naturalistic, to an atmosphere which springs from the sights and sounds of a nature close to reality and perceptible to man.

"Cheest," published on April 5 after Anderson's return to New Orleans, is perhaps the best illustration of Faulkner's adaptation of one of Anderson's fictional techniques; like Faulkner's "The Cop," it is characterized by a first-person revelation and primer-like style not unakin to Anderson's techniques in such stories as "I'm a Fool." On April 26, Faulkner published his review of Anderson's work, referring to "I'm a Fool" as "the best short story in America" and describing the piece as

the tale of a lad's adolescent pride in his profession (horse racing) and his body, of his belief in a world beautiful and passionate created for the chosen to race horses on, of his youthful pagan desire to preen in his lady's eyes that brings him low at last. Here is a personal emotion that does strike the elemental chord in mankind. (p. 91)

Faulkner's "Cheest," like Anderson's story, humorously reveals the pride of a young man, Jack Potter, absorbed with the world of horses, who tells his story in first-person; the viewpoint is skillfully handled so as to give further psychological insights into the character of the persona-narrator. Potter has the same kind of swaggering personality and callow belligerence as Anderson's protagonist. There are more detailed similarities, too. Potter, like Anderson's hero, meets a girl in the company of her girlfriend, and attempts to impress her by showing off in the most obvious way; in both characters, the traits of brashness and arrogance become prisms through which the reader sees the more basic qualities of youthful ignorance, arrogance, and insecurity. Both stories involve two couples who double-date; both heroes treat their girls to an evening dancing at cabarets; and, finally, both stories feature a horse race as an important central action. In a general way the center of action about a horse race, the method of narration, and an occasional line such as "a little child shall beat them to the wire . . ." (p. 94) anticipate parts of *The Reivers,* which in turn may suggest the possibility of relating an Anderson influence over the span of thirty-seven years of Faulkner's literary career to the 1962 novel; but the differences between the early sketch and the last major work are so vast as to make the point of hardly more than passing interest.

All this is not to say that a clear line can be drawn before which Faulkner was experimenting ineffectually with various literary techniques and after which he abandoned them and attempted to emulate Anderson. Faulkner's New Orleans sketches and poems continued to reveal strong relationships with his own earlier work. Pastoral images of *The Marble Faun* reappear in the character of the Priest in "New Orleans" ("starry meadows . . . faint dewed grass," p. 39); in "The Cobbler" ("the belled flocks among the sunny hills long after the valley itself was in shadow!" p. 43); and in "Home," ("in the meadows where quiet cattle grazed or stood knee-deep in the water," p. 79). Similar aspects of nature are echoed in "Out of Nazareth" ("how green the trees were, and the grass, and the narcissi and hyacinths like poised dancers," p. 101); and even more specifically in striking avian images ("the broken flight of golden birds," p. 131, and "a bird . . . like a buzzard, drawing endless black circles on a blue sky," p. 157). More concise relationships with *The Marble Faun* can be seen in cognate phrasing; to illustrate, the Artist in "New Orleans" speaks in monologue of "this dream within me in marble" (p. 47), and in "The Liar," four men sit on a porch "in easy amity" (p. 171), a familiar image in not only *The Marble Faun,* but also *A Green Bough.* Finally, similar thematic overtones between *The Marble Faun* and the sketches are evident. "Damon and Pythias Unlimited" is characterized by Faulkner as narrator, writing, "I pondered on the mutability of mankind" (p. 61). In "Episode," the old man's experience in viewing life in conditions of both sight and blindness render him "calm as a god who has seen both life and death and found nothing of particular importance in either of them" —a condition suggesting that of the somnolent equanimity of the faun at the end of the poem. The catalepsy of the country wife posing for William Spratling's sketch is associated, too: "it was as if someone had whispered a sublime and colossal joke in the ear of an idol" (p. 190).

The early poem "Cathay" is faintly echoed in the Wealthy Jew of "New Orleans" as he reflects upon man's "Destiny, foaming out of the East where . . . centuries ago his ancient Phoenician ancestors breasted the uncharted fabulous seas with trading barques" (p. 37). The *Mississippian* poem "Naiads' Song" is recapitulated in the personification of "trees . . . like poised dancers" (p. 101). There are many mirrorings of "Nocturne" in the sketches, among them the "cold stars" (p. 38); a "flung rose . . . under the evening star" (p. 43); "The stars are cold" (p. 44) of "New Orleans"; and "the cold, cold stars" (p. 157) of "Sunset." The image of a girl "like music of a hundred fiddles become one white and scarlet flame" (p. 133) in "The Cobbler," and "the hot black gaze . . . like a blade spitting him against the wall, like a pinned moth" (p. 181) in "The Liar" are images closely corresponding to the earlier "Nocturne."

The emphasis on unattractive details of scenery, Juan Venturia's "dumped trash and tin cans" (p. 123) in "The Rosary," recapitulates the same details of Faulkner's earlier prose sketch "The Hill";[19] and his reference to "the luxuries and vices of an age as the Baptists teach us" (p. 61) in "Damon and Pythias Unlimited" harks back to Faulkner's disfavor "of striving, of whipped vanities . . . of the drying spittle of religious controversy" in "The Hill."

It is not surprising that traces of Faulkner's *A Green Bough* should be particularly evident in a number of the sketches, for by 1925 he had just prepared the volume under the title of *The Greening Bough*. Thus, Magdalen, a prostitute in "New Orleans," relates her story of sad aging and regret: "maybe its [sic] I that aint like I was once" and "sometime a thousand worms, feeding upon this body which has betrayed me, feeding, will live" (pp. 48-49). She concludes with "Was there love once? I have forgotten her. Was there grief once? Yes, long ago. Ah, long ago" (p. 49). Poem XXXIII of *A Green Bough*, the theme of which is regret or dead love, begins with the stanza

Did I know love once? Was it love or grief,
This grave body by where I had lain,
And my heart, a single stubborn leaf
That will not die, though root and branch be slain?

(p. 57)

Similarly, Faulkner in the sketch of the Tourist in "New Orleans" likens the city to "A courtesan" (p. 49) and her surroundings, while poem XXXV of *A Green Bough* begins with "The courtesan is dead, for all her subtle ways" (p. 58), although in this latter poem the courtesan personifies the vanishing of warm summer as "winter's lean clean rain sweeps out her room." Finally, the theme of affirmation through praise of the earth's refreshing beauty expressed in "Out of Nazareth" (pp. 106-110, a sketch dealing with a poet of the earth) is condensed in poem XLIV of *A Green Bough.*

Faulkner continued to apply the French Symbolist techniques exhibited in his earlier work, especially images involving faint suggestion, synesthesia, motion, color, and music. Thus in "Mirrors of Chartres Street" one reads of a police wagon at night "clanging among the shivering golden wings of street lights" (p. 56); in "Home" of a "sky . . . rumorous with dawn" (p. 79); in "The Rosary" of a tune "spilling the dusty sparrows tumultously from the eaves" (p. 128), and in "Country Mice" of a car ride through the countryside of Louisiana which "rushed by us in a fretful, indistinguishable green" (p. 194).

Even the familiar themes of the past and the struggle to identity with its accompanying tensional images appear again. In addition to those touched upon in my relating of what appears to be Faulkner's biographical aspects rendered by Anderson in "A Meeting South" (especially the remarks on the Southern poet's "great-grandfather") and of the sketches to *The Marble Faun,* "Cathay," and "Naiads' Song," one finds a description of the statue of Andrew Jackson presented in familiar cataleptic imagery in "Out of Nazareth": "he bestrode his curly horse in terrific arrested motion" (p. 101). A more universal past and present vie as East and West in "Yo Ho and Two Bottles of Rum": "the East raised its implacability bodiless as mist against the West and civilization and discipline" (p. 219).

It would be difficult to contend that Anderson is *the* dominating influence in the seventeen sketches; nor do I wish to suggest that other influences are not operative. One finds innuendoes of Cervantes' Rosinante in the reminiscence of the Beggar in "New Orleans": "The knight still would ride forth, but his steed is old and not sure of foot any more" (p. 47). Conrad's influence appears to be deeper. There are echoes of "Heart of Darkness" in the Longshoreman of "New Orleans" in such images as "the great trees sailing like ships up the rivers of darkness" (p. 44). But the echoes of "Youth" are even stronger in "Yo Ho and Two Bottles of Rum," commencing early in the sketch with a reference to the ineffectual ship *Diana* (p. 211), which, after encountering difficulties, "rolled and wallowed on" (p. 219). The ship's destination is the East: "out of Canton, bound for Bangkok" (p. 214), and the lyricism of the anticipated East, as it appears to the Westerner, echoes memorable portions of "Youth":

There is something eternal in the East, something resilient and yet rocklike, against which the Westerner's brief thunder, his passionate, efficient methods, are as wind. (p. 217)

Again, "Mr. Ayers looked from face to quiet face, remote and expressionless as so many idols . . ." (p. 217): then "the East raised its implacability bodiless as mist against the West and civilization and discipline. They were all going ashore . . ." (p. 219); and "The sun was red and implacable as a furnace mouth" (p. 220). One distinction between the two pieces lies in the intolerable nature of the cargoes of the ships: in "Youth" it is a smoking freight in the ship's hold; in Faulkner's sketch it is the putrefying body of Yo Ho. However, both features serve as *tour de force* focal points about which the action revolves, and both devices are laden with explosive possibilities. Housman's manner is suggested in "Home" with the sentence, "Thinking, indeed, lays lads underground" (p. 74); and the *Shropshire Lad* is mentioned as belonging to the natural poet and quoted in "Out of

Nazareth" (p. 104). A faint hint of imagery from the chapter titled "Sunset" in Melville's *Moby-Dick* can be found in Faulkner's Magdalen in "New Orleans." Both Ahab and Magdalen are looking out windows, both have aching heads, and both reflect upon their youth in images of gold:

MELVILLE	FAULKNER
The gold brow plumbs the blue . . . . 'Tis iron . . . not gold. 'Tis split, too. . . . Oh! *time was,* when as the sunrise nobly spurred me, so the sunset soothed. [Italics added.]	"God, the light in my eyes, the sunlight . . . crashing in my poor head. . . . *I can remember when* I found days gold, but now the gold of day hurts my head." (p. 48) [Italics added.]

Similarly, O'Neill's Yank of *The Hairy Ape* anticipates Faulkner's Jean-Baptiste in "Home" with the question: "How much longer would he be free, to walk the earth . . . be uncaged? Perhaps tomorrow he would clasp steel bars like a caged ape, panting for freedom" (p. 75). Swinburne's devices of allusion and imagery reappear in the Priest of "New Orleans": "The twilight . . . stirring among the lilacs and shaking spikes of bloom, ringing the soundless bells of hyacinths dreaming briefly of Lesbos. . . ." (pp. 38-39).

But the general direction of Anderson's influence on Faulkner can be most clearly illustrated in Faulkner's increasing tendency to turn to prose, to write of familiar, down-to-earth subjects; and, eventually, to return to and to find the substance of his literature in his own region, even in the circumstances of his own life and family background. There are several aspects of the sketches which anticipate these evergrowing developments in Faulkner's writing. The most obvious is the previously treated "The Liar." In addition, two of the sketches, "Out of Nazareth" and "Episode," consist of first-person reporting; in the first of these one may see specific traits and larger motifs which foreshadow *The Sound and the Fury, Light in August,* and *A Fable.* Finally, and of lesser significance, Jean-Baptiste's reflection in "Home" on "the joy he had felt in handling high explosive in a shell factory" (p. 78) may reveal a tenuous thread of mutual experience connected to

Faulkner's employment in 1918 at the Winchester arms factory at New Haven; and the knowledge of New Haven and Yale which the narrator reveals in "Country Mice" harks back to Faulkner's rooming with Phil Stone during the same period at New Haven.[20]

Soldiers' Pay was written in about two months at the urging of Anderson. Thus, there can be little doubt that Anderson was a strong motivating force behind Faulkner's literary creation. Both the legendary and factual information concerning the publication of the book by Horace Liveright, Anderson's publisher, bear out Anderson's interest and Faulkner's close contact with him even more.[21] As they had hailed Anderson's work before, critics greeted Faulkner's first novel as a distinctly impressionistic work. Perhaps one of the most directly prominent adaptations of Anderson's methods by Faulkner in *Soldiers' Pay* was his use of the girl character who is keenly aware of her sexuality and freedom. Anderson had given to such characters a special kind of tenderness and sensitivity, a kind of dreamy yearning for "a far off joy and eventual fulfillment"; and yet they have "passion without body, and sexuality without gaiety and joy . . . ."[22] Thus Rosalind of "Out of Nowhere into Nothing" is vibrantly aware of her sex as she stands nude:

Rosalind's cheeks were flushed. She made an odd and lovely figure standing nude before the glass in her room. . . . She was so much alive and yet not alive. Her eyes shone with excitement. She continued to turn slowly round and round. . . . She also had found out something about life. Her body was still the body of what was called a virgin. . . . (pp. 204-205)

It is through just such a deep consciousness of their sexual experiences that Anderson's characters perceive life and its ramifications. Faulkner's typical post-war girl, the Cecily of *Soldiers' Pay,* becomes the same kind of figure of desire, a pattern of the new woman aware of her sexual freedom:

her lax hand between them grew again like a flower: it was as if her whole body became her hand. The symbol of a delicate, bodyless lust . . . her body . . . crushed softly about with her fragile clothing.

Her long legs, not for locomotion, but for the studied completion of a rhythm carried to its *nth*: compulsion of progress, movement; her body created for all men to dream after. (p. 224)

The similarity of the two passages lies not so much in the phraseology as in the purpose of the girl-character: in the work of both men she is a brooding thing, a symbol rather than someone to be remembered for herself, a symbol of a newly independent, youthful desire, freshly experienced in the new, unrestrained atmosphere of independence itself.

Even with the general cognates of theme, characterization, and style, the Anderson influence on *Soldiers' Pay* is indirect rather than direct. One finds more direct Anderson influences in both *Mosquitoes* and *Sartoris*.

Neither Faulkner's nor Anderson's biographers have ever worked out in detail Anderson's part as source and influence for *Mosquitoes* (1927).[23] The action deals with a group of New Orleans artists of the Vieux Carré who have been persistently herded aboard the *Nausikaa,* the yacht of a socialite, Mrs. Maurier. A five-day voyage over Lake Pontchartrain ensues, during which the artists—whose spirit is best represented by a famous writer, Dawson Fairchild, and a taciturn sculptor, Gordon—persist in being tardy to meals, remaining below deck drinking and playing cards, and being altogether unco-operative with Mrs. Maurier, who yearns to realize her preconceived notion of what a yacht party should be. She finally relents in helpless confusion while the art group engages in long, sometimes-amusing, always-interesting conversations. During the five days the hostess's niece disappears in a swamp with the young steward, where they are set upon by flights of mosquitoes. The novel concludes in the Vieux Carré, where it began.

The most obvious Anderson source in the novel is the character Dawson Fairchild, of whom Sherwood Anderson is apparently the prototype. As Anderson was, Fairchild is "an American of a provincial midwestern lower middle class family" (p. 241). He describes American life "as American life is" (p. 243). He is "a man in all the lusty pride of his

Ohio Valley masculinity" (p. 209). If the fictional character agrees with the model, then Faulkner portrays Anderson as a "novelist, resembling a benevolent walrus too recently out of bed to have made a toilet" (p. 33), as having a "burly jovial voice" (p. 44), and as not minding the heat:

"I like it, in fact. Like an old racehorse, you know. He's willing enough, you know, but in the cool weather when his muscles are stiff and his bones ache, the young ones all show him up. But about Fourth of July, when the sun gets hot and his muscles loosen up and his old bones don't complain any more, then he's good as any of 'em." (p. 49)

Such comments probably are not intended as a disparagement of Anderson, but rather give a balance of reality and humanity to the portrait.

Even though the resemblances between Faulkner's Fairchild and Anderson are curiously similar, perhaps even convincing, the tall-tale evidence makes Anderson an indisputable influence and source of material extending beyond character parallels alone. In 1953 Faulkner wrote of the tall tales that he and Anderson had worked on together:

During those afternoons when we would walk about the old quarter, I listening while he talked to me or to people—anyone, anywhere— whom we would meet on the streets or the docks, or the evenings while we sat somewhere over a bottle, *he, with a little help from me, invented other fantastic characters. . . . One of them was supposed to to be a descendant of Andrew Jackson, left in that Louisiana swamp after the Battle of Chalmette, no longer half-horse half-alligator but by now half-man half-sheep and presently half-shark, who—it, the whole fable—at last got so unwieldly and (so we thought) so funny, that we decided to get it onto paper by writing letters to one another such as two temporarily separated members of an exploring—zoological expedition might. . . .*[24] [Italics added.]

In *Mosquitoes* Faulkner had Fairchild tell the following story about some half-horse, half-alligator creatures that General Jackson used in the battle of New Orleans "down there in those Chalmette swamps":

"in some way the breed got crossed with alligators. And so . . . Old Hickory . . . had 'em round up as many of those half-horse half-alligators as they could, and he mounted some of his infantry on 'em and the British couldn't stop 'em at all." (p. 68)

Later in the novel, Faulkner wrote,

"Old man Jackson"—Fairchild continued—"claims to be a lineal descendant of Old Hickory . . . he thought up the idea of taking up some of this Louisiana swamp land and raising sheep on it . . . the sheep learned to swim pretty well. . . . Finally . . . Claude—Al's brother . . . went right in the water and grappled for 'em . . . old man Jackson quit the sheep business and went to fish ranching . . . pretty soon [Claude] got to where he'd stay in the water all day . . . Claude's eyes . . . kind of shifted around to the side of his head and his mouth spread back a good way, and his teeth . . . got longer. . . . Pretty soon after that, though, there was a shark scare at the bathing beaches along the Gulf Coast. It seemed to be a lone shark that kept annoying women bathers, especially blondes; and they knew it was Claude Jackson. He was always hell after blondes." (pp. 277-281)

There is no mistaking the relationship between fact and fiction, or that Faulkner made use of this particular tall tale, about which Faulkner wrote, "he [Anderson] with a little help from me, invented. . . ." Faulkner's use of this material, which Anderson unquestionably had a hand in, takes Anderson beyond influence or source and virtually into the realm of collaboration. The force of Anderson's guiding hand in this portion of *Mosquitoes* is borne out further by Faulkner again, who wrote, speaking of the letters containing the tall tale, this exchange of dialogue between Anderson and himself concerning Faulkner's reply to Anderson's first letter:

He [Anderson] said:—
"Does it satisfy you?"
I said, "Sir?"
"Are you satisfied with it?"
"Why not?" I said. "I'll put whatever I left out into the next one."
Then I realized that he was more than displeased: he was short, stern, almost angry. He said:—
"Either throw it away, and we'll quit, or take it back and do it over." I took the letter. I worked three days over it before I carried it back to him. He read it again, quite slowly, as he always did, and said, "Are you satisfied now?"

"No sir," I said. "But it's the best I know how to do."

"Then we'll pass it," he said, putting the letter into his pocket, his voice once more warm, rich, burly with laughter, ready to believe, ready to be hurt again.[25]

From this passage one might assume that even the portions of the tall tale which Faulkner wrote were read over and criticized by Anderson; and in at least this particular circumstance revised by Faulkner at Anderson's insistence.[26]

The probability of Sherwood Anderson's being the model for Dawson Fairchild is consistent with the strong suggestions of other prototypes, too, including those based on the characters Colonel Ayers, Pete, and Gordon, the darkly brooding sculptor, who suggests Faulkner himself, his artistic medium altered. Other elements of *Mosquitoes* could be related to the influence of Anderson, but these are quite general in nature: the strange combination of the realistic, the impressionistic, the mystical; the psychological investigations of his characters, not nearly so prevalent in *Soldiers' Pay;* and isolated segments of style such as the use of slang and archaisms.

But Anderson was only one influence, albeit the most dominating one. Among the others are Aubrey Beardsley, Thomas Beer, James Branch Cabell, T. S. Eliot, Aldous Huxley, James Joyce, H. L. Mencken, Mark Twain, and Oscar Wilde.

Thematically *Mosquitoes,* perhaps more than its predecessor, *Soldiers' Pay,* lacks the rich depth of life, the tragedy and lovely enigma of human existence which Anderson portrayed in *Winesburg, Triumph,* and *Horses.* Faulkner did, however, manage to express a haunting love of the Southern land, although the direction of his thinking, at least on the surface, was towards a cynical despair. The action, characterization, and theme of *Mosquitoes,* despite its satirical elements, show that the author was still identifying with the world-weary, sensitive young men of the *fin de siècle* tradition. But the fictional resources of Faulkner's north-central Mississippi area, not the themes of sophistication for which Huxley was already famous, had been observed by Anderson as the strongest potential in Faulkner. As a consequence, Anderson told him: "You've got too much talent. You can do it too easy, in too many different ways. If you're not careful, you'll never write anything."[27] Anderson told Faulkner that a writer "has first got tc be what he is, what he was born," and

"It dont matter where it was, just so you remember it and aint ashamed of it. Because one place to start from is just as important as any other. You're a country boy; *all you know is that little patch up there in Mississippi where you started from.* But that's all right too. It's America too; pull it out, as little and unknown as it is, and the whole thing will collapse, like when you prize a brick out of a wall. . . . *All America asks is to look at it and listen to it and understand it if you can. Only . . . the important thing is to believe in it even if you dont understand it, and then try to tell it, put it down.* Because tomorrow America is going to be something different, something more and new to watch and listen to and try to understand; and even if you cant understand, believe." (p. 28) [Italics added.]

But although he had learned a lot from Anderson as writer, by the summer of 1925 Faulkner's dream that caused him to quit the postmastership at the University of Mississippi and leave Oxford was still carrying him farther from, not closer to, what Anderson referred to as "that little patch up there in Mississippi." He had come to New Orleans bent on going to Europe, and he would go. Faulkner and his friend, the artist William Spratling, with whom he would soon collaborate on *Sherwood Anderson and Other Famous Creoles,* sailed for Europe in the summer aboard the freighter *West Ivis.*

VIII

Soldiers' Pay:
Detour Through Decadence

Faulkner was a keen observer and wide reader, and although his inventions were often powerful, he seems never to have invented more than he had to. He was also an intuitive and instinctive thinker. When he read the French Symbolists, he discovered in them a philosophical basis akin to his own—one involving an *intuitional* perception. For with these writers, the intuitional perception is a very real thing, encompassing the fictive transfer of the senses from life to the page—the senses of sight, sound, smell, taste, and touch, but especially the power of suggestion.

In this context one should recall that Faulkner had excelled in French at Ole Miss. He had composed the *Marble Faun* poems and received $15.00 for "L'Apres-Midi d'un Faune," published in the *New Republic* August 6, 1919. The poem was reprinted in the college weekly newspaper, *The Mississippian,* in late October. During the next seven months he published a total of thirteen poems, at least six of them demonstrating concurrent interests in the French language and the techniques and philosophical attitudes of the decadents and French Symbolists, especially Paul Verlaine.

The idea that Faulkner's early poetry was "schoolboyish" need hardly be denied; but, standing alone, the view is misleading. The difference between *juvenilia* and mature work is obvious enough, but "schoolboy plus Verlaine" is another matter—an important one within the developing pattern of Faulkner's work.

Faulkner's early prose and poetry owe much to the *fin de siècle,* or, more accurately, the decadent tradition of which it partook; but exactly what that tradition is requires some further review. A clarified concept of decadence and Faulkner's employment of some of its various aspects should serve to illuminate in new ways the meaning of his first novel, *Soldiers' Pay,* its significance as a phase of his literary development during the period of its composition in 1925, and its relationship to the whole process of Faulkner's maturation as a literary artist.

Baudelaire was among the first French writers to point out the vagueness of the literary term *décadence,* writing in a letter to Jules Janin that it was a convenient means by which educators could hide their ignorance—a vague word by which anyone could conceal his laziness and lack of curiosity. Baudelaire's *Les Fleurs du Mal* and Huysmans' *À Rebours* were regarded as decadent because of the subject matter they treated. To trenchant guardians of literary propriety, decadence was a flamboyant pennon of wickedness, a shameful decline of what is wholesome. We know now that those who condemned, for example, *Fleurs du Mal,* were often moral *esprits simplistes* who had oversimplified their literary judgments to the extent that they could appreciate neither the work's revelations of conscience nor its evocations of tormented beauty.

In a second and more meaningful sense, the word decadence was used to indicate a literary style, principally the suggestivity of words, a skillful obliquity of connotation wrought by such devices as synesthesia which produced an intensely original power of language.

One finds strong distinctions between the politico-historical understanding of decadence, and the esthetic or literary concept of decadence. Historians tend to admit no other idea of decadence than that of natural death; but although civilizations may be born, grow to maturity, weaken, and die somewhat in an organic sense, a serious question exists as to how accurate the analogy holds for the fine arts. Holbrook Jackson in *The Eighteen Nineties* emphasized that the *fin de siècle* literature was neither completely decadent nor hopeless. On the contrary, "decadence was often decadence in name only" and "would have been better named regeneration"; for it was a time of vitality, too, in which literature was often in opposition to customs and conventions that were looked upon as being relatively permanent. Thus, decadence was a kind of Janus-faced anomaly:

En fait, la "décadence" offre un double aspect: *elle est à la fois une fin et un commencement.* Elle marque bien un terme en ce sens qu'elle clôt un âge qui, depuis longtemps déjà, trahissait une certaine lassitude, semblait marcher vers l'épuisement. Mais elle est aussi un point de départ, et il semble que ce soit la sa véritable signification. La lutte contre le victorianisme a fait apparaître l'étroitesse des vieilles formules, trop étriquées pour répondre aux aspirations des temps nouveaux. Peu à peu, les écrivains se dégagent de l'emprise du passé, poussés par le besoin de découvrir d'autres voies. Des doctrines émergent, diffuses, flottantes encore, mais qui laissent entrevoir l'art de l'avenir.[1] [Italics added.]

Beginning with Edgar Allan Poe, Oscar Cargill has traced the decadent movement, mentioning the characteristics of *egotism, obscurity, necrophilia* ("Lust for the bodies of the dead," or an emphasis upon death itself), *perverseness, artificiality,* and *synesthesia* as a consciously employed literary device.[2] The decadent movement eventually mingled with the French Symbolist movement through Stéphane Mallarmé, who established his leadership with his masterpiece "L'Après-midi d'un Faune" (1876).[3]

The list of characteristics of the decadent movement could be extended, but my purpose is not to be inclusive. Rather, I wish to emphasize the vagueness of the term as a generalization; to recognize its various interpretations,[4] especially those which are extreme and inaccurate; and to clarify the term as

much as possible in a few words. Finally, it is my intention to
sketch in some of those characteristics which are both generally
accepted and functionally related to Faulkner's first novel.
Among them are the following:

1. a thematic questioning of Victorian optimism accompanied by a
    spiritual and moral disillusionment, rebellion, perverseness, an
    emphasis on pleasure and death;
2. a mockery of sentimentality and an exaltation of feminism, "the
    new woman";
3. a breakaway from traditional novel forms and a subtilizing refine-
    ment of experimental technical devices, including synesthesia,
    novelty versus monotony, and other innovations.

The decadent influences upon Faulkner's early work included
Hart Crane, Eliot, Mallarmé, Poe, Dante Gabriel Rossetti,
Swinburne, and Wilde. Keeping in mind the influences on
Faulkner's early work, one should add the names of Aiken,
Baudelaire, and Verlaine to this group. Like Wilde, who wrote
in his "Preface" to *The Picture of Dorian Gray* a defense of
the doctrine of art for art's sake, Faulkner stated,

An artist is a creature driven by demons. He doesn't know why they
choose him and he's usually too busy to wonder why. He is completely
amoral in that he will rob, borrow, beg, or steal from anybody and
everybody to get work done. . . . The writer's only responsibility is to
his art. . . . Everything goes by the board: honor, pride, decency,
security, happiness.[5]

Whatever the relationship of his sense of métier to that of
Wilde or any other decadent, his first novel, *Soldiers' Pay*,[6]
best illustrates his treatment of a fictional situation with the
characteristics, devices, and philosophical underpinnings of
decadence. On one level the novel is a dramatic rendering of
two contending groups, soldiers and civilians, and of the various
conflicts that occur when the two encounter each other after
World War I. To particularize the tragedy of those conflicts
and to explore the manifold meanings of life and death,
Faulkner presented the reader with a grotesquely disfigured
returning hero, Lieutenant Donald Mahon of the Royal Air
Force, who lives in a moribund world of semi-oblivion. On

his way home by train to Charlestown, Georgia, he meets
Private Joe Gilligan, Cadet Julian Lowe, and Margaret Powers,
an attractive young war widow. The three, seeing Mahon's
helpless state, decide to care for him. In the course of the trip,
Gilligan, a seasoned veteran, makes love to Margaret, while
young Cadet Lowe, romantically overwhelmed by such things
as war and women, worships her in a childish fashion. In
Charlestown, meanwhile, Mahon's father, an Episcopalian
rector, walks in the garden of his churchyard, unaware that
his son is not dead, but alive and returning. He converses
with Januarius Jones, a fat ex-fellow of Latin "born of whom
he knew and cared not" (p. 40). After the two have retired
to the parsonage, Cecily Saunders, Donald's capricious fiancée,
appears. As the Divine kisses her cheek, "Jones' goat's eyes
immersed her in yellow contemplation" (p. 49). There follows
a blatant scene of attempted seduction by Jones, after which
Cecily escapes his uninhibited advances and flees to the arms
of her current boyfriend, George Farr. Undaunted during her
temporary absence, Jones turns his attentions toward Dr.
Mahon's young housekeeper, Emmy.

At the end of this tragicomic exposition, Gilligan and
Margaret Powers, having packed Cadet Lowe off to his home
in California, enter with Donald Mahon; the two have resolved to remain with the doomed protagonist until the last.
For a time Dr. Mahon retains the illusion that his son will
rally, but the reality of the boy's impending death eventually
pierces even his quaint shell of metaphysical optimism. When
it becomes apparent that Cecily cannot bring herself to marry
Donald, even as a therapeutic gesture, Margaret Powers weds
him out of a sense of expiation for not having loved her first
husband. After Lieutenant Mahon dies, she perversely refuses
to marry Gilligan, whom she deeply loves, because "If I married
you you'd be dead in a year, Joe. All the men that marry me
die, you know" (p. 212). She leaves Charlestown alone.
Throughout the action, Januarius Jones continues his attempts
to seduce Cecily, Margaret, and Emmy; but he succeeds only in
the impalpable realm of contemplation. Cecily, pregnant with
George Farr's child, extricates herself from the conflict by

eloping with him. Margaret leaves. Only Gilligan and Dr. Mahon remain. The book ends as they walk into the dark by "moon-silvered ridges above valleys where mist hung slumbrous . . ." (p. 220). They pause by a tumbledown Negro church to listen to the services.

The French Symbolist influences operate in numerous ways throughout the novel. For Faulkner, they resulted not merely in a few stylistic techniques, but in new ways of looking, experiencing, reacting, and thinking. What he learned was not a juggler's trick, but a philosophical perversity which colored the work with subtly different hues. Because the philosophical underpinning is less obvious than the stylistic mannerisms, it needs to be emphasized. Three recurring images which may serve to strengthen and point up the deeper aspects of decadence are the faun, the worm, and the tower. Although each of these images is treated separately within a division of the chapter, one should realize that all three involve not only a separateness but also a connection. Faulkner himself was working toward a solution of the paradoxes which they represent.

THE ELEMENTAL FAUN

Stéphane Mallarmé's masterpiece of decadence, "L'Après-midi d'un Faune," is characterized by a faun who, in the afternoon on a mountainside, contemplates some nymphs whom he believes he has raped:

> *Ces nymphes, je les veux perpétuer.*
> > *Si clair,*
> *Leur incarnat léger, qu'il voltige dans l'air*
> *Assoupi de sommeils touffus.*
> > *Aimai-je un rêve?*[7]

The doubt increases, and as he plays his flute he is not sure whether he has dreamed the whole event or whether it has actually happened. Venus, the epitome of all his dreams of desire, teases his half-waking consciousness, and he is on the point of capturing the delightful vision when he succumbs to sleep.

It is, of course, not merely coincidental that Faulkner's first published poem was entitled "L'Apres-Midi d'un Faune," [*sic*] and begins on the same note of reverie:

I follow through the singing trees
Her streaming clouded hair and face
And lascivious dreaming knees
Like gleaming water from some place
Of sleeping streams, or autumn leaves
Slow shed through still, love-wearied air. . . .[8]

Mallarmé may well be the source for Januarius Jones' faunal traits in *Soldiers' Pay*. Early in the novel, his face is described as "a round mirror before which fauns and nymphs might have wantoned when the world was young" (p. 41). And if Jones is the faun, then Cecily and Emmy qualify as nymphs, freely running in a natural world. All the formal restrictions of the Victorian age seem to have vanished. Part of the decadent movement was, of course, the advent of the "new woman" who energetically played golf and hockey, rode a horse or bicycle like a man, danced with nervous intensity and wore skirts of ever-increasing brevity. In the whole process, she often slimmed her figure into that of a boyish silhouette. It is Jones who is most aware of the new woman's passional relations and primitive play, and he stares at Cecily, his eyes "bold and contemplative, obscene as a goat's" (p. 155). Caught in Jones' gaze, she is compared to

A poplar, vain and pliant, trying attitude after attitude, gesture after gesture—"a girl trying gown after gown, perplexed but in pleasure." Her unseen face nimbused with light and her body, which was no body, crumpling a dress that had been dreamed. Not for maternity, not even for love: a thing for the eye and the mind. Epicene, he thought, feeling her slim bones, the bitter nervousness latent in her flesh. (pp. 155-156)

The nymphology of Cecily is assured as Jones contemplates her and becomes "a fat Mirandola in . . . nympholepsy . . ." (p. 156). Such a description echoes an earlier statement of Gourmont which clashed with the more conventional Victorian concepts of beauty: he said beauty is "a sexual illusion" rather than "a pure idea," and is "intimately connected with the idea of carnal pleasure. . . ."⁹

As Cecily leaves the parsonage for a scene of teary passion with George Farr, Jones watches from the window. "His round face was enigmatic as a god's, his clear obscene eyes showed no emotion" (p. 62); and just before he has imagined "her long subtle legs, like Atalanta's reft of running" (p. 55). Several allusions to Swinburne can be found throughout the novel. At a party the town's most eligible bachelor, Dr. Gary, dances with a naïve girl and tells her,

> "Dancing with you . . . is like a poem by a minor poet named Swinburne." . . .
> "Swinburne?" She smiled vaguely, watching the other couple, not losing the rhythm, not cracking her paint. Her face was smooth, as skillfully done and as artificial as an orchid. "Did he write poems, too?" (p. 138)

Swinburne's decadent influence is obvious enough in this scene, as in others, but perhaps more important for our purposes are the thematic suggestions of lassitude, blasé attitudes, and artificiality. The Swinburne references, however, most often blend with the faunal character of Jones. Margaret Powers, Joe Gilligan, and the rector are talking quietly outside when Emmy suddenly runs by and darts inside. Then they see Jones, "like a fat satyr, leaping after her, hopelessly distanced" (p. 198). He is actually running until he notices them. His eyes, "clear and yellow, obscene and old in sin as a goat's, roved between them." After some Wildeian repartee on the subjects of running, reducing (Jones is a very heavy faun), and marriage, this exchange occurs:

> "Perhaps Mr. Jones was merely preparing to write a poem. Living it first, you know," Mrs. Mahon [Margaret Powers] offered. Jones looked at her sharply. "Atalanta," she suggested in the dusk.
> "Atlanta?" [sic] repeated Gilligan, "what—"
> "Try an apple next time, Mr. Jones," she advised. (p. 199)

Jones' ferity is illustrated once again as, on a late evening walk, Gilligan pauses, noticing something crawling shapelessly

along "the moony wall of the rectory, from ledge to ledge."
It is Jones attempting to reach Emmy's room:

> "What are you trying to do?" Gilligan asked.
> "Climb up here a little further and I'll show you," Jones told him
> snarling with his yellow teeth.
> "Come away from there, fellow." (p. 217)

Even after Jones is caught, he still tries to heave himself up
the wall to Emmy's window, only to be dragged down and
beaten by Gilligan. Toward the end of the novel, Jones thinks
of the Garden of Eden and several lines from *The Rubáiyát,*
which reached its height of popularity during the last quarter
of the nineteenth century.[10] As Jones is last seen overcome
with the poetic memory of girls, raising "his clear sentimental
tenor" in the moonlight: "Sweetheart, sweetheart, sweetheart,"
one easily remembers Mallarmé's faun dreaming of nymphs,
playing his flute and sighing on the verge of a dream:

> Jones leaned his elbows on a gate, staring at his lumpy shadow at his
> feet, smelling cape jasmine, hearing a mocking bird somewhere, some-
> where. . . . Jones sighed. It was a sigh of pure ennui. (p. 218)

THE DESTROYING WORM

Baudelaire's poem "Une Charogne" ("A Carrion") may be
said to epitomize the decadent *Fleurs du Mal*:

> Rappelez-vous l'objet que nous vîmes, mon âme,
> Ce beau matin d'été si doux:
> Au detour d'un sentier une charogne infâme
> Sur un lit seme de cailloux,
>
> . . . .
> . . . .
>
> Les mouches bourdonnaient sur ce ventre putride,
> d'où sortaient de noirs bataillons
> Le larves, qui coulaient comme un épais liquide
> Le long de ces vivants haillons.
> . . . .[11]

It has been suggested that these lines are but a "powerful
resetting of those which Poe's deranged Ligeia made her
lover recite as she lay dying":

> *. . . But see, amid the mimic rout*
> *A crawling shape intrude!*
> *A blood-red thing that writhes from out*
> *The scenic solitude!*
> *It writhes!—it writhes!—with mortal pangs*
> *The mines become its food,*
> *And the seraphs sob at vermin fangs*
> *In human gore imbued.*

> *. . . And the angels, all pallid and wan,*
> *. . . affirm*
> *That the play is the tragedy, "Man,"*
> *And its hero, the conqueror Worm.*

(See Cargill, p. 183.)

The special emphasis on death as a characteristic of decadence thus has deep roots; and such an emphasis permeates *Soldiers' Pay,* although the motif is often contrasted with the dream-vitality of the faunal image in the comic form of blatant sex. There are two worm images related to the death theme that are difficult to extirpate from the decadent tradition. The first occurs just after Lieutenant Mahon has died:

Sex and Death: the front door and the back door of the world. How indissolubly are they associated in us! In youth they lift us out of the flesh, in old age they reduce us again to the flesh; one to fatten us, the other to flay us, *for the worm.* When are sexual compulsions more readily answered than in war or famine or flood or fire? (p. 204) [Italics added.]

The second reference issues from the lips of the rector, who says these words to Joe Gilligan:

"You are suffering from disappointment. But this will pass away. The saddest thing about love, Joe, is that not only the love cannot last forever, but even the heartbreak is soon forgotten. How does it go? *'Men have died and worms have eaten them, but not for love.'* " (p. 220) [Italics added.]

THE PERVERSE TOWER OF THE SPIRIT

The worm image, a commentary on physical death in contrast to the transient realities of life and sex, is related not

only to a mockery of the sentimentality of romantic love, but
also to a deeper questioning of Victorian optimism and is,
as it were, a paradoxical affirmation of that spiritual and
moral disillusionment characteristic of the decadent movement.
This perverse affirmation of what may be looked upon as a
kind of negation is an attitude as pervading as that of the
obscene and riotous faun, although it is much more subtle.
It finds expression close to the beginning and at the end of
the novel. The opening scene of Chapter II finds the rector
speaking to Januarius Jones:

"Good morning, young man." His shining dome was friendly
against an ivy-covered wall above which the consummate grace of a
spire and a gilded cross seemed to arc across motionless young clouds.
Januarius Jones, caught in *the spire's illusion of slow ruin*, murmured: "*Watch it fall, sir.*" The sun was full on his young round
face. . . . "It was ever my childish delight to stand beneath a spire
while clouds are moving overhead. *The illusion of slow falling is
perfect.*" (p. 40) [Italics added.]

The conversation continues with a kind of Wildeian repartee,
Dr. Mahon on the defensive, Jones contending that people
not only "do not deserve salvation, but . . . do not particularly
desire it" (p. 40). The faunal Jones, as has been illustrated,
lives in a physical world which emphasizes physical pleasures.
The fact that he is "lately a fellow of Latin in a small college"
is consistent with his frantic Pagan activities throughout the
novel as well as with the faunal concept. He lives always
where sensation is essence, and thus it is fitting that he be
the one to note the church spire's "illusion of slow ruin" and
to challenge not only the rector's spiritual concepts, but, on
a broader level, the Victorian optimism inherent in orthodox
spiritual concepts. At the end of the story, as the rector walks
with the basically decent and more orthodox Joe Gilligan,
who is disappointed in love, he says,

"Circumstance moves in marvellous ways, Joe."
"I thought you'd a said God, reverend."
"*God is circumstance, Joe. God is in this life. We know nothing
about the next. That will take care of itself in good time.* 'The Kingdom of God is in man's own heart,' the Book says."

"Ain't that a kind of funny doctrine for a parson to get off?"
(p. 220) [Italics added.]

Dr. Mahon has lost his son and Joe has lost Margaret Powers.
Both men are suffering from "division and death." They
walk on together until their attention is attracted by services
at a Negro church:

The singing drew nearer and nearer; at last, crouching among a clump
of trees beside the road, they saw the shabby church with its *canting
travesty of a spire*. Within it was a soft glow of kerosene serving only
to make the darkness and the heat thicker, making thicker the im-
minence of sex after harsh labor along the mooned land; and from
it welled the crooning submerged passion of the dark race. *It was
nothing, it was everything*. . . . (p. 221) [Italics added.]

As the Negro voices well into ecstasy, not the question of, but
what appears to be man's intuitive spiritual need is put into
choric words:

Feed Thy Sheep, O Jesus. All the longing of mankind for a Oneness
with Something, somewhere. . . . (p. 221)

Beneath the "canting travesty of a spire" Gilligan and the
rector "turned townward under the moon, feeling dust in their
shoes" (p. 221).

A summary of these three focal images of decadence—the
faun, the worm, and the tower—seems to be in order. Through
the faun, Faulkner appears to contend that the new animalic
man, like the new woman, is, if not as much of an illusion or
dream as life itself, then at least as transient; for the worm
reminds one that the faun as well as the man must die.
Decadence mingles with symbolism, and the latter renders the
deeper portions of the novel to the reader. At this point we
might recall Farmer's statement that decadence had been "but
an incident in the development of symbolism, with which it
ended by mingling itself." *Soldiers' Pay* is profuse with the
French Symbolist techniques often associated with the manner
and devices of literary decadence, including synesthesia, oblique
suggestion, and highly refined expression.[12] The image of the
tower may first appear to perplex the reader, for the juxta-

positions of the rector and Jones, the tower and the faun, the church and the naturalistic man are highly perverse. The spire, of course, may symbolize the values of organized religion, and, to be sure, Faulkner attacked them; but just as the faun frolics and the worm feasts, the tower points toward heaven still. The spires of our churches may seem to fall, or lean awry even to the point of travesty, but they are still the most eloquent symbols of man's striving to reach above the dust which he cannot escape. Thus, through a kind of decadent perversity, revealed in the ultimate device of clashing juxtapositions, Faulkner, like a Victorian iconoclast, shattered the surface formalism of religion; yet simultaneously, like Dr. Mahon himself in his more serious moments, he affirmed man's deeply intuitive, eternal search for spiritual meaning.

Thus, much of the symbolism one finds in *Soldiers' Pay* goes beyond the skillfully employed technical devices of the decadents: of synesthesia, refined images and expressions subject to elaborately free association, and mere shallow, suggestive symbols such as the faun and the worm. The tower partakes of the artist's unconscious dimensions, of what is indeed an affirmative association closely related to local color (*e.g.,* the Negro church) and having little to do with decadence from either a historical or stylistic view. This is simply to recognize, as in his early poems such as "Cathay" and *The Marble Faun,* that Faulkner's unconscious power as a writer dominated the absorbing technique of the moment—here that of the decadents, which he obviously employed, and which has so often and erroneously been associated with a *Weltanschauung* of negativism.

Although the substantive legacy of perversity, which Faulkner gained through the influence of the French Symbolists, was to remain in the corpus of his work, to limit the significance of *Soldiers' Pay* to the subject matter, themes, and technical devices of the decadents would be a generalization as glaring as condemnation of Wilde's *Dorian Gray* on moral grounds. In other words, Faulkner did not suddenly become "a decadent" in 1925, when he wrote *Soldiers' Pay;* rather, what he saw in the post-war disillusionment—the outmoded chivalric notions of war, the dubiousness of Victorian optimism, the sentimental exaltation of feminism and the new woman, spiritual and moral ennui, hypocrisy, the *taedium vitae* of all men who have lived too close to death too long, and the emphasis on pleasure and death itself—all combined to lend themselves to the decadent treatment with which Faulkner had been experimenting and which, by 1925, he had substantially absorbed.

Soldiers' Pay, like the New Orleans sketches, continues to reveal strong relationships with his earlier work, both technically and thematically; and, most particularly, it reveals a continuing interest in regionalism and the devices of local color. Perhaps too much has been said of the *fin de siècle* aspects of this novel because of a general unawareness of the unitive aspects of his previous work, begun in the spring of 1919 with the composition of the *Marble Faun* poems. Yet, the threads of connection are strong and obvious. A major setting of the action in *Soldiers' Pay* is the rectory garden (p. 40), in which Jones is introduced with his emphatic faunal traits. The pre-war Donald is also described as "a wild thing" with "the passionate serene alertness of a faun" (p. 58), and Emmy's story of their love in the moonlit fields, replete with water images (pp. 88-89), repeats strongly similar moods and images of *The Marble Faun,* as do George Farr's nocturnal activities as he anticipates a tryst with Cecily ("he became one with the earth, with dark and silence," p. 165). Other Romantic images of nature in *The Marble Faun* seem to reappear in *Soldiers' Pay* (see pp. 56, 57, 89, 108, 166, 210). The familiar personification of trees as young girls, especially poplar trees, recalls one of the dominant images of *The Marble Faun* and finds its way into the novel no less than nine times (see pp. 43, 56, 59, 66, 144, 185, 196, 198, 202). Other related images, though of some importance in further demonstrating the sequential development of Faulkner's emerging artistry, are too numerous to detail in this chapter.

The relationship of the novel to Faulkner's first published poem, "L'Apres-Midi d'un Faune," which appeared in August, 1919, is obvious enough. Faulkner's first sketch, "Landing in

Luck," published in the *Mississippian* in November, 1919, anticipates in its persona of the callow Royal Air Force cadet the more detailed treatment of the inexperienced Cadet Julian Lowe and some technical aspects of Lieutenant Donald Mahon's flying activities in *Soldiers' Pay*. The novel also echoes the earlier *Mississippian* poems "Naiads' Song" and "Fantouches" [*sic*], both published in February, 1920. The connection with "Naiads' Song" is very similar to that of *The Marble Faun*, having its basis in nature imagery, woodland lanes and dreamy pools of water (pp. 88-89). But the nexus with "Fantouches" [*sic*] is precise and direct. The poem concludes, "La lune ne grade [*sic*] aucune rancune"; Jones in the novel repeats substantially the same line with the same misused idiom: *"La lune en grade aucune rancune"* (p. 93). Both lines, published approximately six years apart, appear in similarly sardonic contexts.

Similarly, "Nocturne," published in the spring of 1921, anticipates *Soldiers' Pay* in a number of ways. Among them, one notes the image of the white candelabra (pp. 57, 195); the terpsichorean image in juxtaposition with those of darkness and metaphorical severed flesh ("from the outer darkness . . . watching her slim body cut by a masculine arm," p. 135); and the most strikingly cognate phrasing ("A man's face spitted like a moth on a lance of flame," p. 181).

Faulkner's disapproval of "Mr. Vachel Lindsay with his tin pan and iron spoon," expressed in his review of February, 1921, is reiterated in *Soldiers' Pay* in his description of a Negro schoolteacher

who could take a given line from any book from the telephone directory down and soon have the entire present personnel chanting it after him, like Vachel Lindsay. (p. 81)

Further relationships between the young hero of *Soldiers' Pay* and the "Tieless casual" of Faulkner's obscure sketch "The Hill" (March 1922) can be seen.[13] Mahon is described through a pre-war photograph by his father: "You will notice that he has neither coat nor cravat" (p. 48). Again, "He would never wear hat nor tie: his mother could never make him" (p. 58);

"He would never have a hat or a coat" (p. 87); and, like the "Tieless casual" of "The Hill," Mahon liked to "go off into the country by himself" (p. 87).

It is hardly surprising that the echoes of *A Green Bough* should be strong in the novel, for *The Greening Bough* (the original title of the volume) was prematurely announced in early 1925, not long before *Soldiers' Pay* was written. The epigraph of *Soldiers' Pay* with the minor changes of italics and quotation marks becomes the fourth stanza of poem XXX of *A Green Bough*. Several details of the novel suggest poem I: first, in the semi-oblivion of the protagonist, existing in a state of living death; second, in the almost cruel inquisitiveness and shallow sympathy of the inquiring women (p. 23); third, in the reiteration of pity, "Oh, the poor man" (p. 126); and fourth, in the phrasing expressed under similar circumstances of soldiers in isolation from the civilian society to which they have returned, "The two of them sat in silent comradeship" (p. 23), close enough to the poem's "We sit in silent amity." The French line, which first appeared in Faulkner's "Fantouches" [*sic*] and reappears in *Soldiers' Pay* slightly altered, *"La lune en grade* [sic] *aucune rancune"* (p. 93), still contains the same incorrect verb usage *"grade"* in what would appear to be the expression "garder rancune" ("to owe a grudge"); of further significance, Faulkner's typescript for poem XXXII, which he presented to his friend Sam Gilmore, was also entitled "La Lune ne Grade Aucune Rancune," the idiomatic error persisting. The perverse repetition of the French line may well point to Faulkner's source. In his first book, *Prufrock and Other Observations* (1917), T. S. Eliot in the poem "Rhapsody on a Windy Night" wrote these lines:

> *"Regard the moon,*
> *La lune ne garde aucune rancune. . . ."*

Eliot's debt to Jules Laforgue's similar lines from "Complainte de cette bonne lune" is obvious enough:

> *"—La, voyons, mam'zelle la Lune,*
> *Ne gardons pas ainsi rancune. . . ."*

Faulkner had very likely read Eliot's "Rhapsody on a Windy Night" and simply lifted the line "whole cloth" for his own purposes in various contexts, never bothering in the process to correct the transposed letters in what should be *garde*.[14]

The following illustrates the close paralleling of Faulkner's poetry and prose:

POEM XVII	SOLDIERS' PAY
o atthis	*"Atthis," he said.*
for a moment an aeon I pause	*"What did you call me?"*
plunging	*He told her: " 'For a moment,*
above the narrow precipice of thy	*an aeon, I pause plunging above*
breast	*the narrow precipice of thy breast'*
	and on and on and on. Do you
what before thy white precipice	*know how falcons make love?*
the eagle	*They embrace at an enormous*
sharp in the sunlight and cleaving	*height and fall locked, beak to*
his long blue ecstasy. . . .	*beak, plunging: an unbearable*
	ecstasy." (pp. 157-158)

The faunal images of poem XLI reappear throughout the novel, especially in the Sybaritic activities of Jones, who is more satyr than faun. Emmy's gazing as "she tasted the bitter ashes of an old sorrow" (p. 115) harks back to the synesthetic linking of the theme of disappointment in love with the senses: in poem XXXII, "paris/tastes his bitter thumbs"; and in poem XXXV, "still is there/An old sorrow sharp as wood-smoke on the air." Similarly, the linkage of human passion with equine images of the wind

(beneath the gold and mute cacophony of stars . . . . a rock against which waves of trees broke, and . . . stars were golden unicorns neighing unheard through blue meadows, spurning them with hooves sharp and scintillant as ice . . . neighing soundlessly from dusk to dawn . . . had seen her, . . . [pp. 135-136])

faintly suggests poem XXXVI of *A Green Bough*. Finally, the closing poem XLIV (also known as "If There Be Grief"), quoted in its entirety in Chapter VI, is recapitulated through both phrasing and theme in *Soldiers' Pay*:

Fair days, and *wet days in which rain ran with silver lances over the lawn,* in which *rain dripped* leaf to leaf while birds still sang in the hushed *damp greenness* under the trees, and made love and married and built houses and still sang; *in which rain grew soft as the grief of a young girl grieving for the sake of grief.* (p. 197) [Italics added.]

Many of the New Orleans sketches were probably written during the composition of *Soldiers' Pay;* and cognates of phrasing, images, themes, and motifs are hardly surprising. To consider Faulkner's sketches in chronological order, one finds in "New Orleans" (January-February 1925) the general attitude of the prostitute Magdalen echoed in Emmy's reflections on sorrow and disappointment in love, particularly in the "bitter ash" image (SP, p. 115). The "courtesan image" employed in reference to the city of New Orleans in the sketch of the same name (pp. 45-50) reappears in relation to Cecily in the novel (SP, p. 161).

"Mirrors of Chartres Street" (February 8, 1925) foreshadows with its avian images of light, "golden wings of street lights" (p. 56) and "the light of golden pennons flapping across the dawn" (p. 57) Faulkner's employment of "lights were shimmering birds on motionless golden wings" in the novel (p. 17). Again, the sketch with such phrases as "his eyes as wild and soft as a faun's" (p. 53) anticipates the novel's photographic description of its hero before the war, "with the serenity of a wild thing, the passionate serene alertness of a faun" (p. 58).

"Cheest" (April 5, 1925) features such localisms in the dialogue of the jockey-hero as "Whatcher want?" (p. 93) employed frequently in *Soldiers' Pay* as, for example, in Cadet Lowe's "Say, whatcher drinking, anyway?" (p. 7). The jockey's belligerent ignorance and veneer of callow self-confidence toward "skirts" are strongly echoed in Cadet Lowe's manner of behavior early in the novel, his immature posturing toward the "Janes" of his acquaintance, and his manner of stating himself in his letters to Margaret Powers with ungrammatical blindness to his own faults.

Just as the natural poet of "Out of Nazareth" (April 12, 1925) carries as one of his few personal possessions a "battered 'Shropshire Lad' " (p. 104), Lieutenant Mahon's personal effects returned to his father include "a cheap paper-covered 'Shropshire Lad'" (p. 48). The title of the sketch "The Kingdom of God" (April 26, 1925) reappears in the text of *Soldiers' Pay* (p. 220). And, finally, "Episode" (August 16, 1925) employs the image of an inscrutable, somewhat detached "idol" in relation to reactions of characters to climactic situations (cf. "Episode," pp. 189-190, to SP, pp. 153, 159).

In summary, then, strong relationships between *Soldiers' Pay* and Faulkner's earlier work can be traced consistently back to the composition of the *Marble Faun* poems in April, May, and June 1919.

By 1925, Faulkner's literary development was undergoing changes perhaps more obvious than the continuing consistencies of subject matter, theme, and technique in his work. One of the most salient changes was at the same time one of the most paradoxical and complex. The inordinate degree to which Faulkner continued throughout his life to romanticize his own World War I experiences will serve to illustrate the point; for paradoxically, it may seem, with the character of Cadet Julian Lowe in *Soldiers' Pay,* Faulkner made the youth's romantic conceptions of war—not completely dissimilar to his own early views—clearly laughable. Cecily Saunders, too, is made to suffer the brunt of humor for her pitifully unrealistic attitude toward war:

Why, I tell you I seen that letter: all the old bunk about knights of the air and the romance of battle, that even the fat crying ones outgrow soon as the excitement is over and uniforms and being wounded ain't only not stylish no more, but it is troublesome. (p. 30)

Cadet Lowe, drunk in a hotel room with the wounded and slowly dying Lieutenant Mahon, thinks,

To have been him! he moaned. Just to be him. Let him take this sound body of mine! Let him take it. To have got wings on my breast, to have wings; and to have got his scar, too, I would take death to-morrow. Upon a chair Mahon's tunic evinced above the left breast pocket wings breaking from an initialed circle beneath a crown, tipping downward in an arrested embroidered sweep; a symbolized desire.

To be him, to have gotten wings, but to have got his scar too!
Cadet Lowe turned to the wall with passionate disappointment like
a gnawing fox at his vitals.[15]

These statements and others, even the ones with satirical
relevance, such as "real soldiers never like to talk about themselves" (p. 152), recapitulate through what appears to be an
artist's mellowed retrospection something of the young Faulkner's martial posturing.

Yet, the tragically romantic extension of what Faulkner
may have been—and perhaps what he came closer to being
than we may realize (I have in mind Stone's statement concerning the crash episode, "some talk about a silver plate in
his head")—is possibly exemplified in the character of Lieutenant Mahon, the officer returning to his native South in a
dream-like state. One is indeed reminded of Faulkner's own
homecoming and his appearance while changing trains at
Holly Springs, Mississippi, an anecdote recalled by John Cullen
and quoted in Chapter II: "[He was] standing as still as a
statue in the railroad depot . . . . paying no attention to anybody
or anything. . . ." The paradox presented by the characterizations of Lowe and Mahon relates in all likelihood to Faulkner's
struggle to identity, for it can be further observed in his
increased reliance upon other autobiographical data and his
turning more directly and consistently to the substance of
local color.

The relationships between Faulkner's persona, Lieutenant
Donald Mahon of the R.A.F. (p. 139), and his own life
extend to the treatment of the Negro as literary source.
Donald's Negro mammy refers to herself as "his ole Cal'line,"
and insists upon caring for him: "here yo' mammy come ter
you" (p. 117). Faulkner's dedicatory note in *Go Down, Moses*
(1940) indicates a distinctly possible prototype:

To Mammy
Caroline Barr
Mississippi
(1840-1940)

Who was born in slavery and who
gave to my family a fidelity without
stint or calculation of recompense
and to my childhood an immeasurable
devotion and love[16]

Donald Mahon's carefree pre-war days, his irregular attendance at school, and his long walks in the country and through the woods (p. 84) closely coincide with the young Faulkner's erratic behavior as a student and his long walks about the countryside surrounding Oxford.[17] There are many other parallels of a minor sort between the persona of Mahon and Faulkner himself, for example, the reference to Mahon's features as "fox-faced" (p. 54), which recalls not only photographic resemblances (especially those of the younger Faulkner) but also Stone's statement about Faulkner's sensitivity over his receding lip, an incentive for his growing a mustache. Then again, Mrs. Saunders' statement in *Soldiers' Pay* about returned veterans "who probably won't work anyway. You know yourself how these ex-soldiers are" (p. 70) sounds like a strong echo of statements made about the real "Count No'count," especially a recollection of Faulkner's early postwar years by his Uncle J. W. T. Faulkner II: "He just wouldn't work."[18]

Faulkner's increased reliance upon autobiographical data, far more pronounced in *Soldiers' Pay* than in any of his earlier works of fiction or poetry, bears a further relationship to his growing tendency to turn to the local color of his region. Faulkner's struggle to identity partakes of this tendency as well as of the substance of autobiography employed in the novel. The locale is Charlestown, Georgia, but it could be "any small southern town" (p. 78) and its life, clustered about the county courthouse in the center of the city square is a mirror reflection of the town in "The Hill" (see Chapter V) and what was soon to become Jefferson:

Charlestown, like numberless other towns throughout the south, had been built around a circle of tethered horses and mules. In the middle of the square was the courthouse—a simple utilitarian edifice of brick and sixteen beautiful Ionic columns stained with generations of casual tobacco. Elms surrounded the courthouse and beneath these trees, on scarred and carved wood benches and chairs the city fathers . . . who . . . feared only God and drouth, in black string ties or the faded brushed gray and bronze meaningless medals of the Confederate States of America, no longer having to make any pretense toward labor, slept or whittled away the long drowsy days while their juniors of all ages, not yet old enough to frankly slumber in public, played checkers or chewed tobacco and talked. . . . They passed beneath a stone shaft bearing a Confederate soldier shading his marble eyes forever in eternal rigid vigilance. . . . (pp. 78-79)

The dance scene at the home where, "Through two heavy identical magnolias the lighted porch was like a stage" (p. 136), the drug store scene with George Farr and Cecily as trysting lovers (pp. 148-151), and the gossiping town journeys of Mrs. Burney "cramped and neat in her meticulous airproof black, holding her cotton umbrella like a flag" (p. 179) give the southern town a distinctive as well as a representative aura of validity. So do such unlike local color details as the singing Negroes holding services in their "shabby church with its canting travesty of a spire" (p. 221) and the intricate maneuverings involved in drinking from a jug of moon liquor (p. 215). Even the description of Donald Mahon's funeral procession roots the action into a distinct locale, functionally strengthening its verisimilitude:

(The procession moved slowly across the square. Country people, in town to trade, turned to stare vacuously, merchant and doctor and lawyer came to door and window to look; the city fathers, drowsing in the courthouse yard, having successfully circumvented sex, having reached the point where death would look after them instead of they after death, waked and looked and slept again. Into a street, among and between horses and mules tethered to wagons, it passed, into a street bordered by shabby Negro stores and shops, and here was Loosh standing stiffly at salute as it passed. "Who dat, Loosh?" "Mist' Donald Mahon." "Well, Jesus! we all gwine dat way, some day. All roads leads to de graveyard.")[19]

Faulkner's problem of identity with his ancestry and his region continued to serve as a kind of catalytic agent, producing its effects upon both his life and his work. He must have experienced an extraordinary tension in his attempts to identify with his great-grandfather and his martial heroics (the dominating symbol of the past) on the one hand, and the newly emerging South with its anti-traditional and sometimes amoral values on the other. The desire for romantic war experiences which drove Faulkner to enlist as a cadet in the R.A.F. in Canada, as well as the fabrication of war heroics through both misleading statements and omitted corrections, was motivated primarily by a conscious wish to escape the barrenness of southern life surrounding him and an unconscious necessity to identify with the Old Colonel (see Chapters II, III). Thus Faulkner, in some of his moments of reflection on his training experiences in Canada and the coming of the Armistice at just about the time he was to receive his wings, must have felt as cheated by fate as Cadet Julian Lowe in *Soldiers' Pay*: "Had I been old enough or lucky enough, this might have been me, he thought jealously" (p. 19), looking at Mahon.

But Cadet Lowe—like the real young Faulkner in many ways—cannot be the hero of this novel. His suffering is only a romantic and counterfeit suffering; it is not genuine as is Mahon's. Once Lieutenant Mahon enters upon the scene, Cadet Lowe not only is not needed, but Margaret Powers tells him, "you would only be in the way" (p. 38). He goes home then to relatively remote California, and his only other presence in the novel is epistolary, serving the purpose of comic relief. The Faulknerian identity shifts as Mahon becomes the tragic center around which the action of Cecily and her "jellybeans" and other anti-traditional representatives or hopelessly apathetic moralists revolve.

Cadet Lowe and Lieutenant Mahon, then, pose a double and conflicting identification for the artist. On the one hand, Faulkner very likely identified himself consciously with the callow Lowe; but, on the other hand, he continued to identify himself through the persona of Lieutenant Mahon, perhaps more unconsciously than consciously, with his heroic great-grandfather and the man's martyred ideals.[20]

I do not wish to imply—using Kenneth Burke's terminology—an "essentializing mode of interpretation" toward the many facets of Faulkner's psyche, to isolate from that cluster of problems only one problem with the result of subordinating all others, and, thus, to seem to "explain the complex in terms of the simple."[21] A man, author or not, discovers his individuation through his work to be sure, but also in his daily problem solving, in his relations with family and friends, and in meeting *reality* situations. My point here, of course, is not to list all such problems, much less to treat them, but rather to center upon significant autobiographical elements which may illuminate Faulkner's motivations in selecting certain aspects of the past and adapting them to the uses of fiction.

One may ask how Faulkner could, even unconsciously, identify himself with the dead hero (Mahon) rather than a living tyro (Lowe). Admittedly, an artist uses all of his experience, actual and vicarious, to clothe his invented characters, and he need not, as such, "identify" with them. But Lieutenant Mahon, "glorified" into semi-oblivion by war, symbolically possesses a kind of atavistic significance: a conscious sense of traditional values which Faulkner possessed in common with the Old Colonel.[22] To one aware of such values the heroic doom of Mahon is meaningful: it is preferable to the shallow, materialistic, and amoral existence of the Cadet Lowes, the Mrs. Saunderses, and the jellybeans with their glued hair, who are as so many baubles to be worn on Cecily's bracelet. Indeed, Mahon's doom, tragic as it is, has involved action, movement, and vitality, which transcend the apathy and ineffectualness of people with conventional values who merely dream their lives away or take one of a variety of philosophical refuges, such as the rector. The local color of "Charlestown," which could be "any small southern town," even Jefferson (or Oxford), is the appropriate backdrop upon which to play out the action:

. . . *Afternoon lay in a coma in the street,* like a woman recently loved. Quiet and war: nothing now that the lover has gone away. *Leaves were like a green liquid arrested in mid-flow, flattened and spread; leaves were as though cut with scissors from green paper and pasted flat on the afternoon: someone dreamed them and then forgot his dream.* . . . Monotonous wagons drawn by *long-eared beasts* crawled past. Negroes humped with sleep, portentous upon each wagon and in the wagon bed itself sat other Negroes upon chairs: *a pagan catafalque under the afternoon. Rigid, as though carved in Egypt ten thousand years ago. Slow dust rising veiled their passing, like Time.* . . . (p. 105) [Italics added.]

To be sure, the catalepsy, the frozen moment, the suspension of time are as striking as their imaginal counterparts in "Nocturne" or "The Hill."[23] Yet, there is also a distinct difference, which is closely related to Faulkner's literary development. Here, the tension which characterizes the earlier images is significantly reduced. Indeed, there is a virtual absence of that polarity which contributes to the tension. The writer seems to have acceded to his material. It is as if the problem of identity has been esthetically, if only momentarily, resolved, somewhat as a piece of a jigsaw puzzle is fitted into its surrounding pattern. The suspension and slow movement, as it were, belong in context.

IX

Sartoris:
Home Again

Faulkner's 1925 voyage to Europe took almost a month, but it was no pleasure cruise. His ship, the *West Ivis,* was a freighter and lay at anchor at Savannah from July 11 through July 14 to take on cargo. On August 2, Faulkner disembarked at Genoa. During the remainder of the month, he traveled over northern Italy. He spent some time at an inn, the Peace d' Oro in Pavia, and lived with the peasants in the hamlet of Sommariva close to Lake Maggiore. By late September, he had traveled through Switzerland and was living in Paris at 26 rue Servandoni, not far from the Luxembourg Gardens, where he spent much of his free time.[1] A photograph from this period reveals a mustached and bearded Faulkner *de profil.*[2] His suit, complete with buttoned vest, appears to be of rough tweed, and a dark tie is drawn to a neat thick knot against a white collar. The rather bleak-eyed young man appears to be sitting on a bench, his legs crossed. His right arm is braced on the back or rail of the bench, and the fore-finger of the hand hooks the stem of a pipe held to his lips. He seems to have taken on a kind of vaguely British mien of the Left Bank, and looks the part of an expatriate posing for a portrait to be printed on the dust jacket of his latest novel.

However, he later refused to claim any identity with the expatriate group of the 'Twenties in Paris, stating, "I don't remember a single Southerner that had any part in it." Although he professed that he was not interested in "literature nor literary people" at the time—that "I was a tramp then"—he did state that he knew about Joyce: ". . . I would go to some effort to go to the café that he inhabited to look at him. But that was the only literary man that I remember seeing in Europe in those days."[3]

Faulkner's European experiences did not last long, and he was back in the United States by late 1925 and spent the Christmas season at home in Oxford. Aside from some of the last New Orleans sketches, a few poems and notes, the only significant writing of the period was a novel, tentatively entitled *Elmer,* which he never finished; one important aspect of the work is the fact that the protagonist lived as a boy in a place called "Jefferson, Mississippi."[4]

After his return from Europe Faulkner began work on a novel or story which he entitled "The Devil Beats His Wife," but he very soon abandoned it. His friend and literary agent, Ben Wasson, used the title for a novel of his own, published in 1929. By the autumn of 1926, Faulkner announced the publication of *Mosquitoes* (1927). During the spring of the same year he served in the capacity of golf professional for the Oxford Country Club and won an inscribed pipe for shooting a hole in one. During the summer he worked in a lumber mill, injuring a finger; but of more immediate interest, he lived for a time in Pascagoula, working as a fisherman on a schooner during the day and at night writing *Mosquitoes.*[5] On page 464, the last page of the typescript of the novel, is the note "Pascagoula, Miss/1 Sept 1926" (Meriwether, p. 64). It is quite likely that good portions of the spring and summer, if not those of the previous winter after his return from Europe, were spent in writing the novel. Faulkner returned to Oxford for a short stay in the autumn of 1926, but spent the winter in the Vieux Carré. He and his traveling companion aboard the *West Ivis,* William Spratling, published *Sherwood Ander-*

son and Other Famous Creoles in New Orleans in December, 1926. Faulkner's "Foreword" was a delightful bit of parodistic whimsey, but Anderson did not appreciate it. He was sensitive about such things, especially from writers whom he took the trouble of getting published. Faulkner had meant no harm. Certainly he had harbored no notion of declaring a stylistic independence from Anderson, as Hemingway had attempted to do with his parody of Anderson in *Torrents of Spring.* With Faulkner it was apparently all innocent fun. He enjoyed Anderson's primer-like style, and he was seized with the *outré* idea of mimicking his preceptor.

Soldiers' Pay and *Mosquitoes* both sold poorly, and by the time that Faulkner finished *Sartoris* Horace Liveright had canceled their contract. The 594-page carbon typescript of *Sartoris,* then entitled *Flags in the Dust* and approximately a fourth longer than the published version, bears a note on the last page of the text: "Oxford, Miss/29 September 1927" (Meriwether, pp. 64-65). The manuscript was finally published by Harcourt, Brace in June, 1929, nearly two years after its completion. Several events combined to make this a critical period during Faulkner's career. First, his expectations had been understandably high. He had published a volume of poetry, the New Orleans pieces, and two novels which had received several favorable reviews, even if they had not made him much money. He had finally begun to think himself a successful writer. Moreover, he was contemplating marriage with Estelle Oldham, his childhood sweetheart, who had divorced her first husband and returned to Oxford. The two were to be married the same year that *Sartoris* was published, 1929.

The delay in publication had been bad enough, but when the book was poorly received by the public Faulkner's dejection was deep. Phil Stone recalled this period of his friend's life vividly. "We thought we really had a book there!" Then he explained how difficulties and delays plagued them:

Finally, *Sartoris* was published, and disappointed us. I can take you to the very place where we stood. Bill said, "I'll *never* get any money, *never* any recognition—"

"I told him he would! 'Write what'll please you,' I said."
Stone smiled, shaking his head incredulously. "You know, I
almost didn't believe it myself then, but I told him anyway.
And he got started, too." Stone told Faulkner that it was
obviously not intended that he be a "popular writer," and
that he should write for himself and those who had literary
taste and "who surely would some day recognize his talent":
" 'I had in mind Flaubert. . . . Instead of catering to an
audience he wrote for the ages, and of course the ages discovered him.' "[6]

Then Faulkner wrote *The Sound and the Fury*. The bound
carbon typescript contains on page 392 the date "October
1928" (Meriwether, p. 65), although the book was not published until one year later; it was apparently written between
the time of the rejection of *Sartoris* by Liveright and its ac-
ceptance by Harcourt, Brace. *Sanctuary*, about which perhaps
too much has already been said by too many critics and by
Faulkner himself, was in all likelihood composed between
January 29 and May, 1929. *As I Lay Dying* followed quickly.
One manuscript of 107 pages bears the date "25 October
1929" on its first page and "11 December 1929" on p. 107,[7]
a dating which would bear out Faulkner's statement that the
book "was written in six weeks . . . because I knew from the
first where that was going."[8] Thus, within the same year that
Sartoris was published Faulkner had written a significant
portion of his major work.

When I asked Phil Stone what happened to Faulkner between
Mosquitoes (1927) and *The Sound and the Fury* (1929), his
answer was an astonishingly simple "He was writing all the
time."

Sartoris,[9] however, seems to have been the turning point in
his fictional career. When questioned about the advisable
sequence of reading his books, Faulkner answered that it would
be best

to begin with . . . *Sartoris* that has the germ of my apocrypha in it.
A lot of characters are postulated in that book. I'd say that's a good
one to begin with.[10]

The book is, of course, an important volume: it initiates the Yoknapatawpha saga. Here we encounter the Sartoris, Benbow, and Snopes families in the town of Jefferson, Mississippi. The Negroes are there, too—Simon and his family, and within these crosscurrents of class and race are the germinal conflicts between the ghosts of a colorful heroic past, and the displaced Southerners of a pale susceptible present. Faulkner stated that he was halfway through the book when

I discovered that writing was a mighty fine thing . . . You could make people stand on their hind legs and cast a shadow. I felt that I had all these people, and as soon as I discovered it I wanted to bring them all back.[11]

Sartoris is divided into five parts. In the first, the reader is introduced to old Bayard Sartoris, who converses with a contemporary of his father and hence an even older man, Will Falls, who has walked in to town from the county poor farm. The presence of old Bayard's father, Colonel John Sartoris, is felt in the very office of the bank by both men. "He was far more palpable than the two old men cemented by a common deafness to a dead period . . ." (p. 27). Will Falls has returned a pipe of the old Colonel's to Bayard: "A po'house ain't no fitten place for anything of his'n. . . . And I'm gwine on ninety-fo' year old" (p. 28). The aging Negro Simon picks up Bayard in the carriage that the banker favors "with a testy disregard of industrial progress" (p. 28). Simon is more a Sartoris himself than a mere servant or employee and, like old Bayard, he smokes a cigar. As the two drive to the Sartoris home, Simon tells Bayard that his grandson, also named Bayard, is home from the war and that he jumped off the blind side of the two o'clock train "like a hobo" (p. 30). At the Sartoris home outside Jefferson we meet old Bayard's aunt, eighty-year-old Virginia Du Pre, a relater of Civil War stories "taking on a mellow splendor like wine" (p. 33). We learn of old Bayard's eponym, Colonel John Sartoris' brother and an aide-de-camp of Jeb Stuart, who recklessly threw his life away for a jar of anchovies. Yet, when Aunt Jenny tells the story, recounting having danced a valse with Jeb Stuart in Baltimore in '58, "her voice [is] proud and still as banners in the dust" (p. 40). In his own bedroom, old Bayard's mind recapitulates the conversation with Will Falls, particularly the story of the old Colonel's daring escape from the Yankees at this very house and, oddly juxtaposed, the succinct story of old John Sartoris' death and his statement of proleptic resignation: "Redlaw'll kill me tomorrow, for I shall be unarmed. I'm tired of killing men" (pp. 43-44). In the remainder of the section, Simon picks up Aunt Jenny from Belle Mitchell's party. She and old Bayard meet at home where they discuss the wild young Bayard, who has still not come home. That night Bayard's grandson emerges from the lilac bushes by the garden fence, a tall figure in moonlight, and mounts the veranda. To his grandfather he relates the circumstances of the death of his younger brother John Sartoris, also a pilot, shot down by the Germans. The first section ends with efficient Aunt Jenny making young Bayard drink a glass of milk and go to sleep.

In the second part, we see more of post-war Jefferson and, in particular, the Sartorises and their Negro servants. Simon and Elnora's son, Caspey, also has returned from the war. He flaunts his uniform and tells about the new ways: "War unloosed de black man's mouf" (p. 73); and it is not until old Bayard clouts him through the doorway with a piece of stove wood that Simon's words sink in: "I kep' tellin' you dem new-fangled war notions of yo'n wa'nt gwine ter work in dis place." Simon's logic is one of simple pride in his race: "Whut us niggers want ter be free fer, anyhow? Ain't we got ez many white folks now ez we kin suppo't?" (p. 89). As Aunt Jenny clips larkspur in her garden, the heroine of the novel, Narcissa Benbow, is introduced. As the two enter the Sartoris parlor, the presence of the old Colonel is once more real. Young Bayard remembers the furniture as looming with "ghostly benignance" (p. 71). When Narcissa meets Bayard in the parlor, she remembers once more his "leashed cold violence" (p. 83). The action shifts, and young Bayard returns from Memphis, seventy miles away, with a new car. Old Bayard tries to keep his grandson from driving recklessly by going with him on his mad rides about the countryside. In another scene old Bayard opens the family trunk which contains the personal effects of the old Colonel, his brocaded uniform, a rapier, a cavalry saber, a pair of silver-wrought dueling pistols in a rosewood case, a blue army forage-cap of the 'Forties and a Mexican machete, and a "long-necked oil-can such as locomotive drivers use" (p. 95), which is a silver trophy with the date "August 9, 1873." But old Bayard is looking for the family Bible in which he enters the names and death dates of young John Sartoris and young Bayard's widow and infant son who died a year before. In the remainder of this part of the novel, Jenny takes old Bayard to the town's new physician, Dr. Alford, to have a troublesome facial wen examined; but just as Dr. Alford suggests operating immediately, the old family doctor Lucius Peabody intercepts them, leads old Bayard away, and tells him to leave the wen alone. In another scene, one of the Snopes family who has managed to gain a position in the Sartoris bank writes anonymous love letters to Narcissa through an amanuensis, young Virgil Beard. Again, the ghostly presence of the old Colonel is felt as Simon putters about the homeplace, and his younger son, Isom, notes, "Pappy out dar talkin' to Ole Marster again" (p. 112). Simon's strange monologue reveals that he is disturbed at the way things have changed. As counterpoint to Simon's pathetic mood, Bayard takes him for a daring ride in his new car, but the old Negro is so frightened that he gets out and walks home. Young Bayard, ashamed and restless, meets a member of the MacCallum family who invites him out to the country for a hunt. They drink, discuss the days of other hunts before the war, and the war itself. Bayard, having drunk too much, almost gets into a fight in a drug store, but MacCallum coaxes him away. Still, Bayard's violent nature is not to be suppressed; he insists on riding an untamed stallion bridled with nothing more than a rope hackamore, is thrown, and knocked unconscious. Dr. Peabody bandages him and brings him around, but Bayard will not go home. Instead he goes riding and drinking in the country. In a memorable scene, Bayard, his friends, and Negro musicians drink moon liquor; they ride over the hills in cold silver moonlight, stop in the shadows to serenade Narcissa, and disperse at the courthouse, where, according to Aunt Jenny's orders, a policeman arrests Bayard.

Horace Benbow's return from the war introduces the third part of the novel. His sister, Narcissa, meets him, and the two discuss the Sartorises. "Funny family," Horace observes. "Always going to wars, and always getting killed" (p. 153). Horace is a sensitive, intelligent, well-read, formally educated (Sewanee and Oxford) young man, who verbalizes like a poet. Described as a lawyer "principally through a sense of duty to the family tradition" (p. 160), he is soon "Easily into the routine of days between his office and his home" (p. 163). An affair is revealed between Horace and Belle Mitchell. For a time young Bayard improves his ways, but he finally wrecks his car in a creek. Two Negros eventually rescue him and take him back to Jefferson in their wagon. As his body mends, Narcissa nurses him and their relationship deepens. When he is on his feet again, he makes another reckless gesture in a car, after which a passionate love scene ensues with Narcissa. Two other scenes are of major interest in the section, one involving Will Falls, who applies a home-remedy ointment to old Bayard's wen. The two discuss the old Colonel and the heroics of "ancient phantoms" once again. As the pauper predicts, the wen drops off old Bayard's face a few days later. The section concludes with the skulking Snopes breaking into the Benbow home and stealing the letters which Narcissa has indiscreetly saved.

Part Four opens with a comical local color episode. Simon's church committee comes to the Sartoris home requesting a return of the funds with which he was entrusted and no longer has. When asked what he did with the money, Simon repeats, "Hit's all right. . . . I jes' put it out, sort of" (p. 236). A pastoral autumn interlude follows, containing passages which are strong echoes of Sherwood Anderson's "A Meeting South."[12] Narcissa and Bayard have married, and Narcissa is pregnant with a baby whom, as Miss Jenny reiterates, "We'll name . . . John" (p. 238). Some of the local color scenes include a description of a mule-powered cane mill, a kind of lyrical tribute to the mule itself (pp. 239-240), harvest scenes in moonlight and firelight, a vivid 'possum hunt, a happy Thanksgiving dinner with a ponderously laden table. Yet, Bayard increasingly isolates himself from Narcissa. Even as she clings to his "rigid body," there is "a ghost between them" (p. 253). The idyllic interlude ends as Bayard, again driving recklessly, precipitates his grandfather's heart attack. Escaping to the country on horseback, Bayard attempts to purge himself in the winter hunts at the MacCallums. The images of winter are coldly effective; but even the frigid nights of sleep fail to assuage the sense of guilt Bayard feels as the result of the deaths of old Bayard and his younger brother, John, in whose place, he thinks, *he* should have been killed. Images of cold and death dominate these bucolic scenes. He spends Christmas Eve in a Negro's stable, making himself a nest in the hay. The Christmas scene which follows the next day, as Bayard shares his jug of liquor with the Negroes and they their Christmas dinner of 'possum, yams, gray ash cake, and coffee with him, is local color of artistic purity.

Part Five commences with a letter to Narcissa from Horace, who has apparently gone away with Belle Mitchell. Still attempting to escape his guilt, Bayard has left Jefferson, while at home Narcissa and Miss Jenny receive rare post cards. The sense of the past pervades Narcissa's thoughts as she feels that Aunt Jenny "is trying to make me one of them; to make my child just another rocket to glare for a moment in the sky, then die away" (p. 300). When Bayard tests the airplane of a wild-eyed inventor, he finally discovers the death he has been seeking. Ironically, on the day the baby is born, Aunt Jenny receives the news of Bayard's death. In a proud display of controlled grief the old lady avows, "Thank God that's the last one. For a while, anyway" (p. 309). Simon, however, is really the last Sartoris to die, in a gesture of bathos rather than pathos: he is found in the home of a young Negro woman, his "grizzled head crushed in by a blunt instrument anonymously wielded" (p. 309). The novel concludes with Aunt Jenny's visit to the cemetery where she hovers benignly over the marbled arrogancies of the Sartoris inscriptions: last

of all the old Colonel's statue stands above her, his head
"lifted a little in that gesture of haughty pride which repeated
itself generation after generation with a fateful fidelity . . ."
(p. 313). Back at the Sartoris homeplace, Narcissa informs
Aunt Jenny that her baby's name is not "John," but "Benbow
Sartoris." Narcissa plays the piano. Aunt Jenny asks, "Do you
think you can change one of 'em with a name?" (p. 317),
and this rhapsodic passage follows:

The music went on in the dusk softly; the dusk was peopled with
ghosts of glamorous and old disastrous things. And if they were
just glamorous enough, there was sure to be a Sartoris in them, and
then they were sure to be disastrous. Pawns. But the Player, and the
game He plays . . . He must have a name for His pawns, though.
But perhaps Sartoris is the game itself—a game outmoded and
played with pawns shaped too late and to an old dead pattern, and
of which the Player Himself is a little wearied. For there is death
in the sound of it, and a glamorous fatality, like silver pennons
downrushing at sunset, or a dying fall of horns along the road to
Roncevaux. (p. 317)

Within the novel one finds a continuing reliance upon
devices and themes used and developed in Faulkner's previous
work; these can be traced back to the composition of the
Marble Faun poems, ten years before *Sartoris* was published.
Romantic descriptions of nature converge with a frequently
pastoral mode. Garden scenes are interspersed throughout
the novel, and the familiar images of moonlight, flowers,
birds, bees, and the protean girl-plant recur.[13] As in the
earliest volume, marble images themselves combine with the
color image of gray to emphasize the themes of mutability
and the past. Thus, as Aunt Jenny visits the Jefferson cemetery,
she finds "marble shapes bearing names" (p. 312) over which
"doves crooned their endless rising inflections" (p. 313). In
Bayard's freezing sleep at the MacCallums, in which he is
rigidly suspended in a kind of purgatory between life and
death,[14] he is surrounded with gray images (pp. 273-274)
unmistakably related to the past and to death. Even the trees
and homely shapes are "like sad ghosts in the chill corpse-
light" (p. 273). Sleep, as for the marble faun, is an escape

from Bayard's tension: "It comes to all . . . his tired heart comforted him, and at last he slept" (p. 274). And finally, when Narcissa reads to the bedfast young Bayard and the shadows lengthen, she is "lost from mutable things" (p. 224).

One finds echoes of the *Mississippian* works throughout the novel. Bayard's semi-oblivious attention to Buddy MacCallum's story suggests linkages to the images and theme of the early poem "Cathay":

It was a *vague, dreamy sort of tale,* without beginning or end and filled with stumbling references to places wretchedly mispronounced— you got *an impression of people, creatures without initiative or background or future, caught timelessly in a maze of solitary conflicting preoccupations,* like bumping tops, against an imminent but incomprehensible nightmare. (p. 271) [Italics added.]

Like the "Wanderers" of "Cathay," Buddy MacCallum, a countryman, can be viewed in the pastoral context of the shepherds tending their flocks among the ruins of a vanished civilization; but Bayard, identifying with the "initiative" and "background" of Colonel John Sartoris, is caught in the tensional clash between two unreachable identities. The 1921 poem "Nocturne" anticipates the terpsichorean and papier-mâché imagery of the Christmas dance imagined by Bayard with its paper bells and paper streamers, and, in the midst of his reverie, the silhouetted image of "yellow flame . . . stenciled on the twilight" (p. 293). Echoes of Faulkner's first local color prose piece, "The Hill," are obvious in the technical use of sun and shadow to indicate slow movement, as Bayard and the Negro go toward town, "Out of the sun they descended into violet shadow" (p. 293). Again, one detail of the town described in "The Hill," the "reverberation of an anvil," is repeated in *Sartoris* (p. 154). The sleepy town in "The Hill," a familiar place with its courthouse columns "discolored and stained with casual tobacco," and an occasional house with "a thread of smoke balanced precariously upon a chimney," anticipates Jefferson in *Sartoris* with its courthouse, its tobacco-chewing countrymen (p. 153), and over the trees in the twilight "a column of smoke stood like a balanced plume" (p. 135).

The techniques and themes of the *Green Bough* poems are reëchoed in *Sartoris*. The negative verb coinages of poem XXVI ("Unprobes," "unblend," "undrown") anticipate the equally unusual noun coinages of the novel: "unassertion" (p. 163), "unillusion" (p. 175), and "unemphasis" (p. 194). Just as "paris/tastes his bitter thumbs" in poem XXXII, Horace Benbow of the novel can "play to any cue at a moment's notice while the younger men chew their bitter thumbs in the wings" (p. 174). The feminine figure of poem II (p. 14) playing the piano in the room at dusk is recapitulated in several details as Narcissa plays the piano in the novel (pp. 317-318). The earth motif of poem XLIV is anticipated in Bayard's "submerged . . . monotony of days" as, for one of the few times, he is charmed into a routine of activities close to the earth (p. 182).[15]

Similarly, the New Orleans sketches suggest images, devices, and themes which appear in *Sartoris*. The Caesar image of "Mirrors of Chartres Street" (p. 57) is recast in the novel while Simon watches over the Thanksgiving table "as Caesar must have stood looking down into Gaul" (p. 252). In "The Rosary" a tune "spilling the dusty sparrows tumultously from the eaves" (p. 128) anticipates the pictorial scene of an Indian maiden holding a guitar and a rose while "dusty sparrows sat on the window ledge . . ." (p. 108) in *Sartoris*. As the jockey in "Cheest" takes a girl's garter "kind of for luck or something" (p. 96), so is Bayard just before he takes off in the inventor's plane offered "a woman's garter" (p. 306). Similar to Johnny's girlfriend in "The Kid Learns" who *wails* "O-o-o-oh, he sc-scared me s-o" (p. 165), Bayard's Narcissa *moans,* "You scared me so bad" (p. 218). Finally, the religious motif with its parallel to Christ in "Out of Nazareth" emerges again more indirectly as Bayard sleeps in the hay of a stable on Christmas Eve (pp. 288-289).

A great many parallels of character, scene, and French Symbolist imagery involving synesthesia, faint suggestion, and highly refined expression exist between *Soldiers' Pay* and *Sartoris*. With a slight turn Cecily Saunders' description becomes those of young Bayard's two wives, first Narcissa's, then in Aunt Jenny's mind as she looks beyond the veil of time and life itself, Caroline White's:

CECILY	NARCISSA, CAROLINE
her lax hand between them grew again like a flower . . . as if her whole body became her hand . . . her hand unawaked . . . crushed softly about with her fragile clothing . . . vain and pliant, trying attitude, gesture after gesture . . . . her body which was no body, crumpling a dress that had been dreamed . . . . Epicene, he thought, feeling her slim bones, the bitter nervousness of her flesh. (pp. 155-156)	the caller tall in a white dress beside her . . . all the impalpable veil of the immediate . . . a girl with a bronze swirling of hair and a small, supple body in a constant epicene unrepose, a dynamic fixation like that of carven sexless figures caught in moments of action, striving, a mechanism all of whose members must move in performing the most trivial action, her wild hands not accusing but passionate still beyond the veil impalpable but sufficient. (p. 68)

As Bayard and his friends of the night sing below Narcissa's window, her thoughts are cast in the words Cecily might have used, "Why in the world are those jellybeans serenading me?" (p. 143). With little difficulty the sophisticated dance scene of *Soldiers' Pay* could furnish the props and atmosphere for the social gathering at Belle Mitchell's in *Sartoris*. Such surface similarities follow into the minutiae of local color: in *Soldiers' Pay* Gilligan's host shows him how to drink corn liquor from a jug,

Crooking his first finger through the handle the man raised the jug with a round back-handed sweep to his horizontal upper arm . . . his mouth met the mouth of the vessel. . . . "That's how she's done," he said. . . . (*SP*, p. 215)

The action in the early novel anticipates the one in the later (cf. p. 131). Similarly, "Loosh," the returned Negro army veteran in *Soldiers' Pay*, whose grandmother is old Mammy Callie, suggests Caspey in *Sartoris*, also a returned veteran in uniform intimately connected with the soldier-hero's family. Even Faulkner's eloquent tribute to the stolid mule (pp. 239-240) in *Sartoris* is faintly suggested by the sensitive outline in the early novel (p. 105). Close to its ending, each novel has a cemetery scene with sunlight, cedars, and singing doves: in *Soldiers' Pay*, "doves were cool, throatily unemphatic among the dead" (p. 206), and in *Sartoris*, "Across the spaced tranquillity of the marble shapes the doves crooned their endless rising inflections" (p. 313). In the same way, the frequent devices of the French Symbolists so richly employed in *Soldiers' Pay* reappear with equal frequency in *Sartoris*.[16]

But the thematic repetitions of *Soldiers' Pay* are even more obvious in *Sartoris*. The theme of youthful disappointment in war, evident in the character of Cadet Julian Lowe in *Soldiers' Pay*, reappears in a slightly different cast in *Sartoris*, for even though he has not been wounded young Bayard, unlike Lowe, has seen war. Thus, when old Bayard asks him if he is all right his grandson snaps, "Why not? Takes damn near as big a fool to get hurt in war as it does in peacetime" (p. 60). Again, young Bayard speaks of the glory, immortality, and doom of war:

Not of combat, but rather of a life peopled by young men like fallen angels, and of a meteoric violence like that of fallen angels, beyond heaven or hell and partaking of both: doomed immortality and immortal doom. (p. 122)

Bayard is so stricken by the glamor of death which surrounds him that he, more deeply and irrevocably than Cadet Lowe of course, yearns to identify with it:

"Hell," he said, lying on his back, staring out the window where nothing was to be seen, waiting for sleep, not knowing if it would come or not, not caring a particular damn either way. Nothing to be seen, and the long, long span of a man's natural life. Three score and ten years to drag a stubborn body about the world and cozen its insistent demands. Three score and ten, the Bible said. Seventy years. And he was only twenty-six. Not much more than a third through it. Hell. (p. 148)

The thematic coupling of love and danger can be readily observed in Narcissa's attraction toward Bayard; she sits nursing him, "and looked at his bold, still face and the broken travesty of him and her tranquil sorrow overflowed in pity for him"

(p. 217). And after he has promised her that he will drive carefully and then with Narcissa in the car speeds madly down a hill and across a narrow bridge, brushing Death, she comes to him: "her crazed hands were on his face and she was sobbing wildly against his mouth" (p. 227).

In *Soldiers' Pay* Faulkner wrote of an air force veteran who is brought home to die in a small southern town. In *Sartoris* a young aviator who has seen combat returns to a southern town to fill out a pattern of identity which, he feels, requires his death; and through a self-destructive compulsion, he achieves his goal. I have treated other similarities of technique and theme. If there are such strong relationships between the two novels—involving action, technique, and theme—then what are the differences? Olga W. Vickery has pointed out that in *Sartoris* Faulkner was engaged in "the making of a myth." Thus, the

thematic action . . . takes place not over a period of months but in a time span covering four generations, flanked by the Civil and First World Wars and by the two John Sartorises.[17]

Not only is the theme of *Sartoris* more all-encompassing than that of *Soldiers' Pay,* but also at least two important tendencies noted in the earlier novel have taken on distinction and become more intricately related to dominant thematic purposes. These are (1) the increased reliance upon autobiographical materials, and (2) the placing of action into the context of familiar local color. Faulkner was writing about what he knew, as Anderson had urged him to. The use of autobiographical materials is most obvious in his choice of characters. The old Colonel, John Sartoris, has many of the features of Faulkner's real great-grandfather, Colonel William C. Falkner. Like the real Old Colonel, his fictive counterpart carries after his death a legendary ghostliness capable of haunting his descendants from the time they are old enough to hear the glamorous legends from others and to feel their ancestor's haunting presence in carefully preserved rooms. Like Colonel Falkner, Colonel John Sartoris fought in the Mexican

War, saw heroic action in the Civil War, built a railroad and himself a monument, killed too many men, won a race for the legislature, and was shot down shortly thereafter on a street while weaponless. Both Colonel John and his prototype had sons who inherited their titles of "Colonel," sold their railroads, became lawyers and bankers, were notoriously deaf, and had reputations for testy dispositions. The parallels extend into the minute detail of their libraries, which contain such Romantics as Dumas. Phil Stone remembers the Young Colonel, J. W. T. Falkner, "sitting out at the corner of his bank in the shade on summer afternoons." The action was not unusual, for hundreds of Southerners—town loafers and merchants alike—did the same. Still, for whatever significance the parallel may have when weighed with all the others, Colonel Bayard Sartoris has "a tilted chair in the bank door" (p. 117).

Horace Benbow is another fictional creation bearing some similarities to a real person: Phil Stone himself. There are, of course, the general character traits of the well-bred young lawyer whose traditional family profession is law, the gift for brilliant speech ("flaming verbal wings," p. 175, is not an inappropriately exaggerated metaphor), and the formal education (Stone graduated from Ole Miss and Yale). However, a more remarkable parallel is to be found in a device of local color, a description which Faulkner very likely drew from fact. In guiding me about the ruins of his family homeplace, Phil Stone pointed to the front lawn from the street, the portion below the curving driveway, and told me a story of how his father had plowed up the flowering terrace and landscaped a greensward where once jonquils, narcissi, and gladioli had grown, but how the flowers nevertheless continued to grow through the lawn every spring thereafter and color the greensward. Faulkner described the Benbow place in *Sartoris* as follows:

The drive ascended to the house and curved before it. . . . About the oak and from the . . . drive descending, lawn flowed streetward with good sward broken by random clumps of jonquils and narcissi and gladioli. Originally the lawn was in terraces and the flowers a formal bed on the first terrace. Then Will Benbow, Horace's and Narcissa's father, had had the terraces obliterated. It was done with plows and scrapers and seeded anew with grass, and he had supposed the flower bed destroyed. But the next spring the lawn was stippled with bloom in yellow, white, and pink without order. (pp. 155-156)

Faulkner relied heavily on his experiences and repeated himself again and again. He apparently used local reality whenever he could and seldom invented what reality provided.

Young Bayard Sartoris has a number of the young Faulkner's traits. Not only is he a descendant of a great-grandfather and grandfather much like Faulkner's own, but his own father is strikingly avoided, perhaps because he is too colorless in comparison to his forebears. When asked about the absence of Bayard's father in the novel, Faulkner replied that there was nothing written about him because nothing dramatic happened in that period from 1870 to World War I.[18] To recapitulate, Faulkner's attitude toward his own father was respectful but unfamiliar. "Dad's square," he said.[19] Young Bayard avoids thoughts of his father, and the man never appears as a character. Neither does his mother except as a minor reference (p. 82). Rather, Bayard's grandfather and great-great-Aunt Jenny serve as his parents. Even the Falkner family trait of walking "very straight" is carried over to old Bayard's carriage, a "stiff erectness which, as a countryman once remarked, if he ever stumbled, would meet itself falling down" (p. 29). Aunt Jenny does not escape the trait either: "that straight, grenadier's back of hers which gave the *pas* for erectness to only one back in town—that of her nephew Bayard" (p. 49). Again both Sartorises and Falkners have a reputation of extraordinary pride:

But those folks, thinking there wasn't anybody quite as good as a Sartoris. Even Lucy Cranston . . . acting like it was divine providence that let her marry one Sartoris and be the mother to two more. Pride, false pride. (p. 82)

Like young Faulkner, Bayard hunts and roams the countryside on foot and by car; similarly, he wears parts of his uniform as he treks through the country; and both are fascinated with airplanes and acts of daring. Narcissa mentions Bayard's swinging by a rope off a water tank and diving into a swimming pool (p. 80), and Bayard's death flight in the untested airplane is narrated with technical skill (pp. 306-307). The first incident, with its emphasis on dangling from a rope at a dangerous height, reflects at least some aspects of Faulkner's painting the steep tower and roof of the law building at the University of Mississippi after his return from the war, ''swinging from a rope as he smeared on the black paint.''[20] Faulkner's interest in flying during the 1920's was still strong, and a member of the Vieux Carré art colony recalls that Faulkner "was a bit hipped on the subject of flying," was in close association with the stunting "Gates Flying Circus," and that "Nobody *else* in our crowd had gone looping-the-loop in a bucket seat and open cockpit over the Mississippi River."[21] Both fictional incidents of daring, then, have at least some possible associations in autobiographical facts.

Just as Colonel John Sartoris had a younger brother (Bayard) killed in the Civil War in an act of derring-do, returning to a Yankee encampment for a jar of anchovies, young Bayard has a younger brother John killed in World War I in an action similar in its foolish daring: "He was drunk . . . or a fool" (p. 60), Bayard tells his grandfather, recounting the incident. Now the action has come almost full circle. Even the old Colonel who outlived his war was a figure of epical achievement before he was shot down in the street. Bayard is a drifter; divided from a dead and dying age, his only route to identity is death. Thus, it has been said that the dream of John Sartoris' glory

becomes progressively more destructive as it takes on all the force of a categorical imperative for Colonel John Sartoris' descendants. Spontaneous reactions to experience are replaced by imitative rituals in which form becomes more important than meaning. The final result is apt to be either an outbreak of violence or complete paralysis. At its most extreme, devotion to the dead and their design can mean a complete denial of one's own life.[22]

The theme of the past is most evident in the ghostly presence of the old Colonel, whether it arise from the conversations of

old Bayard and Will Falls, Aunt Jenny's tales of martial
heroics, the Sartoris parlor set apart like a museum of rich
memory, old Bayard's rummaging through the trunk containing
his father's personal effects, Simon's monologues with the "Ole
Marster," Aunt Jenny's desiring to name the new baby "John"
and perhaps unconsciously to repeat the fatal pattern, her
constant caviling at Sartoris arrogancies, and, in the cemetery,
her acquiescence to the old Colonel's looming example of
glamor and doom set down inescapably for all the Sartorises.
Every one of the five parts of the novel deals in some way
with the old Colonel, and, although he actually enters the
action only through the narrated memories of other characters,
as in the first section, he is often far more palpable than those
who are bodily present.

Past and present are frequently juxtaposed in subtle dramatic renderings, as, for example, in Faulkner's treatment of
Myrtle, the nurse of the up-to-date young Dr. Alford in Part
Two. Myrtle in her "small cubbyhole . . . of Spartan but suave
asepsis" (p. 98) asks Aunt Jenny, "You have an appointment?"
—but after Aunt Jenny ignores the question and tells her to
"run and tell Dr. Alford Colonel Sartoris wants to see him."
she replies, "Yessum, Miss Jenny," and obediently follows the
directions of her elders and, thereby, the dictates of the established social pattern of the past. The clash between new and
old becomes more obvious when the old family doctor, "Loosh"
Peabody, leads the young Colonel away from Dr. Alford and
advises against an operation. Dr. Alford's office becomes
emblematical of the modern world of nondescript, impersonal
efficiency while Dr. Peabody's office, with its roll-top desk,
dusty litter, and stack of paper-covered nickel novels, represents
the identifiable, more slowly moving, and personal world of
the past. One encounters similar clashes in the attitude of the
MacCallum patriarch who "ain't never got over Buddy being
in the Yankee army," and "Claims he ain't coming to town
again until the Democratic party denies Woodrow Wilson"
(p. 120). The disparity between the past and present is
emphasized once more when Will Falls recounts the stories
of the old Colonel to the half-deaf Bayard and Faulkner refers

to Will Falls' "days into which few who now trod that earth could enter with him" (p. 199).

Young Bayard tries in what amounts to frustrating desperation to fit his own life to the fatal, outmoded Sartoris pattern. Swinging by rope from the high water tank, riding the fierce unbridled horse, bolting his car wildly over the countryside, and testing the unproved plane are all so many immolations performed as ritual to a formalized past in which he feels he cannot otherwise share. He tries to escape this kind of fatal identity through his marriage to Narcissa, but he knows their love is only a temporary respite from the ultimate sacrifice: "the temporary abeyance of his despair and the isolation of that doom he could not escape" (p. 248). Again, after precipitating old Bayard's heart attack, he tries to escape into the country, hunting with the MacCallums, but he always encounters the sense of isolation and tension that leaves him in frustrated suspension between the intolerable present and the unreachable past. Familiar cataleptic images occur throughout the novel. Even the old houses in the town "emanated a gracious and benign peace, steadfast as a windless afternoon in a world without motion or sound" (p. 155). As Narcissa, bewitched by love into the fated Sartoris pattern, looks down into her garden, she is likened to "a night animal or bird caught in a beam of light and trying vainly to escape" (p. 223). After his flight to the country, Bayard, guiltily convinced that he has caused both the death of his grandfather and his brother, is imprisoned in cold much as Ugolini in Dante's *Inferno* suffers eternal imprisonment in ice up to his neck for having betrayed his kindred (pp. 270-274). Bayard's attempt to escape his doom ends only when he meets it with a kind of resigned willingness in the airplane crash.

Perhaps the major distinction between *Sartoris* and all of Faulkner's previous works is that the familiar themes of his own struggle to identity and his sense of obligation to his Southern past—traceable through every major phase of his work from its beginning in 1919 to the published advent of the Yoknapatawpha series in 1929—are placed into the contexts of identifiable autobiographical materials and recognizable aspects of local color. In writing *Sartoris*, Faulkner came home to his roots; and, like the best of his mature production, the book is rooted in the northern Mississippi area that he knew best. For the first time in his literary career, Faulkner had acquired the technical maturity to express what he had come to understand was his material.

X

Epilogue:
A Retrospect

The previous biographies concerning William Faulkner—such as those of Coughlan, Howe, Millgate, Miner, and O'Connor—have presented many helpful facts about his life and offered various critical approaches to his work. John Faulkner's portrait *My Brother Bill* and Murry Falkner's memoir *The Falkners of Mississippi,* though affectionate panegyrics, have shed some new light, especially into the years when the brothers were growing up in Oxford. As a result, anyone interested in Faulkner is in a position to know certain facts about his early life and literary development: he published two volumes of poetry; he spent some time at the University of Mississippi and did some writing for campus publications; and he had a colorful ancestry, most notably a great-grandfather who became a kind of legend. Similarly, other bits of information are generally known. Young Faulkner was an imaginative child and erratic adolescent, quitting high school his sophomore year. Later, as a trainee for the Royal Air Force in Canada during World War I, he participated in some uncertain "heroics," perhaps one unauthorized flight involving a crash, although the whole matter remains vague, contradictory, and officially unsubstantiated. At home again in Oxford, Mississippi, he became something of a town character—sometimes the monocled, dapper "Count No'count," sporting his cane—and then again the ragged, barefoot wanderer of the countryside, who squatted on the floor of "Mack" Reed's drug store to read magazines. He was a self-educated genius, who, with the help of a local lawyer, Phil Stone, published his first book of poetry, *The Marble Faun* (1924). Such fragments of information about Faulkner's life are common knowledge; but, too often, they have been played up in such a way as to make him appear eccentric and his behavior unaccountable. Thus, the total impression which biographers have given of Faulkner is one of a very odd person.

With this book, I have tried to provide the relationships between such facts and Faulkner's life, the behavior and the man, the work and the mind which produced it. When these relationships are supplied, Faulkner becomes less of an oddity and more explainable both as a person and an artist. Works of art are composed by people who are living, and there is, consequently, an inevitable relationship between a given piece of art and the artist who executed it, however tenuous that relationship may be. I have therefore approached Faulkner's life and early work from two viewpoints—the esthetic and the psychological, my intention being that the two approaches act as reflecting mirrors, the psychological illuminating Faulkner's work, and the work itself illuminating his personal attitudes and motivations during this period of his life. I have endeavored to move back and forth between the life and the work not in disconnected parts, but rather in an effort to define those parts and to relate them to the larger, more meaningful pattern of the man-artist himself.

The background of my approach, perhaps, needs further amplification. While at Oxford, Mississippi, I was permitted to examine the Faulkner materials at the University library and, in the town, was granted several interviews. Both the research and interviews have increased my understanding of Faulkner's early work and, to some extent, added new information to the previously available knowledge of his life; but the most valuable aspect of my experience in Oxford was the sense of connection gained between the isolated facts and anecdotes already written about and the larger context of Faulkner's early life. This sense of connection seemed gradually to give shape to the patternless bits of information and to make Faulkner believable as a person and his work illuminating in ways not previously recognized.

All the elements discussed in previous chapters seem, in retrospect, to have been necessary and valuable in clarifying Faulkner's literary and personal development. The treatment of his family background and the period of his life up through his enlistment in the Royal Air Force in 1918 reveals the emerging themes of the past and his struggle to identify as he was drawn, on the one hand, toward that past—and, on the other, toward a more personal individuation in the South of his day. The ensuing conflict of identities helps to explain a pattern of recurring tensional images, first appearing in 1919 in Faulkner's earliest published works. These images can be traced throughout his early work and related to the themes of the past and the conflict of identities.

Particularly strong relationships existed between the young Faulkner and both his great-grandfather Colonel William Cuthbert Falkner, the most predominant ancestral influence, and his grandfather John Wesley Thompson Falkner. However, before he could transmute these familiar prototypes into the consciously communicated *personae* of literary art, it was first necessary to write poetry. "I'm a failed poet," Faulkner said. "Maybe every novelist wants to write poetry first, and finds he can't. . . ." He then turned from poetry to prose, and then from his decadent phase of the mid-Twenties toward an increased reliance upon autobiographical materials placed into the context of a more concrete local color. The Falkner family tradition imposed upon him a unique problem of identification, which he ultimately solved; but, conversely, he had the advantage of the ancestry, and having had it impressed upon him so deeply as a child, it was there all the time—a reservoir of material. Desiring to identify with the past, while at the same time being actively disjoined from it by time and the events of history, he began to prepare himself to deal with it imaginatively and, consequently, immersed himself in a series of literary experiences. Thus, the dominant themes of the past and his struggle to identity found outlet in his writing, and can be traced as they appear in various forms throughout every major phase of his early work from its beginning in 1919 up through the published advent of the Yoknapatawpha series, *Sartoris* (1929).

Similarly, the unspectacular facts of Faulkner's training experiences in World War I and the fictional expansions of them which he himself fostered and never bothered to correct become understandable when related to Faulkner's deep imperative to identify with an ancestry that was replete with martial heroism. The war experience in 1918 came along at just the right time for him. Without it he could not have projected so effectively back into the military past of his great-grandfather; if he had been older, he might have been more deeply affected, his cognitive artistry thwarted and deprived of its rich resources of the past. At any rate, his art as well as his life would have been different. He was touched by the war in a minimum way, but that seems to have been enough.

For purposes of this biography, Faulkner's early work has been treated chronologically according to composition: the poems of *The Marble Faun;* the University pieces, most of which were published in the campus weekly, *The Mississippian;* the poems of *A Green Bough;* the New Orleans sketches, poems, and criticisms, most of them published in *The Double Dealer* and the *Times-Picayune;* and the first three novels, *Soldiers' Pay, Mosquitoes,* and *Sartoris.* This material reveals a variety of influences at work in Faulkner's literary development, most notably the French Symbolists, who were to help Faulkner to become a regional writer with a difference. I have isolated, analyzed, and traced recurring images, devices, themes, and motifs as they appear from one work to another, thus giving some concept of the continuing development of Faulkner's techniques during this period; at the same time, I have related various aspects of the significant individual works to their counterparts in the other works of the period covered by this biography, thus placing each piece into the context of a larger developmental pattern.

In addition, I have traced a large number of other influences in Faulkner's early work, beginning with the Romantics. Even though "Cathay" is not a particularly good poem, it is a typical piece and indicates that Faulkner was experimenting with sensuous imagery in a profusion exceeding even that of Keats or Shelley, two of the most pronounced influences on his poetry. The significance of the poem is, of course, basically developmental, but Faulkner had to write it, for that was his way of assimilating the Romantic and French Symbolist influences which were to prepare him to profit from literary experiences to come. Faulkner's critical articles published in *The Mississippian* throw light on biographical facts and help, incidentally, to clarify through internal evidence the chronology of Faulkner's first New York trip, probably in the summer of 1921.

The two most important contemporary influences on Faulkner were Phil Stone and Sherwood Anderson. Phil Stone acted as friend and Maecenas to Faulkner, and he strongly influenced his protégé's reading. If Faulkner had met the French Symbolists in a college course, they might have been dead for him; but he met them through the sympathetic eyes and mind of Phil Stone, who himself had assimilated them. Without Stone's exposure to the Romantics, the French Symbolists, and the *avant-garde* works, Faulkner would probably have been writing jingles for the college yearbook. Various specific patterns of phrasing in Faulkner's prose echo some of those in Stone's published work, suggesting the possibility of a technical, stylistic influence. Faulkner relied quite heavily upon Stone's editing of his manuscripts up through *Sanctuary* (1931), and he continued to check his local color lore with Stone, especially that pertaining to the Snopeses, as late as *The Reivers* (1962). Thus, the literary friendship with Stone brought Faulkner more fully and ambitiously into creative experience, and then sustained him editorially until Faulkner reached artistic maturity. When he and Stone went to New Orleans in the winter of 1924-1925, Faulkner was ready to benefit from Anderson's influence. He looked up to Anderson but, by no means, felt inferior. Indeed, in some ways he felt equal to Anderson, and, in general, Anderson accepted him as an equal. The events surrounding their friendship in New Orleans, the publication of *Soldiers' Pay* (1926), their collaboration on the tall tale which substantively emerged in *Mosquitoes* (1927), and the collaboration itself indicate a mutual, professional respect.

Finally, by the time Faulkner wrote *Sartoris,* he had developed a style which met the need of the local material and, at the same time, the standards of the *avant-garde.* He became a regional writer, but subtly, through a series of necessary experiences—the Phil Stone friendship, the New York trip, the Anderson influence, the sojourn in Europe, and the discipline learned through various works of literary apprenticeship. Faulkner had the material all along, but he had to get a perspective with which to treat it: a recipe by which the emotional depth of the material could be realized. When he went back home to what Anderson called "that little patch up there in Mississippi where you started from," he took with him a mature cognitive artistry with which he could shape the substance of the past into a myth of his own, first for men and then for man. In a peculiar way, then, everything that happened to Faulkner, from the generations of his preconscious past to his individuation as a writer in Oxford, Mississippi, seems to have been necessary. Everything, as it were, prepared him for the next event.

A long tradition of regional realism has existed in America, but no other regional writer so successfully contrived to make out of his native soil a literature so rich in local color and so universal in its appeal. William Faulkner created a myth in the dimension of literary art—a world at once his own, yet larger than himself and his own South, one partaking of the timeless existence of man's noblest strivings from the dark, reachless past to the light of each man's self-discovery.

Notes

1. The whole matter of the designation and spelling of the family name from the Old Colonel to William is inconsistent, complex, and often contradictory. Some reference works list "Harrison" as Faulkner's middle name. Most biographies have failed to mention his middle name altogether. Faulkner signed his legal documents "W. C. Falkner." His closest friend, Phil Stone, interviewed by me (Oxford, Mississippi, 2:30 P.M., July 27, 1962), stated that Faulkner was named *"Cuthbert* from the beginning, *the same as his great-grandfather,"* and explained the younger Faulkner's attempt to change it: "He couldn't stand the name." This first conversation with Stone will be designated as Interview No. 1 in future references. John Faulkner (*My Brother Bill: An Affectionate Reminiscence,* New York, 1963), states that Faulkner signed his name "W. C. Faulkner" (pp. 12, 211), and states that one of the Nobel laureate's grandsons "is named for Bill—William *Cuthbert Faulkner* Summers" (italics added), pp. 243-44. Faulkner himself wrote of "My great-grandfather, *whose name I bear"* (italics added) in a letter dated December 8, 1945, in Malcolm Cowley, *The Faulkner-Cowley File: Letters and Memories, 1944-1962* (New York, 1966), p. 66.

Over against this evidence of the name "Cuthbert," especially as it applies to the Old Colonel, Michael Millgate, *The Achievement of William Faulkner* (New York, 1966), p. 1, gives "Clark" as the Old Colonel's middle name. G. T. Buckley, "Is Oxford the Original of Jefferson in William Faulkner's Novels?" *PMLA,* 76, No. 4, Pt. 1:449, September 1961, writes "Christy," although neither author explains the source of his designation.

Little doubt exists that the original spelling of the family name was "Fa*u*lkner," and that the Old Colonel dropped it to avoid confusion with another family of "Faulkners" whom "he did not like" (John Faulkner, *My Brother Bill,* p. 210). Even so, much scholarly energy has been expended in explaining the variant spelling of the family surname. To illustrate, Ward L. Miner, *The World of*

William Faulkner (Durham, 1952), p. 57, notes: "When the contemporary novelist's first book, *The Marble Faun* [1924], was published, a misprint made Falkner into Faulkner, and so it has remained." William Van O'Connor, *William Faulkner*, University of Minnesota Pamphlets on American Writers, No. 3 (Minneapolis, 1960), p. 4, explains the spelling distinction parenthetically: "The *u* was added to the family name by the printer who set up William's first book." That the family name was originally spelled with the *u*, however, is further supported by John B. Cullen and Floyd C. Watkins, *Old Times in the Faulkner Country* (Chapel Hill, 1961): when Faulkner was a boy, the family still spelled its name "without a *u*, but William has restored the letter *dropped by his great-grandfather*" (p. 3, italics added). Robert Coughlan, "The Private World of William Faulkner," *Life*, Pt. 2 (October 5, 1953), p. 128, reports that the great-grandfather dropped the *u* sometime after 1872 and before 1880, for, as the family story went, there were "some no-good people named Faulkner down around Pontotoc," and the Old Colonel did not want to be confused with them. James B. Meriwether, *The Literary Career of William Faulkner* (Princeton, 1961), p. 7, notes, "William Faulkner apparently first added the 'u' to his surname while in the RAF, and afterward retained it as his 'literary' signature." In my own research, however, I found Faulkner's name spelled "Falkner" as a signature to all his *Mississippian* poems published while he was a student at Ole Miss after the war, 1918-1919. Carvel Collins, "Faulkner at the University of Mississippi," *William Faulkner: Early Prose and Poetry* (Boston, 1962), pp. 10-13, treats the problem with convincing thoroughness, stating that the "u" appeared in the name "intermittently some years before the publication of *The Marble Faun*," first when Faulkner signed his name with the "u" while working for an arms factory in Connecticut from April to June, 1918. Collins concludes, "the answer to the question Who Put the 'u' in William Faulkner's Name? is William Faulkner." In general Faulkner's own treatment of the matter in Malcolm Cowley, *The Faulkner-Cowley File*, pp. 66-67, is in agreement with that of Collins, except that he adds, "Maybe when I began to write, even though I thought then I was writing for fun, I secretly was ambitious and did not want to ride on grandfather's [*sic*] coat-tails, and so accepted the 'u', was glad of such an easy way to strike out for myself. . . . The above was always my mother's and father's version of why I put back the 'u' which my great-grandfather, himself always a little impatient of grammar and spelling both, was said to have removed. I myself really dont know the true reason."

Considering all the evidence, one could assume that the original family name was spelled "Faulkner," that the Old Colonel changed it to "Falkner" in the 1870's; and that even though most members of the family retain the altered "Falkner," both William and John brought the name full-circle to its original designation, "Faulkner." This footnote is only a brief summary of a portion of what has been written on the subject. Perhaps never in the history of literary scholarship have so many letters of the alphabet been written, spoken, and parried to determine the correct designation of only one letter. Faulkner's final statement to Cowley on the matter, "I still think it is of no importance, and either one suits me" (p. 67), seems to be the prime wisdom.

2. *Mississippi: A Guide to the Magnolia State*, Federal Writers' Project (New York, 1938), p. 254. Hereafter referred to as *Mississippi*. Also see Robert Cantwell, "The Faulkners: Recollections of a Gifted Family," *New World Writing*, No. 2 (New York, 1952), p. 307.

3. Adwin Wigfall Green, "William Faulkner at Home," *Sewanee Review*, 40:294-295, Summer 1932.

4. See the prefatory history of Oxford and Lafayette County in "Tour of Pre-Civil War Homes in Oxford, Mississippi," published by the Oxford-Lafayette County Chamber of Commerce, 1962. Other early settlers were the Joneses, Phippses, Kendalls, Pegues, Thompsons, Andrews, Duncans, Avents, Triggs, Fees, Neilsons, and Howreys.

5. See John F. Kennedy, "Lucius Quintus Cincinnatus Lamar," *Profiles in Courage*, Cardinal ed. (New York, 1959), pp. 34-35.

6. For further details of Oxford local color, see Joseph G. Baldwin, *The Flush Times of Alabama and Mississippi* (New York, 1853).

7. For these statistics and other aspects of Oxford's history, see Medford Evans, "Oxford, Mississippi," *Southwest Review*, 15:50-53, Autumn 1929.

8. Malcolm Cowley entered this quotation in his notebook after a conversation with Faulkner in October, 1948, pub. in *The Faulkner-Cowley File*, p. 112.

9. The Colonel's monument with its life-sized statue in the cemetery at Ripley, Mississippi, gives the date of birth "1825." However, the alternate date 1826 is given by Ward L. Miner, *The World of William Faulkner* (Durham, 1952), p. 57, and Robert Cantwell, "Introduction," *The White Rose of Memphis* (New York, 1953 ed.), p. viii, whose material is thorough and valuable, lists 1826. But Frederick J. Hoffman, *William Faulkner* (New York, 1961), p. 13, gives 1825. Following the date on the Falkner gravestone in Ripley, William Van O'Connor, *William Faulkner*, p. 4, states 1825, as does Buckley, n. 15, p. 449. Hoffman supports Cantwell in the designation of the family's place of origin as Knox County, Tennessee.

Faulkner himself maintained that the "place of our origin" was "a hamlet named Falkner just below [the] Tennessee line" (Cowley, *The Faulkner-Cowley File*, p. 66). Millgate, *The Achievement of William Faulkner*, gives neither the year of birth nor the birthplace of Colonel Falkner, although he quotes the entire paragraph from Faulkner's letter to Cowley regarding the great-grandfather, and lets it stand in context (p. 1), excepting a footnote in which he observes that "Falkner . . . does not appear to have been the family's 'place of . . . origin' " (n. 1, p. 295).

10. Robert Coughlan, "The Private World of William Faulkner," *Life*, pt. 1 (September 28, 1953), p. 127. Miner differs as to the reasons for his departure, maintaining that the father died and the family as a whole returned to Tennessee, from where, at the age of *seventeen*, the young man went to Ripley (p. 57). *Mississippi: A Guide . . .* bears the statement that he "was a barefoot boy of ten who had walked the several hundred miles from Middleton, Tenn." (p. 457). Actually, Ripley is only twenty-two miles from Middleton.

11. Cantwell, "Introduction," pp. ix-xii. Coughlan, pt. 1, pp. 312-13, is very likely in error concerning the sequence of events during this period of the Old Colonel's life, suggesting that he married Holland Pearce, that they had a son, and that she died *before* the Mexican War, after which he returned and, as a local hero, led a "grand ball" with Elizabeth Vance, a visiting belle with whom he "fell in love," the same little girl who had befriended him so long ago that dusky evening when he arrived in Ripley. Cantwell, "Introduction," p. xiv, gives the second wife's name as Elizabeth Vance Houston, and mentions that she was born in Alabama in 1834.

12. Cantwell, "The Faulkners . . ." pp. 312-14.

13. Miner, p. 57. *Mississippi*, p. 458. Phil Stone, "William Faulkner, the Man and His Work," *Oxford Magazine*, vol. 1, no. 2 (1934), p. 13, gives as a reason for the replacement a comment attributed to William Faulkner and states, "the men of the Second Mississippi Regiment did not relish the hard discipline which his great-grandfather meted out to them and deposed him. . . ." The band of irregulars which the Colonel organized was initially known as the First Mississippi Partisan Rangers, but later became the Seventh Mississippi Cavalry.

14. For some of these and other interesting facts concerning this famous railroad, see G. T. Buckley, "Is Oxford the Original of Jefferson in William Faulkner's Novels?" *PMLA*, 76, no. 4, pt. 1:450, September 1961. Also note Thomas L. McHaney, "The Image of the Railroad in the Novels of William Faulkner, 1926-1942," unpub. master's thesis (Univ. of North Carolina, 1962) for other details.

15. Cantwell, "Introduction," pp. v, ix; also "The Faulkners . . ." p. 312.

16. All following references to the text are found in the rev. ed. pub. by Coley Taylor (New York, 1953), introd. Robert Cantwell. Page references are indicated after quotations.

17. Cantwell, "The Faulkners . . ." pp. 304-05. These statements, despite their illumination, illustrate ways in which Faulkner could be misleading. Actually, the Colonel did write two other books after *White Rose: The Little Brick Church* (Philadelphia, 1882), intended as an answer to *Uncle Tom's Cabin;* and *Rapid Ramblings in Europe* (Philadelphia, 1884), inspired by a European trip in the summer of 1883. Concerning the Old Colonel's naming the stations after Scott's characters, no such names are evident today. Ingomar was one of the stops, but it was named not for a Scott character but for the Colonel's own in *White Rose.* Also see Buckley, fn. 5, p. 447.

18. Cantwell, "The Faulkners . . ." p. 305.

19. Cantwell, "The Faulkners . . ." p. 305.

20. Coughlan, pt. 1, pp. 130, 134. Phil Stone, "William Faulkner, the Man and His Work," *Oxford Magazine,* vol. 1, no. 2 (1934), pp. 14-15, gives further details concerning J. W. T. Falkner's legal and political career. The Young Colonel moved to Oxford in the late 1880's where he was Assistant United States Attorney for the Northern District of Mississippi under Judge Charles B. Howrey.

21. Pages 4-5. Cullen, a Lafayette County farmer, was a professional cement finisher by the time he was sixteen. Having known the Falkner family since his childhood, he provided many personal experiences for *Old Times in the Faulkner Country,* written in collaboration with Floyd C. Watkins.

22. Coughlan, pt. 1, pp. 133-34.

23. The second-oldest brother, less than two years separated him from William. For Murry's personal reminiscence of William see "The Wonderful Mornings of Our Youth," in *William Faulkner of Oxford,* eds. James W. Webb and A. Wigfall Green (Louisiana State University Press, 1965), pp. 9-22. The editors note that Murry served overseas in both world wars and was wounded in France during the first (p. 9). Murry was also a flying enthusiast, along with William, John, and Dean. He recently published *The Falkners of Mississippi: A Memoir.* Baton Rouge, 1967. The book deals more with the close-knit Falkner family than with the Nobel Prize winner himself; however, the humanity of William is revealed in the reas-

suring depiction of him as a healthy, richly imaginative child of a proud "autonomous" family of the American South. We are provided with a nostalgic picture of the cultural backdrop upon which Faulkner drew heavily for his Yoknapatawpha saga, but the memoir tells us little of his motivations, intense personal crises, and the development of the cognitive artistry which he must have experienced in order to transmute the substance of local color into great art. As biography, the book adds to, but does not supersede John Faulkner's *My Brother Bill*.

24. W. M. Reed, "Mr. Mack remembers 'Bill,' " *The Oxford Eagle*, July 12, 1962, sec. 1, p. 7. Mr. Reed states that Faulkner visited his drug store "approximately 120 times a year for nearly four decades" (p. 1). Concerning the injury which Mr. Reed noted, Faulkner was apparently thrown from his horse on Sunday morning, June 17, 1962; see James W. Webb, "William Faulkner Comes Home," in *William Faulkner of Oxford*, p. 209, who recounts Faulkner's appearance at a party at the home of Professor and Mrs. Green on the same afternoon when Faulkner walked painfully with the aid of a cane.

25. Cullen, p. 7.

26. Paul Flowers, *The Commercial Appeal* (Memphis, Tennessee), July 7, 1962, p. 1.

Chapter II

1. "William Faulkner, the Man and His Work," *The Oxford Magazine*, vol. 1, no. 3 (1934), p. 9.

2. Adwin Wigfall Green, "William Faulkner at Home," *Sewanee Review*, 40:298, Summer 1932. Faulkner also made this statement in the context of a "smart-crack" to Marshall J. Smith in "Faulkner of Mississippi," *Bookman*, 74:412, December 1931.

3. Robert Cantwell, "The Faulkners: Recollections of a Gifted Family," *New World Writing*, no. 2 (New York, 1952), p. 305.

4. In *Old Times in the Faulkner Country*, written in collaboration with Floyd C. Watkins (Chapel Hill, 1961), p. 3. Longer references to this source will be indicated by page numbers in parentheses after quotations.

5. Bill Hudson, "Faulkner before 'Sanctuary,' " *The Carolina Magazine*, 69:12, April 1935.

6. Phil Stone, "William Faulkner, the Man and His Work," no. 3, p. 4.

7. John Faulkner, *My Brother Bill* (New York, 1963), pp. 97-100. These stories have been "colored" with the passage of time. Just as Phil Stone's treatment of the painted chicken episode varies from John Faulkner's (cf. pp. 39-40), even the two brothers Murry and John differed in their details of what was probably the same "fact" of a balloonist who eventually landed, cursing and drunk, on the chicken house of the Falkner lot. See Murry Falkner, "The Wonderful Mornings of Our Youth," in *William Faulkner of Oxford,* eds. James W. Webb and A. Wigfall Green (Baton Rouge, 1965), pp. 12-17, for full details. John Faulkner recalls a "parachutist" whose balloon fell on and broke through their hen-house roof; the father of the boys was so enraged that, when a pig grunted, he turned and immediately shot it between the eyes (pp. 114-16).

8. Robert Coughlan, "The Private World of William Faulkner," *Life,* pt. 2 (October 5, 1953), pp. 133-34.

9. Marshall J. Smith, "Faulkner of Mississippi," *Bookman,* 74:416, December, 1931.

10. Cantwell, "The Faulkners . . ." p. 306.

11. Frederick L. Gwynn and Joseph L. Blotner, eds., *Faulkner in the University* (Charlottesville, 1959), "Session Twenty-Eight," First-Year English Course, April 28, 1958, p. 249. Further references to direct quotations of Faulkner noted in this work will be indicated by the shortened title *"University,"* and page numbers in parentheses after quotations.

12. Cantwell, "The Faulkners . . ." p. 306.

13. Hudson, p. 12.

14. "Verse Old and Nascent: A Pilgrimage," *Salmagundi* (Milwaukee, 1932), p. 34. Originally pub. in *Double Dealer,* 7:129-31, April 1925.

15. Faulkner, "Foreword," *The Faulkner Reader* (New York), p. x. The edition is dated through its copyright "1954 by William Faulkner"; the "Foreword" itself is signed "New York, November, 1953" (p. xi). Faulkner specified "a story of the time of King John Sobieski, when the Poles, almost single-handed, kept the Turks from overruning Central Europe," thus indicating the historical novel *Pan Michael,* first published in 1893 and translated from the Polish by Jeremiah Curtain. It is the third of a trilogy including *With Fire and Sword* and *Deluge.* Faulkner in a letter to Malcom Cowley dated November 1, 1948, wrote that he had read the book "when I was about sixteen I suppose" (Malcolm Cowley, *The Faulkner-Cowley File,* p. 115). Also cf. Joseph Blotner, "Introduction." *William*

Faulkner's Library—A Catalogue (Charlottesville, 1964), p. 12. Upon Faulkner's death, the book was in his library, pub. Philadelphia: Henry Altemus, 1898, trans. by Samuel A. Binion; it bears the autograph, "J. W. T. Falkner/Oxford/Miss."

16.   Lavon Rascoe, "An Interview with William Faulkner," *Western Review,* 15:301, Summer 1951.

17.   Rascoe, p. 302. R. M. Allen, "Faulkner at the University of Mississippi, Spring, 1947," specifies the same years as those Faulkner noted in one of the classes. The document, mimeographed from Allen's notes, is signed and dated "Indianola, Miss., May 12, 1954," p. 3, in the Faulkner Collection, "Miscellaneous Ephemeral Material," Princeton University Library, Princeton, New Jersey.

18.   Carvel Collins, "About the Sketches," *William Faulkner: The New Orleans Sketches* (New Brunswick, 1958), p. 13. It would seem that another statement made by Faulkner may appear to be misleading, ". . . if I could go back to say 1920 when I started writing. . . ." in Gwynn, *University,* "Session Eight," Undergraduate Course in Contemporary Literature, March 13, 1958, p. 65. In context, however, it seems apparent that Faulkner was speaking generally and referring primarily to a date indicating a seriousness of purpose rather than to a specific date of composition.

19.   As the influences relate to Faulkner's poetry, see Chapters III-V. In addition to those I have treated, see Richard P. Adams, "The Apprenticeship of William Faulkner," *Tulane Studies in English,* XII (1962), 113-156.

20.   Phil Stone, Interview No. 2 (Oxford, Mississippi), 10:00 A.M., July 28, 1962. Mr. Stone demonstrated this ritual to me as I sat among the ruins of the Stone homeplace. He bent over close to my face, looked into my eyes, and brushed both sides of my forehead with his fingers. Cullen, p. 13, says that Faulkner hunted with Colonel Stone's camp "while he was just a boy, and he killed a deer when he was only fifteen or sixteen years old."

21.   Gwynn, *University,* "Session Five," the English Club, March 7, 1957, pp. 29-30. This incident suggests Book Four of *The Hamlet* and, almost literally, Part III of *The Bear.* A third inconsistency appears in John Faulkner, *My Brother Bill,* pp. 158-59, who recalled Pittsboro as the source of "Spotted Horses," where William and his Uncle John Falkner stayed at a boardinghouse; in the evening "some men brought in a string of calico ponies wired together with barbed wire," and they were auctioned off the next morning. After the men had pocketed their money and gone, the buyers attempted to get their bargains, but "Someone left the gate open and those ponies

spread like colored confetti over the countryside." William was on the porch when one of the ponies ran across it and "had to dive back into the hallway to get out of its path. He and Uncle John told us about it the next day, when they got home."

22. Cullen, p. 44. Cullen adds that Boon Hogganbeck's accompanying Isaac McCaslin to Memphis for liquor is a factual account from the Stone Camp, which was located just west of Batesville. Some other interesting comments related to Faulkner's hunting stories are mentioned on pp. 27, 28-29, and 43. Also see Cynthia Grenier, "The Art of Fiction: An Interview with William Faulkner—September, 1955," *Accent*, 16:167-77, Summer 1956.

23. The poem first appeared in *A Green Bough* as XVIII (New York, 1933), p. 40. It was reprinted in *Mississippi Verse*, ed. Alice James (Chapel Hill, 1934) along with several other poems from *A Green Bough*: XVI, XXXV, XIX, XLIV, XX, and XIV, pp. 31-35.

Chapter III

1. Phil Stone, interviewed by me (Oxford, Mississippi), 10:00 A.M., July 28, 1962. The street is now named Washington Avenue. The verandaed mansion, along with most of Stone's splendid library and some of Faulkner's original manuscripts, was destroyed by fire over two decades ago, but the ruins are still there. This second interview with Stone, which took place on the grounds, will be designated in further references as Interview No. 2.

2. Interviewed by me (Oxford, Mississippi), 10:00 A.M., July 27, 1962. Mrs. Calvin S. Brown of Oxford, Mr. Reed told me, had given him the information concerning the afflicted child.

3. Recorded by me (Fullerton, California), 8:00 P.M., January 22, 1960. Stallings, coauthor of *What Price Glory?* (1924) and author of the World War I novel *Plumes* (1925), knew Faulkner when both worked for the movies in Hollywood.

4. Lavon Rascoe, "An Interview with William Faulkner," p. 303.

5. The family has shown little desire to clarify this matter or any others—at least, not through a published statement. At the time of my conversation with John Faulkner (Oxford, Mississippi), 7:45 P.M., July 26, 1962, he was close-mouthed about his brother and himself, saying only, "Twenty-five or thirty years ago my brother and I made an agreement not to discuss our work or each other." His comments in *My Brother Bill*, pp. 136-39, are general: Faulkner

limped when he got off the train in Oxford, for he had flown his Camel through the roof of a hangar and had to get down on a ladder raised from the inside. Concerning this frequently repeated story, Emily Whitehurst Stone, wife of Phil Stone, recalls an interview with Faulkner in 1930, pub. in a revealing essay "Some Arts of Self-Defense," *William Faulkner of Oxford,* in which he talked of his Royal Air Force days in Canada: "We crashed through the hangar roof, upside down. There we were, hanging from our belts with our heads down in the plane, craning our heads back and looking down at the ground" (pp. 96-97), giving further credence to the "crash legend," except for the "tall tale" texture of the anecdote, which Faulkner embellished further for his listeners, "to drink whiskey while you were hanging upside down" was "a sort of a hard thing to do," and "I died that time." Apparently in an effort to get Malcolm Cowley to revise a biographical note, with the crash legend set in France, Faulkner wrote four letters to Cowley, pub. in *The Faulkner-Cowley File,* stating only that he "went to RAF" (Dec. 8, 1945, p. 67); "when the war was over" (Dec. 24, 1945, p. 74); "belonged to RAF 1918" (ca. early Jan., 1946, p. 77); and "Was a member of the RAF in 1918" (Jan. 21, 1946, p. 82)—becoming forcefully insistent in the final letter. On Feb. 1, 1946, he wrote again concerning the war experience, stating that he objected to the original text "because it makes me out more of a hero than I was," and, in an explanatory tone, "The mishap was caused not by combat but by (euphoniously) 'cockpit trouble'; i.e., my own foolishness; the injury I suffered I still feel I got at bargain rates. A lot of that sort of thing happened in those days, the culprit unravelling himself from the subsequent unauthorized crash incapable of any explanation as far as advancing the war went, and grasping at any frantic straw before someone in authority would want to know what became of the aeroplane, would hurry to the office and enter it in the squadron records as 'practice flight'. As compared with men I knew, friends I had lost, I deserve no more than the sentence I suggested before: 'served in (or belonged to) RAF'. But I see where your paragraph will be better for your purpose, and I am sorry it's not nearer right" (pp. 83-84). Murry C. Falkner wrote in "The Wonderful Mornings of Our Youth," *William Faulkner of Oxford,* p. 20, "I can almost hear now as he chuckled in recounting how, to celebrate the Armistice, he fortified himself with some good drinking whiskey, took up a rotary motored Spad and spun it through the roof of a hangar." Murry Falkner's further note, "He took flying lessons for his civilian pilot's license under Captain Vernon Omlie at the old Memphis airport" (p. 21) may indicate not only a legal technicality to be met, but also the possibility that Faulkner had not mastered flying. Michael Millgate, "William Faulkner, Cadet," *University of*

Toronto Quarterly, XXXV (Jan. 1966), 117-132, has accumulated some impressive evidence, including that of two men who attended the School of Military Aeronautics with Faulkner in Toronto; much of the evidence points to the probability that Faulkner never "learned" to fly in the RAF, although, of course, a crash into a hangar could still have been possible, perhaps during an unauthorized flight; however, no record of such a crash has been found. Consistent with Stone's statement that he and Faulkner had learned to speak with a British accent, Mr. Albert Monson, a Canadian, recalls that "Faulkner gave an impression of being English" and that "He was just an outstanding little fellow" (p. 123). Faulkner's honorary commission as a second lieutenant was in effect from the time of his demobilization, but was not announced in the *London Gazette* until March 9, 1920, 2911; however, "Official R.A.F. records" . . . make it clear that Faulkner did not qualify for "wings" or "a flying badge" (p. 131), in spite of the fact that he was photographed wearing "wings" shortly after his return to Oxford. For further details, see Gordon Price-Stephens, "Faulkner and the Royal Air Force," *Mississippi Quarterly,* XVII (Summer 1964), 123-128.

6. Stone, "William Faulkner, the Man and His Work," *Oxford Magazine,* vol. 1, no. 2 (1934), p. 11.

7. *The Mississippian,* ed. Professor Erwin (University, Mississippi), pp. 2, 7.

8. Interview No. 1. However, Stone did not withhold information concerning what he felt to have been his contribution to the success of his protégé. He told me that he "read proof of Bill's work up through *Sanctuary."* I asked him if he made corrections, and he answered, "Yes, and wrote in whole lines." O'Connor, *The Tangled Fire of William Faulkner* (Minneapolis, Minnesota), p. 21, notes that "Stone . . . wrote that he had put up the money to pay the Four Seas Company of Boston for publishing *The Marble Faun* . . . to get Faulkner before the public." Other statements have shed additional light on the Stone influence, among them Edith Brown Douds' "Recollections of the Bunch," pub. in *William Faulkner of Oxford,* in which she writes, "Phil . . . was interested in seeing Bill write down the stories which he could tell aloud so well. To say that Phil 'encouraged' Bill, as so many biographers do, is gross understatement. He cajoled, browbeat, and swore at him; he threatened and pleaded; encouragement came later" (p. 50). When Faulkner brought the manuscript of his first novel, *Soldiers' Pay,* to Phil Stone's office, "My chief reaction at the time was to be shocked at how badly it was punctuated. I offered to repunctuate it, and Bill said he didn't care, *so I did"* (p. 51, italics added). Also, James W. Webb and A. Wigfall Green, eds., *William Faulkner of Oxford,* note that the

"Sallie," of whom her close friend Mrs. Douds writes, is now Mrs. Baxter Elliott, "who acted as secretary for Phil Stone and typed *and helped to edit* William's manuscripts . . ." (p. 49, italics added). Concerning the broader aspects of Stone's influence on Faulkner, Joseph Blotner, "Introduction," *William Faulkner's Library—A Catalogue* (Charlottesville, 1964), notes that Faulkner did "an enormous amount of reading" (p. 3), was absorbed with "literary technique," and, further, that Stone had doubtless provided a portion of that reading; Blotner includes an appendix (pp. 123-27) of "a partial list of orders Stone placed with the Brick Row Bookshop in New Haven, Connecticut," although the list gives no information concerning "other books Stone may have ordered during the early and middle 1920's" (p. 6).

9. Boston, p. 51. The title page of the edition at Princeton University bears Faulkner's signature in small, cramped handwriting and the date "19 December 1924." All further references to *The Marble Faun* will be indicated by page numbers in parentheses after quotations. The original edition of *The Marble Faun* was issued at Boston, December 15, 1924.

10. George P. Garrett, "An Examination of the Poetry of William Faulkner," *Princeton University Library Chronicle,* 18, no. 3:124-35, Spring 1957. Harry Runyan, "Faulkner's Poetry," *Faulkner Studies,* 3, nos. 2-3:23-29, Summer-Autumn 1954. I am excepting Phil Stone's "Preface" to *The Marble Faun,* of which I shall say more in Chapter V. John McClure reviewed Faulkner's *Marble Faun* in "Literature and Less," *New Orleans Times-Picayune,* Sunday magazine sec., January 25, 1925, p. 6, recognizing both the achievement and promise of the work. Other reviews related to *A Green Bough* (1933) are more pertinent to Chapter VI. These include William Rose Benét, *Saturday Review of Literature,* April 29, 1933, p. 565; Eda Lou Walton, *New York Herald Tribune Books,* April 30, 1933, p. 2; Peter Monro Jack, *New York Times Book Review,* May 14, 1933, p. 2; *Nation,* vol. 136 (May 17, 1933), p. 565; and Morris U. Schappes, "Faulkner as Poet," *Poetry,* 43:48, October, 1933.

11. Pages 26-27.

12. For a more detailed working out of Romantic influences in Faulkner's poetry during the fall of 1919 and his following semesters at the University of Mississippi, see the next chapter. The Keats influence has also been noted by Richard P. Adams in an impressive article on the wide reading of Faulkner and the influences upon his work, "The Apprenticeship of William Faulkner," *Tulane Studies in English,* XII (1962), 113-156; specifically, see pp. 118-19.

13. Edmund Wilson, *Axel's Castle* (New York, 1954), pp. 15-16, in support of this point compares Shelley's lyric beginning "O World! O Life! O Time!" with Musset's "J'ai perdu ma force et ma vie," both "curiously similar" in Romantic flavor, with the conclusion that Musset's poem is the more classical, even to the point of using epigrammaticisms, whereas Shelley's is the more "vague," giving us "images unrelated by logic," therefore more consistently symbolical.

14. The thirteen poems printed in the newspaper will be treated in Chapter IV. Four of these are translations from Verlaine: "Fantouches" [*sic*] (Feb. 25, 1920, p. 3); "Clair de Lune" (Mar. 3, 1920, p. 6); "Streets" (Mar. 17, 1920, p. 2); and "A [*sic*] Clymene" (April 14, 1920, p. 3).

15. In a review of "Aria da Capo: a Play in One Act, by Edna St. Vincent Millay," under the column title "Books and Things," *The Mississippian* (University, Mississippi), January 13, 1922, p. 5, col. 1, Faulkner enthusiastically praised the drama and showed his disapproval of Sandburg's work with the remark, "even though . . . Mr. Carl Sandburg sets it [*Aria da Capo*] in the stockyards, to be acted of a Saturday afternoon, by the Beef Butchers' Union."

16. *On Native Grounds* (New York, 1956), pp. 351-52.

17. Daniel E. Schneider, *The Psychoanalyst and the Artist* (New York, 1950), p. 75, emphasizes the artistic gift's "inherent capacity for transformation of the unconscious of the individual into a more or less universalized ('back to reality') consciously communicative work." Cf. Freud's *Wit and Its Relation to the Unconscious*.

CHAPTER IV

1. Stone, Interview No. 1. He mentioned that the Falkner home stood on the present site of the Alumni House, just off the west side of the campus drive. Faulkner's letter to Malcolm Cowley is dated Dec. 8, 1945, pub. in *The Faulkner-Cowley File*, p. 67. The context of the statement, however, is general, and, once again, Faulkner was careless with the facts, stating, "That was in *1920*" (italics added), when, in actuality, his year of entrance into Ole Miss was 1919. See William Faulkner, "Student Record, University of Mississippi," No. 6057 (Oxford, Mississippi). Arthur Wigfall Green, "William Faulkner at Home," *Sewanee Review*, 40:300, Summer 1932, mentions Faulkner's withdrawal from English the second semester with a failing grade, but Faulkner's record gives no information on this point. The notation of Faulkner's withdrawal has been made in pencil in what should be the column for the school year

1920-21, although the column is not dated and no course work has been indicated as having begun in the fall semester of 1920. His age is given as "21" and his name is spelled "Fa*u*lkner, William" (italics added), even though his publications in the campus weekly, *The Mississipian,* during 1919-20 are all signed, as regards the surname, "Falkner."

2. *Poems* (Philadelphia, [n.d.]), pp. 82-84.

3. The poem echoes Verlaine's "Après Trois Ans." Not only is it consistent in form and rhyme, but the melancholy tone and theme of retrospective sadness—the hopeless paradox of love past and yet lasting, physically dead yet spiritually alive—are interesting cognates. The poems differ in that Faulkner's is more particularized and less related to talismanic devices. Both, however, conclude with strong olfactory images.

4. Paul Verlaine, "Fantoches," *Selected Poems,* trans. C. F. MacIntyre (Berkeley, 1948), p. 66. All other quotations in this section in French are taken from this volume, based on Verlaine's *Œuvres complètes,* Tome I (Paris, 1900), and will be indicated by page numbers in parentheses.

5. Cf. Faulkner's typescript of "Cathay" lent for the Faulkner exhibition in the Princeton University Library, May-August, 1957, reproduced in James B. Meriwether, *The Literary Career of William Faulkner* (Princeton, 1961), Fig. 3. Meriwether notes that the typescript "differs slightly from the published version" (p. 8). Actually, there are many changes, the most significant of which are the following: the substitution of "her" for "thee" throughout the poem; the use of lower case in "*fate*" for the personification in 1. 3; the change of "cast" in 1. 6 to "shook"; the adjustment of the inverted "So is it" in 1. 8 to "So it is"; the unifying in 1. 14 of the *arsis* "Still" instead of dropping and indenting it; the substantive change of "Through the span" in 1. 15 to "Through spawn"; the tense change of "They know the[e] not" in 1. 17 to "They knew her not"; and other alterations which I have indicated, the addition of the commas in lines 1 and 13. Interestingly, the typescript retains the misspelled "fortells" in 1. 3. Because of the large number of changes—too many for a typesetter, editor, or proofreader to make, apparently—it seems likely that Faulkner, or someone, revised the poem sometime after it was published in *The Mississippian.*

6. Ward L. Miner, *The World of William Faulkner,* p. 113, presents revealing support in maintaining that Faulkner is like the legendary Antaeus, whom Hercules could not defeat as long as he remained in contact with the ground, his mother; that "as long

as he maintains his intimate associations with Oxford, he maintains his strength as a writer. . . . The more he deprives himself of his artistic roots, the weaker he is as a writer." In a letter dated November 1, 1948, Faulkner wrote Malcolm Cowley that he had read Sienkiewicz "when I was about sixteen I suppose" (see *The Faulkner-Cowley File*, p. 115). Cowley observes the parallel "that Faulkner must have drawn between the heroic but defeated past of Poland and that of the South. It is more than a simple military parallel, for the life of the Polish gentry—with their habit of command, their fierce pride, their chivalric illusions, and their estates on the edge of a wilderness—bore an inescapable resemblance to the life of Mississippi planters before the Civil War. Among Sienkiewicz's heroes, it would be Pan Michael, 'the little knight' who was the bravest swordsman in Poland, with whom Faulkner could most easily identify himself."

To indicate how closely Faulkner identified with his work, see Cynthia Grenier, "The Art of Fiction: An Interview with William Faulkner—September, 1955," *Accent*, 16:173-174, Summer 1956. She quotes him: "I like the idea of the world I created being a kind of keystone in the universe. Feel that if I ever took it away the universe around that keystone would crumble away. . . ."

7. Ch. 1, verse 9. For a psychological work which takes as its thesis a new application of the term, see Gerald Sykes, *The Hidden Remnant* (New York, 1962). The author defines the term "Remnant" as "a group of people who have survived or can survive a great catastrophe . . ." (p. 95). The member of such a group is different from most other people about him for he "tries to fulfill himself without either mass props or minority props . . ." (p. 196). If Faulkner was indeed unconsciously reflecting his own South in a conscious treatment of "Cathay," then his action is in harmony with that of the sensitive artist who is a member of the Remnant, for the "remnant must stand a full exposure to the unconscious . . . because only thus can it attain its full stature" (p. 47). See also the related material in the same work, "The Revolt of the Writers," pp. 165-169. For an interesting review of this book, see Nicholas Samstag, "Elite vs. Substandard Protoplasm," *Saturday Review*, March 10, 1962, pp. 27, 37.

8. C. G. Jung, "Psychology and Literature," *Modern Man in Search of a Soul* (New York, [n.d.]), p. 164, says that "primordial experience" is the ultimate source of the poet's creativity, that it is related through the poet's "collective unconscious," i.e., "a certain psychic disposition shaped by the forces of heredity; from it consciousness has developed . . ." (p. 165). The poet's "disposition involves an overweight of collective psychic life as against the personal. Art

is a kind of innate drive that seizes a human being and makes him its instrument" (p. 169). See also René Wellek and Austin Warren, "Literature and Psychology," *Theory of Literature* (New York, 1956), pp. 71-72. "Inspiration" is a "traditional name for the unconscious factor in creation." Applied to "a shaman, prophet, or poet," it suggests that "he may involuntarily be 'possessed' by some ancestral or totemic spirit-control . . . the work seems written through one" (p. 74).

In connection with these points, Faulkner himself often spoke of being compelled to write, e.g.: "An artist is a creature driven by demons. He doesn't know why they choose him and he's usually too busy to wonder why," in Jean Stein's "William Faulkner," (Interview), *Paris Review,* IV (Spring, 1956), 28-52; reprinted in H. Smith's "William Faulkner vs. the Literary Conference," *Saturday Review of Literature,* July 7, 1956, p. 16. Phil Stone, in a letter to Louis Cochran, dated December 28, 1931, stated in response to an article by Cochran, "With reference to the statement on Page 3 regarding Bill's tenacity of purpose, I rather doubt this. I think he kept on writing because he couldn't help it and not through any determination to succeed. I think he would have quit writing years ago if he could have done it," collected in *William Faulkner of Oxford,* eds. James W. Webb and A. Wigfall Green, p. 226.

9. Edmund Wilson, *Axel's Castle* (New York, 1954), p. 13, points out the relationship between French Symbolism and the device of synesthesia or "a confusion between the perceptions of the different senses." The similarity between the Romantics and Symbolists has been previously mentioned, especially the device of a kind of disembodied imagery. Charles Mauron, "Introduction," *Mallarmé: Poems* (New York, 1951), p. 23, quotes *Divagations* in relation to Mallarmé's purposes of suggestion: "A line, a few brief vibrations, the suggestion is complete."

10. Wellek and Warren, pp. 71-72, say that the device's "attitude and style are characteristic of the Baroque and the Romantic periods. . . ." As has been noted, the device of synesthesia is common to both Romantic and French Symbolist poetry. An example of the confusion of the senses is the reflection of a song in the smile of a pale Vasco in Mallarmé's "Au Seul Souci de Voyager . . .": "Par son chant reflété jusqu'au/Sourire du pâle Vasco." Faulkner's "Cathay" is a strong echo of Mallarmé's poem, complete with a plunging caravel (in the earlier piece "Plongeante avec la caravelle"), although thematically Mallarmé's poem is more limited than Faulkner's.

11. Arthur O. Lovejoy, "On the Discrimination of Romanticisms," *Essays in the History of Ideas* (New York, 1960), pp. 228-253, maintains that individual characteristics cannot accurately be used as

keys to such an amorphous concept, that "Romantic" as a term is "far too rough, crude, undiscriminating" (p. 253). Realizing the limitations which lie in my own approach, I have nevertheless used some of the generally acknowledged delimiting features of the mass of early nineteenth-century poetry, particularly that of Keats and Shelley, at the same time acknowledging that the method is subject to criticisms which are inherent in such useful generalizations. The several characteristics of Romanticism which I have employed are listed with others in Thrall and Hibbard's *A Handbook to Literature,* rev. C. Hugh Holman (New York, 1960), pp. 429-432.

12. Richard Harter Fogle, *The Imagery of Keats and Shelley* (Chapel Hill, 1949), p. 22, attributes the term to Robert Vischer and others, and notes it "could be either a projection of the ego *into* the object or a merging of the ego *with* the object." The point at which such empathy ("one-feeling") becomes identity is, of course, not clear; but a close relationship does seem logical. Jung, *Modern Man . . .,* p. 164, says that the "primordial experience . . . cannot be fathomed, and therefore requires mythological imagery to give it form. . . ." It is a "deep presentiment that strives to find expression."

13. This interview is noted by Robert Coughlan, *The Private World of William Faulkner* (New York, 1954), pp. 52-53. For further information on this period of Faulkner's life, see Calvin S. Brown, Jr., "Billy Faulkner, My Boyhood Friend," in *William Faulkner of Oxford,* pp. 40-48.

14. *Mississippian,* March 17, 1920, p. 4, col. 4.

15. *Mississippian,* February 25, 1920, p. 3. It begins "Ah, fair one, with those dreamy eyes," ends with a reference to a cow, and is signed "Jiggitts & Lester Inc." Another humorous poem "Une Ballade D'une Vache Perdue," May 12, 1920, p. 3, could possibly be a parody of Faulkner's "Une Balad Hedes Femmes Perdues" [*sic*], the essence of humor being the incongruous coupling of French love lyrics and the pastoral mode to celebrate the beauty of Betsy, a cow. The poem is signed "Lordgreyson." In this connection, Emily White-hurst Stone, "Some Arts of Self-Defense," *William Faulkner of Oxford,* p. 99, recounts a story of the only son of a widow from the backwoods who had "taken up with a cow," and the comment made by the narrator, "Do you know, Miss Emily, that pore boy ain't had a lick of sense from that good day to this. It ruint him. Plumb ruint him." Mrs. Stone notes that her husband, Phil Stone, told the story to Faulkner, and the incident appeared later in *The Hamlet.* She also adds that she later discovered that Faulkner "had known about that incident long before I had. Everybody out that way was bound to have known it, and certainly he did."

16. *Mississippian*, March 24, 1920, p. 3, col. 5.

17. One of the parodies, as noted, is signed "Jiggitts & Lester Inc.," another "J." I asked Phil Stone about "Jiggitts," and he said, Interview No. 1, that he was a brilliant man from Canton, Mississippi, who became a lawyer and who died several years ago. A note titled "Jiggit[t]s Plans Extended Tour," *Mississippian*, March 17, 1922, p. 4, mentions that Louis M. Jiggitts was a Rhodes scholar from Ole Miss and was then touring Europe. *Who's Who in America* (1944-45), ed. Albert Nelson, XXIII, p. 1080, corroborates the newspaper information, mentioning that he was a Rhodes scholar from 1920-23. He received a B.A. in Jurisprudence in 1923, returned to Ole Miss and received an LL.B. in 1924. He practiced law in Jackson, Mississippi. *Who's Who in America* (1946-47), XXIV, p. 1207, records his death on March 22, 1945.

18. *Mississippian*, April 7, 1920, p. 1.

19. Interview No. 2. Most of Faulkner's pictures indicate that he succeeded in disguising the trait of a receding lip. One of the photographs which reveals it quite clearly, a profile, can be found in Marshall J. Smith, "Faulkner of Mississippi," *Bookman*, 74:414, December 1931.

20. "William Faulkner at Home," *Sewanee Review*, 40:299, Summer 1932.

21. Coughlan, *The Private World of William Faulkner*, p. 53.

22. "William Faulkner of Oxford, Mississippi," *Writer's Digest*, July 1961, p. 16.

23. *William Faulkner*, p. 6. Edith Brown Douds, "Recollections of William Faulkner and the Bunch," *William Faulkner of Oxford*, pp. 50-51, recalls the name of the car of the period of the early 1920's as "Drusilla."

24. "New Year's Craw," *New Republic*, 93:283, January 12, 1938.

25. Marshall J. Smith, p. 416. The remark about his dismissal may or may not be true. Faulkner's "smart-crack" to the same interviewer in answering a question about his birth leaves room for doubt: "Born? . . . Yes, I was born male and single at an early age in Mississippi. I am still alive but not single. I was born of a Negro slave and an alligator, both named Gladys Rock. I had two brothers, one Dr. Walter E. Traprock and the other Eagle Rock, an airplane." Michael Millgate, *The Achievement of William Faulkner*, p. 9, quotes Elizabeth Prall's statement that "Faulkner didn't keep his accounts straight, but a good accounts secretary did that for him." Stark Young,

with whom Faulkner was living at the time, wrote that Faulkner simply "drifted back South."

CHAPTER V

1. (University, Mississippi), XXV, 214-215.

2. *Mississippian* (University, Mississippi), p. 5.

3. *Mississippian*, May 4, 1921, p. 5.

4. Cf. the analyses of *The Marble Faun*, Ch. II, and "Cathay," Ch. IV.

5. To illustrate, William Van O'Connor, *The Tangled Fire of William Faulkner* (Minneapolis, 1954), p. 19, indicates that the trip was made in 1920; Robert Coughlan, *The Private World of William Faulkner* (New York, 1954), p. 56, notes 1923. O'Connor, in arriving at his date, probably relied upon an assumption which is all too easy to make from Stark Young's statement in "New Year's Craw," *New Republic*, 93:283, January 12, 1938: "Finally *in the summer of 1920*, after the World War, I found Faulkner at Oxford. . . . and I suggested that he *come to New York* and sleep on my sofa . . . till . . . he could find a room. *He did both*" (italics added). But it seems pertinent to observe first that Stark Young composed the statement in 1938, long after the event to which he alluded; and second, that he *did not* mention the actual date of Faulkner's arrival or the duration of the trip. Coughlan's date of 1923 seems to rest on an attempt to juxtapose the sequence of the trip with the winter 1924-25 meeting between Faulkner and Sherwood Anderson in New Orleans. Further, Michael Millgate, in *The Achievement of William Faulkner* (New York, 1966), p. 9, mentions concerning the dating of the New York sojourn only that Faulkner must have taken Young up on his invitation "some time following his withdrawal from the University that November [1920]," and by "December 1921 Faulkner was [back] in Oxford." Carvel Collins, in an unpublished letter to me (January 14, 1969) writes, "Faulkner left Mississippi for the East *in 1921, presumably in late summer or early autumn* . . ." (italics added). His two-volume biography of Faulkner, to be published by Farrar, Straus and Giroux, will very likely illuminate this matter and others as well.

6. Phil Stone, Interview No. 1, also told me that Faulkner went to New York for a period of "about six months" *before* his tenure as postmaster of the University began.

7. O'Connor, *The Tangled Fire* . . ., p. 20.

8. "Verse Old and Nascent: A Pilgrimage," *Salmagundi* (Milwaukee, 1932), p. 37; originally pub. in *The Double Dealer*, 43: 129-131, April 1925.

9. "Verse Old and Nascent," *Salmagundi*, p. 36.

10. See Ch. III. I have already mentioned Stone's part in providing some of the substance and a great deal of the encouragement for Faulkner's treatment of the Snopes materials. Stone, Interview No. 1, said that he prodded Faulkner over and over again, "When are you goin' to write *my* book, Bill?" I gathered that Stone meant not only *The Hamlet*, but also *The Town* and *The Mansion*.

11. The detractory tone of Faulkner's references to Freud and psychoanalysis is important, it seems to me, in establishing the degree of Freud's influence on him. Several critics assume that an influence exists. O'Connor, *The Tangled Fire* . . ., p. 70, quotes a passage from *Miss Zilphia Gant* with the comment that her dreams "seem to come straight out of a Freudian case study"; on p. 162 he applies the term "Freudian milieu" to both "A Rose for Emily" and *Miss Zilphia Gant*. Stanley D. Woodworth, *William Faulkner en France* (Paris, 1959), p. 101, mentions Faulkner's debt to Freud, among others, relating his remark to the use of interior monologue and qualifying it: "De même, bien que Faulkner doive beaucoup . . . à Freud, c'est une dette purement technique." Faulkner, however, in *Faulkner in the University*, Frederick L. Gwynn and Joseph L. Blotner, eds. (Charlottesville, Virginia, 1959), "Session Thirty-Two," Department of Psychiatry, May 7, 1958, p. 268, maintained that he had no idea where he learned his psychology: "Only what I have learned about it from listening to people that do know. What little psychology I know the characters I have invented and playing poker have taught me. *Freud I'm not familiar with*" (italics added). Once again, Phil Stone, Interview No. 1, proves useful. In answer to my question, "What about Faulkner's knowledge of psychology—Freud and Jung?" Stone replied, "He wouldn't read Freud. I tried to get him to. I taught *at* him, but he wouldn't listen. He wasn't interested in psychology." Perhaps critical confusion has resulted from Faulkner's original reference to Freud in this *Mississippian* article and his phenomenal intuitive applications of psychology. Vincent F. Hopper, "Faulkner's Paradise Lost," *Virginia Quarterly Review*, 23:420, Summer 1947, has noted, "The novels are mirrors of 'anyone' in the very specific sense that they contain, to resort to the language of psychoanalysis, the conflict of Ego, Super-Ego and Id, expressed in the half-comprehensible imagery of the dream-state." Thus, it seems quite likely that Faulkner never really studied Freud's work, or even read him with any degree of thoroughness. Rather, he attained his knowledge of psychology indirectly, through conversations with Stone

and others, and intuitively applied what only appears to be a technical knowledge of Freudian methods.

12. Faulkner notes that Mark Twain used the regional materials of the Mississippi River; however, the young critic, either through an over-zealous desire for "literary cleverness" or pure ignorance arising from a lack of close, perceptive reading—probably both— characterizes Mark Twain as "a hack writer who would not have been considered fourth rate in Europe, who tricked out a few of the old proven 'sure fire' literary skeletons with sufficient local color to intrigue the superficial and the lazy." Actually, Twain was acknowledged and admired in Europe long before he achieved serious recognition in America.

13. George P. Garrett, "Faulkner's Early Literary Criticism," *Texas Studies in Literature and Language,* 1:5-6, Spring 1959. Laurence Stallings, interviewed by the Fullerton Junior College Literary Club, recorded by me (Fullerton, California), 8:00 P.M., January 22, 1960, in answer to a question about the quality of Faulkner's writing said, "Brilliant. Why, I remember what Hemingway said about it. . . . 'We might as well all quit!—you and me and Fitzgerald and all of us!' But then Hemingway said, 'After I read about eighty or ninety pages . . . it hits you like a shot of insulin bringing you out of shock [actually, this is either a Stallings or Hemingway misconception, for although insulin may bring a person *out* of a coma, it puts a person *in* shock] and you know he ain't any better. Bill Faulkner don't ever *finish* a book. Never has finished a book.' "

14. Pp. 1, 2. The sketch is unsigned, but the March 17 issue of the *Mississippian,* p. 5, makes the correction, pointing out that the piece should have appeared over the initials "W.F."

15. III, 337. Reprinted in *Salmagundi,* pp. 45-46. Quotations from "Portrait" are taken from *Salmagundi* and are indicated by page numbers in parentheses.

16. New York. Reprinted by Signet Books (New York, 1959). All page references are to the Signet ed. and will be indicated by numbers in parentheses.

17. *The Marble Faun* images: "dark trees like spilled ink" (p. 216); the description of morning as "marbled" (p. 203); romantic nature scenes (pp. 70, 216-218). Other poems: The line *"La lune en grade aucune rancune"* (p. 93) is close enough to that final line of Faulkner's "Fantouches" [*sic*], "La lune ne grade aucune rancune," and contains the same incorrect verb usage "grade" in what should probably be the expression "garder rancune" ("to owe a grudge"). Also see Ch. VIII, n. 14 for further details on the French line. "Noc-

turne": the description of a garden's pear tree as branching, white candelabra, p. 75; and on the same page, the fruit blossoms leaning across a sunny garden wall suggest a similar description in the second paragraph of "The Hill." Finally, the poem "Portrait" is suggested in the detailed scene of "quiet, elm-shaded streets . . . along which girls and boys walked in the evening to and from the picture show" (p. 121).

18. Cf. the fictionalized treatment of the Old Colonel, John Sartoris, to that of the Young Colonel, Bayard Sartoris, in *Sartoris*.

19. Erik H. Erikson, "Reflections on the American Identity," *Childhood and Society* (New York, 1950), p. 273, makes this related observation in a footnote: "In psychoanalytic patients from the upper classes the overwhelming importance of the grandfather is often apparent. He may have been a . . . railroad builder . . . or an unreconstructed Southerner. What these grandfathers have in common is the fact that they were the last representatives of a more homogeneous world, masterly and cruel with good conscience. . . . Their world invented bigger and better machinery like gigantic playthings which were not expected to challenge the social values of the men who made them. Their mastery persists in their grandsons as a stubborn, and angry sense of superiority. Overtly inhibited, they can accept others only on terms of pre-arranged privilege. Unless they are exceptionally gifted, these men of the highest strata join those from the very lowest ones in feeling truly disinherited in American life, which demands that one enjoy the potential promise of an ever more universal identity." Whatever the applications of this general observation to Faulkner, himself—and there are some interesting possibilities which are obvious enough—its broad significance lies in its indication of the feasibility of a grandparent's representing a direction of identity for a grandson, and for reasons which could possibly apply to both Colonel W. C. Falkner and his great-grandson William.

Chapter VI

1. For documented details of this summary, see Ch. II.

2. Meriwether, *The Literary Career of William Faulkner*, p. 23, notes that *A Green Bough* "had been announced early in 1925." In addition, "the dated manuscripts of several of the poems of *A Green Bough* show that they were written in the 1920's, but they were revised and tightened for book publication."

3. George P. Garrett, "An Examination of the Poetry of William Faulkner," *Princeton University Library Chronicle,* 18:129-131, Spring

1957, illustrates Faulkner's concern with revision between the publication of nine of his poems in *Contempo*, vol. 1, no. 17, February 1, 1932, and the appearance of five of these in revised form in *Green Bough* the following year; specifically, he thoroughly examines XXXVI in *Green Bough*, previously published as "Spring" in *Contempo*.

4. See Ch. III. Other studies tend to be fragmentary, such as Frederick L. Gwynn's "Faulkner's Prufrock—and Other Observations," *Journal of English and Germanic Philology*, 52:63-70, January 1953, which is primarily a study of Eliot influences in *Mosquitoes* rather than *Green Bough*. Martha Mayes, "Faulkner's Juvenilia," *New Campus Writing*, no. 2, ed. Nolan Miller (New York, 1957), pp. 135-144, makes only peripheral comments and centers her attention on the *Mississippian* pieces.

5. Concerning the dating of *A Green Bough*, Runyan notes the premature announcement of its forthcoming publication in "February 1925," and speculates that it was withheld probably because of "the poor reception of *The Marble Faun* the year previous, and its eventual appearance to the hope that it would succeed as a book by the then famed author of *Sanctuary*" (p. 24). Bibliographical facts are treated on pp. 25, 28-29; influences on pp. 26-27; and his final evaluation on p. 27. Garrett, "An Examination . . ." p. 124, notes that Runyan's bibliography adds nothing to that compiled by Robert Daniel, *A Catalogue of the Writings of William Faulkner* (New Haven, 1942).

6. *Saturday Review of Literature*, 9:565, April 29, 1933.

7. *New York Herald-Tribune Books*, April 30, 1933, p. 2.

8. *New York Times Book Review*, 82:2, May 14, 1933.

9. Anon., rev., 136:565, May 17, 1933.

10. "Faulkner as Poet," 43:49-51, October, 1933.

11. The outline of literary traditions which follows specifies what I have summarized. Wherever isolated images or mere portions of the individual poem, rather than its prevailing tone, indicate its grouping, I have attempted to specify in parentheses reasons for the poem's placement which might not otherwise be immediately clear:

    a. *Romantics*: I (nature images, pp. 8-9); II ("gold" images, p. 12); III (medieval references, p. 16, pastoral elements, p. 18); VII (pastoral and nature elements, pp. 25-26); VIII; IX; X; XVIII; XX (nature images, p. 42); XXI (medieval references); XXII (topics of love and memory expressed in nature images, p. 44); XXIII (nature images, color, p. 45); XXIV ("name like muted silver bells," p. 46); XXVII ("Philomel" allusion, p. 49); XXX (nature images, p. 53); XXXIII; XLII (medieval, nature images, p. 65); XLIV (earth images, p. 67). Total: 18 poems.

b. *French Symbolists:* II ("Playing a music of lustrous silent gold./ Bathed in gold she sits," p. 12; "Rain as slow as starlight on her breast," p. 14); III ("silver spears of streaming burning hair," p. 16; "breast . . . harped of silver," p. 17; "sucking silver sound," p. 19); VII ("trumpets of sun," p. 25); X (fourth stanza, p. 30); XII ("life . . . taut as silver wire," p. 32); XIV ("hushed and haughty starlight/To stroke his golden hair," p. 34); XIX; XX ("leaves of silence," p. 42); XXII ("clothed in quiet sound," p. 44); XXIII ("wane the windless gardens of the blue;/ . . . a lost green hurt," p. 45); XXV (first line suggests Mallarmé's "L'Apres Midi d'un Faune," p. 47); XXVII; XXVIII ("moons of cold," p. 51); XXXIV ("soft doveslippered eyes," p. 57); XLI; XLIII; XLIV ("silver grief . . . green woods be dreaming," p. 67). Total: 17 poems.

c. *"Conventional" verse forms:*
   1. *Elizabethan forms:* XVI (images and paraphrase, *Macbeth, Hamlet,* p. 37); XXI (paraphrase, *Macbeth,* stanza 3, p. 43); XXXIV; XXXV; XXXVI; XXXVII; XXXVIII; XXXIX; XL; XLI; XLII; XLIII (in its modified form only). The last ten poems listed are modified Italian sonnet forms. Total: 12 poems.
   2. *Housmanesque forms:* VI; XI; XII; XIII; XIV; XV; XXXI. Total: 7 poems.
   3. *Folk ballad:* XIV. Total: 1 poem.
   4. *Miscellaneous conventional forms:* XXIX; V; XLIV. Total: 3 poems.

d. *Moderns, such as Cummings, Eliot, Joyce, Robinson, Yeats:* I; II; III (original images); IV; XVII; XVIII; XXII (images); XXIII (images); XXVI (coinages); XXXII. Total: 10 poems.

12. A more specific charting of the individual influences in *A Green Bough* follows:

a. *Browning:* IX (The final line suggests the conclusion of Browning's "Love among the Ruins," p. 29); X (The first two stanzas faintly echo Browning's "Parting at Morning," p. 30).

b. *Cummings:* IV; XVII; XXXII; XLIII (All emphasize lower case).

c. *de la Mare*: XXV ("The moon" . . . "trod with silver shoon," p. 47, reflects the basic image of "Silver").

d. *Eliot*: I (The poem depicts a tea party, employes mythology, and uses devices which echo Eliot—dialogue, rhythmical patterns, and intense irony); II (cf. "Portrait of a Lady"); V (Note the use of water imagery, dead leaves, and tonal similarities to "The Love Song of J. Alfred Prufrock" and "The Waste Land"); XVI (The "I" of the poem, tired of posturing, converses with a phantom companion, who, in the last stanza, urges him to "drown," a roughly substantial parallel to "Love Song"); XIX (The drowning image, "seamaids red and brown," of the second stanza echoes "Lovesong"); and XXVII ("Sweeney" is suggested, complete with raven, nightingale [Philomel], and dropping ordure).

e. *Housman*: VI; XI; XII; XIII; XIV; XV; XXXI (These poems echo Housman in form, manner, and, to a lesser extent, substance).

f. *Joyce*: IV (stream of consciousness pattern, p. 21).

g. *Keats*: X (The "urn" reference, as well as the theme, suggests Keats' "Ode on a Grecian Urn").

h. *Mallarmé*: XXV (The first line suggests Mallarmé's "Aimai-je un rêve?" in "L'Apres-midi d'un Faune").

i. *Robinson*: XXXVII (The Lilith ref., p. 60, form, and theme suggest "Another Dark Lady").

j. *Swinburne*: XVII (sensuous imagery); XXIV (sensuous imagery related to dream).

k. *Verlaine*: XLI (The octave of the sonnet contains a reference to "The old satyr . . ." p. 64, reminiscent of Verlaine's "Le Faune," beginning, "Un vieux faune de terre cuit. . . .").

l. *Yeats*: XXII (form and substance strongly suggest Yeats' "A Deep-Sworn Vow").

13. In addition to those mentioned in this paragraph, also consider III, X, XXX, XLI, XLIV.

14. There are, of course, many other themes, often complex and overlapping. To indicate the variety of themes in the poetry of *A Green Bough*, I have categorized the poems according to the following divisions:

Love: II, XI, XII, XIII, XVII, XIX, XXII, XXIII (satire),

XXXV (satire, regret), XXXVII (regret), XXXVIII, XL (Total: 12 poems).

Passion: II, VI, XI, XII, XIX, XXIV, XXXVI, XXXIX, XLI, XLIII (Total: 10 poems).

Death: V, VI, VII, X, XV, XVI, XXV, XXXIII, XXXV, XXXIX, XLIV (Total: 11 poems).

Nature: III, VII, VIII, XV, XVII, XVIII, XXV, XXX, XXXVI, XLIV (Total: 10 poems).

Futility or doom: VI, VII, X, XIV, XXVII (misalliance), XXVIII, XXX, XXXI, XXXII (Total: 9 poems).

War and aftermath: I (waste), IV (satire), XXX (cf. *Soldiers' Pay*), XXXI (Total: 4 poems).

Traditional romance: III, XIV, XXI (Total: 3 poems).

Romance of the airman: XVIII, XXV, XXVIII (Total: 3 poems).

Religion: XXXIV, XLII (Total: 2 poems).

Pastoral: VII, IX (Total: 2 poems).

15. For an analysis of the theme of "The Hill," see Ch. V.

16. Cf. the poem's "Behind him day lay stark with labor/Of him who strives with earth for bread;/Before him sleep, tomorrow his circling/Sinister shadow about his head/" with the vignette's "Behind him was a day of harsh labor with his hands, a strife against the forces of nature to gain bread and clothing and a place to sleep." Both pieces use shadows, suggesting something "sinister" in the poem, something of "portent" in the sketch. The poem however, unlike the sketch, specifies two interesting phrases which may possibly have psychological and autobiographical innuendos, "Forgotten his father, Death; Derision/His mother, forgotten by her at last."

17. Faulkner's line has obvious associations with Keats' "Ode on a Grecian Urn," but so does the poem as a whole. Keats, too, employed "pipes and timbrels" and "soft pipes." Keats' second stanza also possesses a similar tension, as of a lover caught in a trance and suspended in time. The fourth stanza mentions a "little town" with silent streets: "and not a soul, to tell/Why thou art desolate, can e'er return." Faulkner probably had little difficulty identifying himself and his own milieu with the images and substance of this masterpiece. When interviewed by Jean Stein, New York City, 1956, pub. in *Writers at Work: the Paris Review Interviews,* ed. Malcolm Cowley (New York, 1959), p. 124, he paid the ultimate tribute to Keats' poem: "If a writer has to rob his mother, he will not hesitate; the 'Ode on a Grecian Urn' is worth any number of old ladies."

18. "Verse Old and Nascent: A Pilgrimage," *Salmagundi* (Milwaukee, 1932), p. 35. Originally published in *Double Dealer,* 43:129-131, April, 1925.

19. Pub. originally as "My Epitaph," *Contempo*, 1:2, February 1, 1932. It was also known as *This Earth* (New York, 1932). Meriwether, *Literary Career of William Faulkner*, p. 24, notes that these versions of the poem and the one in *A Green Bough* "differ slightly." Finally, the poem was reprinted in *Mississippi Verse*, ed. Alice James (Chapel Hill, 1934) as "If There Be Grief," along with six other *Green Bough* poems, pp. 31-35.

20. Sometimes Faulkner's attitude toward Oxford and the South seems ambivalent. Malcolm Cowley, "Introduction to *The Portable Faulkner*," pub. in *William Faulkner: Three Decades of Criticism*, eds. Frederick J. Hoffman and Olga W. Vickery (Michigan State University, 1960), p. 102, says that Faulkner was speaking for himself as well as Quentin when he has the narrator of *Absalom, Absalom!* reply to Shreve McCannon's question "Why do you hate the South?" with an immediate, "I dont hate it," and thinks panting in the cold air, *"I dont. I dont hate it! I dont hate it!"* Undoubtedly Faulkner disliked certain aspects of the South, such as those he noted in his sketch "The Hill," the "whipped vanities . . . lusts . . . the drying spittle of religious controversy"; but these are universal as well as regional faults. Faulkner's feeling toward the South was complex, even early in his development, as I have tried to indicate with an explication of "Cathay" in Ch. IV; but his deep devotion toward the region is evident in such works as poem XLIV in *A Green Bough*. Phil Stone, "William Faulkner, the Man and His Work," *Oxford Magazine*, vol. 1, no. 3 (1934), pp. 4-5, repeats the statement that Faulkner "loves Oxford and its surrounding country dearly, prefers them above all others in the world." Again, Stone recalls that after the publication of *Sanctuary* Faulkner wrote him from New York saying that he "felt sorry for all these millions of people here because they don't live in Oxford" (p. 7).

21. The answer to the question of whether the artistic conception toward his region was consciously or unconsciously present may be an important one in dating the poem. The date of its first publication was February 1, 1932 (in *Contempo*), and it is altogether possible that Faulkner wrote this particular poem after he had made his decision to return to Oxford and concentrate his creative energies upon that region, about 1927.

22. To put the exaggerated details of his eccentric behavior in Oxford during 1923-24 into better focus, William McNeil ("Mack") Reed, interviewed by me (Oxford, Mississippi), 10:00 A.M., July 27, 1962, painstakingly explained some of the much-bandied episodes in these words: "There's *no truth whatever* to all that talk about Bill lounging around the drug store reading the magazines and sponging

off me. Oh, he would come in often and might browse or lose himself for awhile. Usually he stood, checked through the magazines, and made his selection. He usually bought, or if he didn't have the money, he charged. He always had an open charge account here. On two occasions he sat down on the floor, but in those days we didn't have many chairs [a smile here]. He came into the store barefoot once or twice after walking in the woods . . . But Bill rarely came in here barefoot—certainly not more than twice."

23. Collins, "About the Sketches," p. 10. The famous statement upon his resignation, "Now I won't be at the beck and call of every son of a bitch who happens to have two cents," noted by Robert Coughlan, *The Private World of William Faulkner* (New York, 1954), p. 57, and several other writers, has been so frequently reported and, in proportion to other statements, exaggerated, that I hesitate to mention it again, even though it does dramatically represent Faulkner's animosity toward any activity which distracted him from writing.

Chapter VII

1. Sherwood Anderson, *Sherwood Anderson's Memoirs* (New York, 1942), p. 473.

2. 73:269-270, April 1925. Further references to "A Meeting South" will be indicated by page numbers in parentheses after quotations. The piece was also published in *Sherwood Anderson's Notebook* (New York, 1926), pp. 103-121. Several critics suggest the character parallel between Faulkner and David, among them Joseph Warren Beach, "William Faulkner," *American Fiction 1920-1940* (New York, 1941), p. 147; and Irving Howe, *Sherwood Anderson* ([New York], 1951), pp. 159-160.

3. In "Verse Old and Nascent: A Pilgrimage," *Salmagundi* (Milwaukee, 1932), pp. 38-39, Faulkner wrote feelingly of Keats and Shelley: "Shelley dreamed of golden men and women immortal in a silver world in which young John Keats wrote 'Endymion' trying to gain enough silver to marry Fannie Brawne and set up an apothecary's shop. Is not there among us someone who can write something beautiful and passionate and sad instead of saddening?" Again, of Keats' "Odes to a Nightingale, [on] a Grecian urn, 'Music to Hear,' etc.; here is the spiritual beauty which the moderns strive vainly for with trickery, and yet beneath it one knows are entrails; masculinity" (pp. 38-39), originally pub. in *The Double Dealer*, 7:129-131, April 1925—the same month that Anderson's "A Meeting South" appeared in *The Dial*.

4. For this detail we have not only Anderson's *Memoirs*, recount-

ing how Faulkner unloaded his "things," consisting of "six or eight half gallon jars of moon liquor" (p. 473), but also Marshall J. Smith's interview, "Faulkner of Mississippi," *Bookman*, 74:411, December 1931, which begins with this statement: "Sunday morning down in Oxford, Mississippi, I found William Faulkner bottling beer in the kitchen. . . . He was squatting on the floor beside a cracked churn siphoning scummy homebrew out through a piece of hose into second-hand ginger ale bottles."

5. Carvel Collins suggests this in "About the Sketches," *New Orleans Sketches* (New Brunswick, 1958), p. 18. Also, in an unpublished letter to me (January 14, 1969), Collins states, "Faulkner did go to New Orleans *in the fall of 1924 and did meet Anderson then*" (italics added), consistent with my own information. Collins' forthcoming two-volume study on Faulkner will, doubtless, give further details on the meeting. However, James Schevill, *Sherwood Anderson: His Life and His Work* (University of Denver, 1951), p. 194, describes the meeting with a reference to Anderson's "new friend *whom he met in 1925*, a slight, crippled, lazy figure with piercing eyes and a mustache" (italics added). For clarification of Schevill's reference to the "crippled . . . figure," see Stone's statement, mentioned in Ch. III, applicable to the period within six weeks after Faulkner's return from Canada to Oxford: "As far as I could see he wasn't injured at all." It is, of course, possible that Faulkner was injured sometime after the war, although I find no record of such an injury.

6. *Faulkner in the University*, eds. Frederick L. Gwynn and Joseph L. Blotner (Charlottesville, Virginia, 1959), "Session Twenty-Five," Graduate Course in American Fiction, February 21, 1958, p. 231.

7. Collins, "About the Sketches," pp. 14-15.

8. *Faulkner in the University*, p. 230.

9. Faulkner, "Sherwood Anderson," *Atlantic*, 191:29, June 1953.

10. Anderson, *Memoirs*, p. 476, specifically stated that he "made a fight to get the book published . . . going personally to Horace Liveright to plead for the [book]." Schevill, *Sherwood Anderson . . .*, p. 207, notes that "it was largely Anderson's recommendation that got the book accepted as Liveright did not like it."

11. Faulkner, "Sherwood Anderson," *Princeton University Library Chronicle*, 18, no. 3:91, Spring 1957. Originally pub. in the *Dallas Morning News*, April 26, 1925, p. 7.

12. In the *Dallas Morning News*, p. 7.

13. "Sherwood Anderson," *Princeton University Library Chronicle,* pp. 93-94. Further references to this article will be indicated by page numbers in parentheses after quotations.

14. Cf. Faulkner's "Sherwood Anderson," *Atlantic,* p. 27.

15. The sixteen *Times-Picayune* pieces published from February 8 to September 27, 1925, have been collected, along with the *Double Dealer* "New Orleans" sketch, published in the January-February issue, in *New Orleans Sketches,* ed. Carvel Collins (New Brunswick, 1958). All page references to the sketches are taken from this source and appear in parentheses after quotations.

16. *New Orleans Sketches,* pp. 26-30.

17. See my article, "The 'Hemingwaves' in Faulkner's 'Wild Palms,' " *Modern Fiction Studies,* 4, no. 4:357-360, Winter 1958-59.

18. (New York), pp. 171-267. Further page references to *Triumph* appear in parentheses after quotations.

19. For an analysis of "The Hill" see Ch. V.

20. See Ch. III for further details on Faulkner's life during this period.

21. Faulkner in "Sherwood Anderson," *Atlantic,* p. 29, told a story with the kind of exaggeration he was fond of: "I met her [Elizabeth Prall Anderson] on the street. She commented on my absence. I said I was writing a novel. She asked if I wanted Sherwood to see it. I answered, I don't remember exactly what, but to the effect that it would be all right with me if he wanted to. She told me to bring it to her when I finished it, which I did, in about two months. A few days later she sent for me. She said, 'Sherwood says he'll make a swap with you. He says that if he doesn't have to read it, he'll tell Liveright . . . to take it.' " At any rate, the publication of *Soldiers' Pay* was not that simple. See n. 10 in this chapter, and Anderson's letter to Horace Liveright, dated April 11, 1926, in *Letters of Sherwood Anderson,* pp. 154-155, which indicate his personal interest in Faulkner as a writer and his continuing influence with Liveright on Faulkner's behalf.

22. Lionel Trilling, "Sherwood Anderson," *The Liberal Imagination* (New York, 1957), pp. 22-23, 27.

23. New York. The portion of the chapter which follows relating to Anderson and Faulkner's tall tale has been published with minor revisions and some additions in my article "Faulkner, Anderson, and Their Tall Tale," *American Literature,* 34:287-291, May 1962.

24. "Sherwood Anderson," *Atlantic*, p. 28.

25. "Sherwood Anderson," *Atlantic*, pp. 28-29.

26. See my presentation of this evidence in "Faulkner, Anderson, and Their Tall Tale," *American Literature*, 34:287-291, May 1962, and the reply of Walter B. Rideout and James B. Meriwether, "On the Collaboration of Faulkner and Anderson," *American Literature*, 35:85-87, March 1963. To clarify the opposition of views, I suggest a close reading of pp. 28-29 of Faulkner's *Atlantic* article involving a conversation about the fable which they were working out together, Anderson as teacher, Faulkner as student. Also note my subsequent article, "Anderson and Faulkner," *American Literature*, 36:298-314, November 1964, especially n. 26.

27. Faulkner, "Sherwood Anderson," *Atlantic*, p. 28.

Chapter VIII

1. Albert J. Farmer, *Le Mouvement Esthétique et "Décadent" en Angleterre—1873-1900* (Paris, 1931), p. 384. Thus, "In fact, the 'decadence' offers a double aspect: it is at once an end and a beginning. It marks well an end in the sense that it closes an age which, for a long time already, betrayed a certain lassitude, which seemed to move toward exhaustion. But it is also a point of departure, and it seems that would be its true significance. The fight against Victorianism revealed the narrowness of its old forms, too curtailed to respond to the aspirations of the new times. Little by little, the writers disencumbered themselves from the effort of the past, compelled by the need to discover new paths. Doctrines emerged, different, afloat anchorlessly, but which allowed a glimpse of the art of the future."

2. In *Intellectual America* (New York, 1941), pp. 185-196. Farmer relates decadence to the Romantic movement in this fashion: "Sur cet âge ingrat, les descendants spirituels de la seconde génération romantique vont bientôt prendre une ironique, une éclatante revanche" (p. 33); thus, "On account of that unfruitful age, the spiritual descendants of the second romantic generation were going soon to take an ironic, a brilliant revenge."

3. Farmer supports this contention: "Notre perspective d'aujourd'hui a réduit ces manifestations à leurs justes proportions. Le 'décadisme' n'a été, on s'en apercoit, qu'un incident dans le développement du symbolisme, avec lequel il a fini du reste par se confondre" (p. iv); thus, "Our perspective of today has reduced these manifestations to their just proportions. The 'decadence' had been, one discovers, but an incident in the development of symbolism, with which it ended by mingling itself."

4. To illustrate, William Gaunt, *The Aesthetic Adventure* (New York, 1945), p. 259, gives a thesis of the "aesthetic man" of the *fin de siècle* which is quite different from that of Farmer, saying that he was indifferent to "religion, morality, education, political principle, or social improvement." He cultivated *l'art pour l'art* just as "the economic man" had "made political economy into a science with its own laws in the early nineteenth century." The movement was "opposed and offensive to Victorian idealism," the essence of which was social service.

Cargill gives us an interesting picture of American decadence of the twentieth century, naming Ezra Pound, T. S. Eliot, Hart Crane, and Archibald MacLeish "as deserving of immortality as . . . Baudelaire, Mallarmé, Rimbaud, and Valéry" (p. 309). He mentions the "bookishness" and "artificiality" of the American decadence, Pound's lack of experience and the vicarious "world of the bibliophile," Pound who went abroad "to gather materials for a doctoral dissertation on Lope de Vega . . . and remained more than a third of a century" (p. 230), his wasted energies and imitations; Amy Lowell's "imagism" and her interest in the relation of melody and verse; Conrad Aiken's "nympholepsy" in *The Charnel Rose* (1918) where "beginning with the lowest order of love, the merely carnal, the theme leads irregularly, with returns and anticipations as in music, through various phases of romantic or idealistic love, to several variants of sexual mysticism; finally ending . . . in a mysticism apparently pure." It is a kind of "dream pursuit" (p. 249). Eliot's "The Waste Land" arrives at the "culmination of Decadence" with its "major theme of the . . . spiritual sterility of contemporary life," and the poet's answer to fear—"death" (p. 259). Cargill goes on to state that "there is nothing mystical about the new Eliot; there is instead in him a resuscitation of the old harsh dogmatism of Archbishop Laud" (p. 268).

5. Interviewed by Jean Stein, New York City, 1956, pub. in *Writers at Work: the Paris Review Interviews,* ed. Malcolm Cowley (New York, 1959), pp. 123-124.

6. Signet ed., New York, April 1959. Originally pub. New York, 1926. References to the book are from the Signet ed. and are indicated by page numbers, and by the initials SP where the lack of the abbreviation might otherwise result in confusion, in parentheses after quotations. I have checked all quotations referred to in this more accessible reprint against those of the first edition and have found them to be consistent.

7. From *Mallarmé: Poems,* trans. Roger Fry (New York, 1951), p. 80; thus, "These nymphs I would perpetuate./So clear/Their light

carnation, that it floats in the air/Heavy with tufted slumbers./Was it a dream I loved?"

8. *New Republic,* August 6, 1919, p. 24.

9. In "The Disassociation of Ideas," *Decadence and Other Essays on the Culture of Ideas,* trans. William Aspenwall Bradley (New York, 1925), p. 30, "This identification of woman and beauty goes so far to-day [*sic*] that we have had innocently proposed to us the 'apotheosis of woman,' meaning the glorification of beauty, with all the promises contained in Stendal's [*sic*] definition taken in its erotic sense. Beauty is a woman and woman is beauty. The caricaturists accentuate the common sentiment by invariably coupling with a woman, whom they strive to render beautiful, a man whose ugliness they stress to the extreme of vulgarity. . . ." Thus, the depiction of Cecily as nymph and Jones as faun becomes a kind of caricature or satire of the associated ideas of beauty and woman in the truly decadent tradition.

10. Farmer, p. 30, links the *Rubáiyát* to the serious, spiritually impoverished decadents. Writing of the decadence, he states, "Il s'agit encore de divergences individuelles, mais les années qui suivent immédiatement 1870 offrent des indices qui laissent deviner que l'heure est proche où la masse prendra conscience de ce que les esprits insolés ont déjà discerné: que le matérialisme ne saurait satisfaire les besoins des âmes; que la science positive a détruit la foi traditionnelle et n'a donné en retour que la torture du doute, ou bien une certitude trop cruelle, à savoir que l'univers est indifférent aux efforts et aux souffrances des êtres. Le *Rubáiyát* de Fitzgerald, où un desespoir sombre se cache sous un epicurism nonchalant, n' avait éveillé aucun écho en 1859, et la seconde édition (1868) avait été egalement négligée; mais la troisième (1872) connaît un commencement de succès, et la quatrième (1879) est enlevée immédiatement." Thus, "It is more a question of divergent individuals, but the years which follow immediately 1870 offer some indications which confide that the hour is growing near when the mass will take conscience of what the lonely minds have already discerned: that materialism will not know how to satisfy the needs of souls; that practical science has destroyed traditional faith and given nothing in return but the torture of doubt, or else a very cruel certainty in the knowledge that the universe is indifferent to the efforts and suffering of human beings. The *Rubáiyát* of Fitzgerald, where a sombre despair hides under a nonchalant Epicurianism, had evoked not an echo in 1859, and the second edition (1868) had been equally neglected; but the third (1872) knew a beginning of success, and the fourth (1879) sold out immediately."

11. *Les Fleurs du Mal,* Barnard ed. (Londres, 1942), IV, 50; thus, "Do you recall the object that we saw, my soul,/That lovely soft morning of summer:/On the side of a path a filthy carrion/On a bed strewn with pebbles. . . ./Flies buzzed over these putrid entrails,/Whence emerged foul hosts/Of larva, which oozed out like a heavy syrup/Along these living, writhing rags."

12. The list which follows is only an indication of several of these devices: "lights were shimmering birds on motionless golden wings, bell notes in arrested flight" (p. 17); "The room . . . was a suggestion of furniture, identically vague" (p. 27); instead of turning out the light, "her arm swept the room with darkness" (p. 32); "the broken meal" (p. 55); "the silence of the house was a clock like a measured respiration" (p. 63); "The divine's face was gray and slack as dirty snow" (p. 65); "Her windy dress molded her longly" (p. 73); "a few thick clouds fat as whipped cream" (p. 80); "rain-perplexed tree" (p. 86); "harp her sorrow on her golden hair" (p. 93); "blurring her slim epicenity, blurring her body with pain" (p. 99); "fragile articulation of her body" (p. 103); "a pale yellow city of symmetrical stacked planks" (p. 109); "a violet silence soft as milk" (p. 114); "The sun flamed slowly across the wistaria" (p. 127); "The syncopation pulsed about them, a reiteration of wind and strings warm and troubling as water" (p. 137); "Music came faint as a troubling rumor beneath the spring night, sweetened by distance" (p. 147); "Furniture was slow unemphatic gleams of lesser dark" (p. 153); "Light in her hair was the thumbed rim of a silver coin" (p. 154); "trumpets in his blood" (p. 156); "he moved but she followed like water" (p. 158); "elastic shadows" (p. 162); "she lay in the soft familiar intimacy of sleep, like a faintly blown trumpet" (p. 168); "rose splashed redly" (p. 172); "spikes of bloom, became with night spikes of scent" (p. 188); "She shuddered, a slim muted flame hushed darkly in dark clothing" (p. 190); "Dusk was a dream of arrested time" (p. 201); and "the dusty sound of sparrows" (p. 205).

13. For similarities of images and phrasing in this piece and others, such as the poem "Portrait" (pub. *Double Dealer,* June 1922), see Chapter V.

14. James B. Meriwether, *The Literary Career of William Faulkner* (Princeton, 1961), p. 90. See fig. 4 for a reproduction of the typescript complete with its French title. Also see T. S. Eliot, "Rhapsody on a Windy Night," *Collected Poems 1909-1935* (New York, 1936), p. 29; Warren Ramsey, *Jules Laforgue and the Ironic Inheritance* (New York, 1953), p. 201, who treats Laforgue as a source for Eliot; George Williamson, *A Reader's Guide to T. S. Eliot*

(New York, 1955), pp. 80-82; and Herbert Howarth, *Notes on Some Figures behind T. S. Eliot* (New York, 1955), p. 107.

15. P. 33. Several other passages similar in tone and indicating the same kind of youthful disappointment at not having seen action or having been romantically mutilated in war can be found in the novel: pp. 34, 37, 38, 112, 120, 130.

16. For more information on this likely prototype, see Bessie Ford, "Faulkners' Servant Not Forgotten," *Commercial Appeal* (Memphis, Tennessee), July 28, 1962, Miss. sec., p. 1. Her tombstone bears the inscription: "Callie Barr Clark. Born 1840. Died 1940. Mammy. Her white children bless her." The article reports John Cullen's remembrance of her standing quietly watching the Falkner and Oldham children play along South Lamar Street. "After Faulkner became a successful writer, they [the Faulkners] built Callie Clark a private room. . . . she felt that the family belonged to her." The article adds, "In all likelihood, Callie was the inspiration of Dilsey . . . in 'The Sound and the Fury.' Cullen says many of the traits of [the] fictitious Dilsey were those found in Callie Clark, especially her devotion to 'her family.' " The Negro mammy in *Soldiers' Pay*, of course, expresses a deep devotion toward "Mist' Donald honey," and in addition to referring to herself as "Cal'line," she also says, "Donald, baby, look at me. Don't you know who dis is? Dis yo' *Callie* what use ter put you ter bed, honey" (p. 118, italics added).

17. See Ch. III, n. 2. Bill Hudson, "Faulkner before 'Sanctuary,' " *Carolina Magazine,* 69:11, April 1935, notes that Faulkner "entered school at the age of eight, made four grades the first two years, began to see the failings of formal education during his third year, and . . . dropped out of school in the tenth grade." For further observations on Faulkner's erratic education, see Chapter II.

18. Robert Coughlan, "The Private World of William Faulkner," *Life,* October 5, 1953, pt. 2, p. 61.

19. Faulkner's treatment of his persona was ironically prophetic. See the first page of the *Oxford Eagle,* July 12, 1962, with the headline "William Faulkner Takes Last Ride Through The City He Loved Most," on the left of which is a photograph of his funeral cortege as it "moved slowly across the square," with onlookers both white and colored standing along the curbs and by parked cars.

20. Daniel E. Schneider, *The Psychoanalyst and the Artist* (New York, 1950), does not, of course, contend that a search for identity makes great art; but he does point out how a great artist "transmutes" through "interpretation and alteration of what is repressed and extant

into a new form" (p. 295), and how that search for identity is "unconscious and relentlessly compulsive" (p. 208). See also the related article, Henry Lowenfeld, "Psychic Trauma and Productive Experience in the Artist," *Art and Psychoanalysis,* ed. William Phillips (New York, 1957); he explains that in such cases the artist's conflicts and tensions "can never be completely resolved in actual life; it represents, in a way, a condition of unavoidable, inherent frustration. This frustration is the source of the artist's fantasy, driving him again and again to forsake disillusioning reality and to create a world for himself in which he, in his imagination, can realize his desires. It forces him to sublimation" (p. 301).

21. In "Freud—and the Analysis of Poetry," *The Philosophy of Literary Form* (New York, 1957), p. 224.

22. George Marion O'Donnell, "Faulkner's Mythology," *Faulkner: Three Decades of Criticism,* eds. Frederick J. Hoffman and Olga Vickery (Michigan State University, 1960), pp. 83-93. Originally pub. in *The Kenyon Review,* Summer 1939, pp. 285-299. O'Donnell takes as his thesis that Faulkner's work is "built around the conflict between traditionalism and the anti-traditional modern world in which it is immersed" (p. 83). He relates *Soldiers' Pay* to this thesis on p. 85, but he does not treat—nor to my knowledge does any other scholar—Faulkner's psychological problem of identity, the struggle to discover his individuation and the part that the past, especially that symbolized by his ancestry, plays in that struggle. This problem of identity runs like a steady current throughout his early work.

23. See Chapter V.

CHAPTER IX

1. Carvel Collins, "About the Sketches," *William Faulkner: New Orleans Sketches* (New Brunswick, 1958), pp. 31-33.

2. See the photograph in *Life* (October 5, 1953), p. 57.

3. In *Faulkner in the University,* eds. Frederick L. Gwynn and Joseph L. Blotner (Charlottesville, Virginia, 1959), "Session Seventeen," May 13, 1957, p. 136; and "Session Eight," March 13, 1958, pp. 57-58.

4. James B. Meriwether, *The Literary Career of William Faulkner* (Princeton, 1961), pp. 13, 81, states as the source of his information an interview with Faulkner on March 12, 1958. Faulkner said that the unfinished novel was "funny, but not funny enough" (p. 81). The 130-page manuscript has four titles: "Elmer," "Elmer and Myrtle," "Portrait of Elmer Hodge," and "Growing Pains" (pp. 13, 81). It

comprises "some of the elements of humor and satire that he was to use in *Mosquitoes*" (p. 13).

5. Noted by Collins in "About the Sketches," p. 33.

6. Coughlan, *The Private World* . . ., p. 75.

7. Meriwether, pp. 65-66. Another bound carbon typescript of 266 pp. contains on p. 265 the following note: "Oxford, Missippi [*sic*]/January 12, 1930." The spelling of the state probably represents the not infrequent elision one may encounter in the pronunciation of a native. Faulkner employed it in the dialogue of the Negro horse trainer Ned in *The Reivers* (New York, 1962).

8. In *Faulkner in the University*, "Session Ten," an interview with visitors from Virginia colleges, April 15, 1957, p. 87.

9. William Faulkner (New York, 1953), Signet ed. Originally pub. by Harcourt, Brace (New York, 1929). Further references to *Sartoris* will be indicated by page numbers in parentheses after quotations.

10. *Faulkner in the University*, "Session Thirty-Six," in a talk with the University of Virginia and community public, May 23, 1958, p. 285.

11. Signet ed., pp. vii-viii.

12. Anderson, "A Meeting South," *Dial*, 73:277-278, April 1925, has his persona David, who bears many similarities to the young Faulkner of the period (see Ch. VII), relate an autumnal description of his father's plantation much like the country Bayard visits. Anderson, however, intersperses his own narrative remarks: " 'In the fall it's best,' he said. 'You see the niggers are making molasses.' Every negro cabin on the place had a little clump of ground back of it where cane grew and in the fall the negroes were making their 'lasses. . . . 'The niggers sing. They laugh and shout. Sometimes the young niggers with their gals make love on the dry cane pile. I can hear it rattle.' "
Faulkner's scene in *Sartoris* is more thoroughly detailed, contains the tribute to the mule (pp. 239-240), and differs, too, in that Narcissa accompanies him, but enough other parallels are present to make one suspect Anderson as source, especially since Faulkner dedicated the novel to him. Pertinent excerpts follow: [In the fall] "the negroes brought their cane and made their communal winter sorghum molasses. . . . the sharp, subtly exciting odor of fermentation and of boiling molasses. Bayard liked the smell of it. . . . Sometimes [the Negroes] sang—quavering, wordless chords in which plaintive minors blent with mellow bass. . . . in shadowy beds among

the dry whispering cane-stalks youths and girls murmured and giggled" (pp. 238-241).

13. For the garden and flower images, see pp. 58, 65, 223, 317; moonlight images, pp. 57, 60, 62, 135, 136, 145, 286; avian images, pp. 137, 194, 313; girl-plant images, p. 49.

14. Richard C. Carpenter, "Faulkner's 'Sartoris,' " *Explicator,* 14: item 41, April 1956, advances the thesis that, after Bayard "doubles his guilt" by precipitating his grandfather's heart attack (being the older, he rather than young John, "should have sacrificed himself to the Sartoris concept of glamorous courage in World War I"), the reader expects "something more or less dramatic to happen." Carpenter then compares Bayard's suffering from deadly cold in the country to Cantos 32 and 33 of Dante's *Inferno* "where the damned—those who have betrayed trust, especially Ugolino, who has betrayed his kindred—are eternally imprisoned in ice to their necks. Bayard has betrayed his family through his aloofness and self-regard." Carpenter then points out that the suffering is unnecessary "from a naturalistic point of view, since he need only accept Buddy MacCallum's offer of warm woolen underwear. . . ." Faulkner's *"leitmotif* is cold."

15. Other parallels between *Sartoris* and *A Green Bough* too numerous to detail in the text are, of course, present. Among them are the following: the thematic relationship involved in man "cozening" his body (*Sartoris,* p. 148 and poem VI); the image of drowning in relation to sex (*Sartoris,* p. 223, and poem XIX); and a parallel of phrasing involving the linkage of sorrow with an image of wood-smoke (in *Sartoris,* p. 238, "an ancient sadness sharp as woodsmoke on the windless air"; and in poem XXXV, "An old sorrow sharp as woodsmoke on the air").

16. A sampling of French Symbolist imagery follows: "in her face was that tranquil repose of lilies" (p. 49); "mellow downward pool of the lamp" (p. 57); "the drifting sharpness of tobacco lay along the windless currents of the silver air" (p. 58); "the silver rippling of the frogs" (p. 60); "treacherously illuminated by the moon" (p. 61); "tragic and transient as a blooming of honeysuckle" (p. 62); "sound like blurred thunder" (p. 114); "alcohol-dulled nerves radiated like threads of ice" (p. 148); "borne aloft on his flaming verbal wings" (p. 157); "Her hand was warm, prehensile, like mercury in his palm exploring softly" (p. 165); "like a chiseled mask brushed lightly over his spent violence" (p. 192); "immaculate linen and a geranium like a merry wound" (p. 193); "edgeless canopy of ragged stars," and "the faint odor of heat" (p. 242); "a field of sedge odorous of sun and dust" (p. 245); "a hickory . . . gleaming like a sodden flame on the eternal azure" and "a swaddling of rain" (p.

253); "florid stone gesture" (p. 258); "ridge on ridge blue as wood-smoke" and "the sun that spread like a crimson egg broken on the ultimate hills" (p. 260); "ruddy invitation" (p. 262); "musical gusts, ringing as frosty glass" (p. 268); "brittle scintillation" (p. 269); "cumulate waves of heat" (p. 281); "red sun that fell like a blare of trumpets into the hallway" (p. 289); "evening was a windless lilac dream, foster dam of quietude and peace" (p. 318). Several of the images use colors in unique arrangements: "he was a trapped beast in the high blue" (p. 181); "the creek rippled and flashed brownly" (p. 183); "in a red doze he clung to the seat" (p. 187); a road "curving redly" (p. 227); and "The road lifted redly" (p. 292).

17. "The Making of a Myth: 'Sartoris,' " *Western Review*, 22:209-210, Spring 1958.

18. *Faulkner in the University*, "Session Twenty-Eight," First-Year English Course, April 28, 1958, pp. 251-252.

19. See Chapter II.

20. Marshall J. Smith, "Faulkner of Mississippi," p. 414, notes a picture of the law school and the statement about Faulkner's rope swinging from the steep tower and roof.

21. Hamilton Basso, "William Faulkner: Man and Writer," *Saturday Review*, July 28, 1962, p. 12, mentions Faulkner's acquaintance with the Gates Flying Circus in New Orleans in the mid-1920's.

22. Vickery, "The Making of a Myth," p. 213.

Bibliography

SELECTED WORKS OF WILLIAM FAULKNER

This bibliography does not include all of Faulkner's publications, but rather selected works functionally related to this book. Numerous bibliographies of Faulkner's work are available; among the best are James B. Meriwether's *The Literary Career of William Faulkner* (Princeton, 1961) and Harry Runyan's *A Faulkner Glossary* (New York, 1964).

"L'Apres-Midi d'un Faune" [*sic*], (poem), *New Republic*, 20:24, August 6, 1919. Reprinted in *The Mississippian*, October 29, 1919, p. 4.

"Cathay," (poem), *The Mississippian*, November 12, 1919, p. 8.

"Landing in Luck," (story), *The Mississippian*, November 26, 1919, pp. 2, 7.

"Sapphics," (poem), *The Mississippian*, November 26, 1919, p. 3.

"After Fifty Years," (poem), *The Mississippian*, December 10, 1919, p. 4.

"Une Balad des Hedes [*sic*] Femmes Perdues," (poem), *The Mississippian*, January 28, 1920, p. 3.

"Naiads' Song," (poem), *The Mississippian*, February 4, 1920, p. 3.

"Fantouches" [*sic*], (poem), *The Mississippian*, February 25, 1920, p. 3.

"Clair de Lune," (poem), *The Mississippian*, March 3, 1920, p. 6.

"The Ivory Tower," (article in answer to parodies of his publications in *The Mississippian*), *The Mississippian*, March 17, 1920, p. 4.

"A Poplar," (poem), *The Mississippian*, March 17, 1920, p. 7.

"Streets," (poem), *The Mississippian*, March 17, 1920, p. 2.

"To the Editor," (letter), *The Mississippian*, April 7, 1920, p. 1.

"A Clymene [*sic*]," (poem), *The Mississippian*, April 14, 1920, p. 3.

"Study," (poem), *The Mississippian*, April 21, 1920, p. 4.

"Alma Mater," (poem), *The Mississippian*, May 12, 1920, p. 3.

"To a Co-ed," (poem), *Ole Miss* (the yearbook of the University of Mississippi), 1919-1920, XXIV, 174.

Review of *In April Once* by W. A. Percy, *The Mississippian*, November 1, 1920, p. 5.

Review of *Turns and Movies* by Conrad Aiken, *The Mississippian*, February 16, 1921, p. 5.

"Co-Education at Ole Miss," (poem), *The Mississippian*, May 4, 1921, p. 5.

"Nocturne," *The* [*sic*] *Ole Miss* (the yearbook of the University of Mississippi), 1920-1921, XXV, 214-215.

Review of *Aria da Capo* by Edna St. Vincent Millay, *The Mississippian*, January 13, 1922, p. 5.

"American Drama: Eugene O'Neill," (article), *The Mississippian*, February 3, 1922, p. 5.

"The Hill," (prose sketch), *The Mississippian*, March 10, 1922, pp. 1, 2. (The piece is unsigned; however, in the March 17 issue, p. 5, the attribution of the sketch is made to "W. F.")

"American Drama Inhibitions," (article in two parts), *The Mississippian*, March 17, 1922, p. 5. Continued March 24, 1922, p. 5.

"Portrait," (poem), *The Double Dealer*, 3:337, June 1922. Reprinted without revision in *Salmagundi*. Milwaukee, April 30, 1932, p. 45.

Review of *Linda Condon, Cytherea,* and *The Bright Shawl* by Joseph Hergesheimer, *The Mississippian*, December 15, 1922, p. 5.

The Marble Faun. (Poems.) Boston [December 15], 1924. "Preface" by Phil Stone.

"Dying Gladiator," (poem), *The Double Dealer,* 7:85, January-February 1925. Reprinted without revision in *Salmagundi.* Milwaukee, 1932, p. 43.

"New Orleans," (eleven short sketches), *The Double Dealer,* 7:102-107, January-February 1925. Reprinted without revision in *Salmagundi.* Milwaukee, 1932, pp. 13-28.

"On Criticism," (article), *The Double Dealer,* 7:83-84, January-February 1925. Reprinted without revision in *Salmagundi.* Milwaukee, 1932, pp. 29-33.

"Mirrors of Chartres Street," (sketch), *New Orleans Times-Picayune,* February 8, 1925, Sunday magazine sec., pp. 1, 6. Reprinted with typographical errors corrected in *William Faulkner: New Orleans Sketches,* ed. Carvel Collins. New Brunswick, New Jersey, 1958, pp. 51-57.

"Damon and Pythias Unlimited," (sketch), *New Orleans Times-Picayune,* February 15, 1925, Sunday magazine sec., p. 7. Reprinted with typographical errors corrected in *William Faulkner: New Orleans Sketches,* ed. Carvel Collins. New Brunswick, New Jersey, 1958, pp. 59-70.

"Home," (sketch), *New Orleans Times-Picayune,* February 22, 1925, Sunday magazine sec., p. 3. Reprinted with typographical errors corrected in *William Faulkner: New Orleans Sketches,* ed. Carvel Collins. New Brunswick, New Jersey, 1958, pp. 71-79.

"Jealousy," (sketch), *New Orleans Times-Picayune,* March 1, 1925, Sunday magazine sec., p. 2. Reprinted with typographical errors corrected in *William Faulkner: New Orleans Sketches,* ed. Carvel Collins. New Brunswick, New Jersey, 1958, pp. 81-90.

"The Faun," (poem), *The Double Dealer,* 7:148, April 1925. Reprinted without revision in *Salmagundi.* Milwaukee, 1932, p. 42.

"Verse Old and Nascent: A Pilgrimage," (article), *The Double Dealer,* 7:129-131, April 1925. Reprinted without revision in *Salmagundi.* Milwaukee, 1932, pp. 34-39.

"Cheest," (sketch), *New Orleans Times-Picayune,* April 5, 1925, Sunday magazine sec., p. 4. Reprinted with typographical errors corrected in *William Faulkner: New Orleans Sketches*, ed. Carvel Collins. New Brunswick, New Jersey, 1958, pp. 91-98.

"Out of Nazareth," (sketch), *New Orleans Times-Picayune*, April 12, 1925, Sunday magazine sec., p. 4. Reprinted with typographical errors corrected in *William Faulkner: New Orleans Sketches*, ed. Carvel Collins. New Brunswick, New Jersey, 1958, pp. 99-110.

"The Kingdom of God," (sketch), *New Orleans Times-Picayune*, April 26, 1925, Sunday magazine sec., p. 4. Reprinted with typographical errors corrected in *William Faulkner: New Orleans Sketches*, ed. Carvel Collins. New Brunswick, New Jersey, 1958, pp. 111-119.

"Sherwood Anderson," (article), *Dallas Morning News*, April 26, 1925, Part 3, p. 7. Reprinted in the *Princeton University Library Chronicle*, 18:89-94, Spring 1957.

"The Rosary," (sketch), *New Orleans Times-Picayune*, May 3, 1925, Sunday magazine sec., p. 2. Reprinted with typographical errors corrected in *William Faulkner: New Orleans Sketches*, ed. Carvel Collins. New Brunswick, New Jersey, 1958, pp. 121-128.

"The Cobbler," (sketch), *New Orleans Times-Picayune*, May 10, 1925, Sunday magazine sec., p. 7. Reprinted with typographical errors corrected in *William Faulkner: New Orleans Sketches*, ed. Carvel Collins. New Brunswick, New Jersey, 1958, pp. 129-134.

"Chance," (sketch), *New Orleans Times-Picayune*, May 17, 1925, Sunday magazine sec., p. 7. Reprinted with typographical errors corrected in *William Faulkner: New Orleans Sketches*, ed. Carvel Collins. New Brunswick, New Jersey, 1958, pp. 135-143.

"Sunset," (sketch), *New Orleans Times-Picayune*, May 24, 1925, Sunday magazine sec., pp. 4, 7. Reprinted with typographical errors corrected in *William Faulkner: New Orleans Sketches*, ed. Carvel Collins. New Brunswick, New Jersey, 1958, pp. 145-157.

"The Kid Learns," (sketch), *New Orleans Times-Picayune*, May 31, 1925, Sunday magazine sec., p. 2. Reprinted with typographical errors corrected in *William Faulkner: New Orleans Sketches*, ed. Carvel Collins. New Brunswick, New Jersey, 1958, pp. 159-167.

"The Lilacs," (poem), *The Double Dealer*, 7:185-187, June 1925. Reprinted slightly revised as *A Green Bough*, I. New York, April 20, 1933, pp. 7-11.

"The Liar," (sketch), *New Orleans Times-Picayune*, July 26, 1925, Sunday magazine sec., pp. 3, 6. Reprinted with typographical errors corrected in *William Faulkner: New Orleans Sketches*, ed. Carvel Collins. New Brunswick, New Jersey, 1958, pp. 169-184.

"Episode," (sketch), *New Orleans Times-Picayune*, August 16, 1925, Sunday magazine sec., p. 2. Reprinted with typographical errors corrected in *William Faulkner: New Orleans Sketches*, ed. Carvel Collins. New Brunswick, New Jersey, 1958, pp. 185-190.

"Country Mice," (sketch), *New Orleans Times-Picayune*, September 20, 1925, Sunday magazine sec., p. 7. Reprinted with typographical errors corrected in *William Faulkner: New Orleans Sketches*, ed. Carvel Collins. New Brunswick, New Jersey, 1958, pp. 191-207.

"Yo Ho and Two Bottles of Rum," (sketch), *New Orleans Times-Picayune*, September 27, 1925, Sunday magazine sec., pp. 1, 2. Reprinted with typographical errors corrected in *William Faulkner: New Orleans Sketches*, ed. Carvel Collins. New Brunswick, New Jersey, 1958, pp. 209-223.

Soldiers' Pay. (Novel.) New York [February 25], 1926. Reprinted, Signet ed. New York, 1959. All references to the Signet reprint have been checked against those of the original edition and found to be uniform.

"Foreword," (parody), *Sherwood Anderson & Other Famous Creoles: A Gallery of Contemporary New Orleans* by William Spratling. New Orleans, 1926. For Faulkner's full text, see William Van O'Connor, *The Tangled Fire of William Faulkner*. Minneapolis, 1954, pp. 22-23.

Mosquitoes. (Novel.) New York [April 30], 1927.

Sartoris. (Novel.) New York [January 31], 1929. Reprinted, Signet ed. New York, 1953. All references to the Signet reprint have been checked against those of the original edition and found to be uniform.

The Sound and the Fury. (Novel.) New York [October 7], 1929.

As I Lay Dying. (Novel.) New York, 1930.

Sanctuary. (Novel.) New York [February 9], 1931.

Salmagundi. (Collection of essays and poems.) Milwaukee [April 30], 1932. "Preface" by Paul Romaine, pp. 7-9.

Light in August. (Novel.) New York [October 6], 1932.

A Green Bough. (Poems.) New York [April 20], 1933.

Absalom, Absalom! (Novel.) New York [October 26], 1936.

The Unvanquished. (Novel.) New York [February 15], 1938.

The Wild Palms. (Novel.) New York [January 19], 1939.

The Hamlet. (Novel.) New York [April 1], 1940.

Go Down, Moses and Other Stories. (Stories.) New York [May 11], 1942.

Knight's Gambit. (Stories.) New York [November 7], 1949.

"Sherwood Anderson," (essay), *Atlantic,* 191:27-29, June 1953. This essay is a personal reminiscence, not to be confused with Faulkner's earlier review of Anderson's work which has the same title, published in the *Dallas Morning News,* April 26, 1925, Part 3, p. 7.

"Foreword," *The Faulkner Reader.* (Miscellaneous collection), ed. Saxe Commins. New York, April 1, 1954, pp. ix-xi. Faulkner's "Foreword" is signed "New York/November, 1953."

A Fable. (Novel.) New York [August 2], 1954.

The Town. (Novel.) New York [May 1], 1957.

The Mansion. (Novel.) New York, 1959.

The Reivers. (Novel.) New York, 1962.

OTHER WORKS

Adams, Richard P. "The Appenticeship of William Faulkner," *Tulane Studies in English,* 12:113-156, 1962.

Alexander, Franz. "The Psychoanalyst Looks at Contemporary Art," *Art and Psychoanalysis,* ed. William Phillips. New York, 1957, pp. 346-365.

Allen, R. M. "Faulkner at the University of Mississippi, Spring, 1947." Signed mimeographed document (Indianola, Miss., May 12, 1954, p. 3) in the Faulkner Collection, box labeled *Miscel-*

laneous Ephemeral Material, Princeton University, Princeton, New Jersey.

[Anderson, Sherwood.] *Letters of Sherwood Anderson,* ed. Howard Mumford Jones. Boston, 1953.

_____. "A Meeting South," *The Dial,* 78:269-279, April 1925.

_____. *Sherwood Anderson's Memoirs.* New York, 1942.

_____. *Sherwood Anderson's Notebook.* New York, 1926.

_____. *Triumph of the Egg.* New York, 1921.

Anon. rev. (*A Green Bough*). *Nation,* 136:565, May 17, 1933.

Baldwin, Joseph Glover. *The Flush Times of Alabama and Mississippi.* New York, 1853.

Basso, Hamilton. "William Faulkner: Man and Writer," *Saturday Review,* July 28, 1962, pp. 11-14.

Baudelaire, Charles [Pierre]. *Les Fleurs du Mal.* Barnard ed. Londres, 1942.

_____. Letter to Jules Janin in "Epigraph," Remy de Gourmont, *Decadence and Other Essays on the Culture of Ideas.* New York, 1921, p. 139.

Beach, Joseph Warren. *American Fiction 1920-1940.* New York, 1941.

Benét, William Rose. (Review of *A Green Bough*), *Saturday Review,* April 29, 1933, p. 565.

Bishop, William Avery. "Tales of the British Air Service," *National Geographic Magazine,* 33:27-35, January 1918.

Blotner, Joseph. *William Faulkner's Library—A Catalogue.* Charlottesville, 1964.

Boyd, Thomas. (Review of *Soldiers' Pay*), *Saturday Review,* April 24, 1926, p. 736.

Brooks, Cleanth. *William Faulkner: The Yoknapatawpha Country.* New Haven and London, 1964.

Buckley, G. T. "Is Oxford the Original of Jefferson in William Faulkner's Novels?" *PMLA,* 76:447-454, September 1961.

Burke, Kenneth. *The Philosophy of Literary Form.* New York, 1957.

Cantwell, Robert. "The Faulkners: Recollections of a Gifted Family," *New World Writing*, no. 2. New York, 1952, pp. 300-315.

_____. "Introduction," Col. William C. Falkner, *The White Rose of Memphis*. New York, 1953, pp. v-xxvii.

Cargill, Oscar. *Intellectual America*. New York, 1941.

Carpenter, Richard C. "Faulkner's 'Sartoris,' " *Explicator*, 14:item 41, April 1956.

Chaze, Elliott. "Visit to Two-Finger Typist," *Life*, July 14, 1961, pp. 11-12.

Collins, Carvel. "About the Sketches," *William Faulkner: New Orleans Sketches*. New Brunswick, New Jersey, 1958, pp. 9-34.

_____. "Faulkner at the University of Mississippi," *William Faulkner: Early Prose and Poetry*. Boston, 1962, pp. 3-33.

_____. Unpublished letter to the author (January 14, 1969).

Coughlan, Robert. "The Private World of William Faulkner," *Life*, pt. 1, September 28, 1953, pp. 118-120 ff.; continued pt. 2, October 5, 1953, pp. 55-58 ff.

_____. *The Private World of William Faulkner*. New York, 1954. Contains most of the material in the *Life* articles above, revised.

Cowley, Malcolm. *The Faulkner-Cowley File: Letters and Memories, 1944-1962*. New York, 1966.

_____. "Introduction," *The Portable Faulkner*. New York, 1946, pp. 1-24. Also pub. in *William Faulkner: Three Decades of Criticism*, eds. Frederick J. Hoffman and Olga W. Vickery. Michigan State University, 1960, pp. 94-109.

_____. "An Introduction to William Faulkner," *Critiques and Essays on Modern Fiction 1920-1951*, ed. John W. Aldridge. New York, 1952, pp. 427-446.

_____, ed. *Writers at Work: The Paris Review Interviews*. New York, 1958.

Cullen, John B. "As I [K]new William Faulkner," *The Oxford Eagle*, July 12, 1962, sec. 2, p. 1.

_____. In collaboration with Floyd C. Watkins. *Old Times in the Faulkner Country*. Chapel Hill, 1961. "Introduction" by Watkins.

Daniel, Robert Woodham. *Catalogue of the Writings of William Faulkner*. New Haven, 1942.

Douds, Edith Brown. "Recollections of the Bunch," *William Faulkner of Oxford*, eds. James W. Webb and A. Wigfall Green. Baton Rouge, 1965, pp. 48-53.

Eliot, T. S. "Rhapsody on a Windy Night," *Collected Poems 1909-1935*. New York, 1936, p. 29. Orig. pub. in *Prufrock and Other Observations*, 1917.

Erikson, Erik H. *Childhood and Society*. New York, 1950.

Evans, Medford. "Oxford, Mississippi," *Southwest Review*, 15:46-63, Autumn 1929.

Falkner, Col. William C. *The White Rose of Memphis*. New York, 1953. Originally pub. in the *Ripley Advertiser*, August 1880; then in book form in 1881. See *The Catalog of Books Represented by Library of Congress Printed Cards* (1943), vol. 46, p. 380.

Falkner, Murry C. *The Falkners of Mississippi: A Memoir*. Baton Rouge, 1967.

————. "The Wonderful Mornings of Our Youth," *William Faulkner of Oxford*, eds. James W. Webb and A. Wigfall Green. Baton Rouge, 1965, pp. 9-22.

Farmer, Albert J. *Le Mouvement esthétique et "décadent" en Angleterre—1873-1900*. Paris, 1931.

Faulkner, John. *My Brother Bill: An Affectionate Reminiscence*. New York, 1963.

————. Telephone conversation with the author. Oxford, Mississippi, 7:45 P.M., July 26, 1962.

"Faulkner, William (Harrison) [*sic*]." *Encyclopedia Americana*, (1954), XI, 63.

"Faunus," and "Faun of Praxiteles," *Encyclopedia Americana*, (1954), XI, 63-64.

Fiedler, Leslie A. "Archetype and Signature," *Art and Psychoanalysis*, ed. William Phillips. New York, 1957, pp. 454-472.

Flowers, Paul. "Storied Oxford Unruffled at 'Curious Bill's' Passing," *The Commercial Appeal* (Memphis, Tennessee), July 7, 1962, p. 1.

Fogle, Richard Harter. *The Imagery of Keats and Shelley*. Chapel Hill, 1949.

Ford, Bessie. "Faulkners' Servant Not Forgotten," *The Commercial Appeal* (Memphis, Tennessee), July 28, 1962, Miss. sec., p. 1.

Freud, Sigmund. "Wit and Its Relation to the Unconscious," in *The Basic Writings of Sigmund Freud,* ed. Dr. A. A. Brill. New York, 1938, pp. 633-803.

Frohock, W. M. *The Novel of Violence in America*. Dallas, 1946.

Fry, Roger, trans. *Mallarmé: Poems*. New York, 1951. "Introduction" by Charles Mauron, pp. 1-43.

Garrett, George P. "An Examination of the Poetry of William Faulkner," *Princeton University Library Chronicle,* 18, no. 3:124-135, Spring 1957.

_____. "Faulkner's Early Literary Criticism," *Texas Studies in Literature and Language,* 1:3-10, Spring 1959.

Gaunt, William. *The Aesthetic Adventure*. New York, 1945.

Geismar, Maxwell. "A Cycle of Fiction," Sec. 77, pt. 5, *Literary History of the United States,* eds. Robert E. Spiller and others. New York, 1959, pp. 1304-08.

_____. *Writers in Crisis*. Boston, 1942.

Gourmont, Remy de. *Decadence and Other Essays on the Culture of Ideas,* trans. William Aspenwall Bradley. New York, 1921.

Green, Adwin Wigfall. "William Faulkner at Home," *Sewanee Review,* 40:294-306, Summer 1932.

Grenier, Cynthia. "The Art of Fiction: An Interview with William Faulkner—September, 1955," *Accent,* 16:167-177, Summer 1956.

Gwynn, Frederick L. "Faulkner's Prufrock—and Other Observations," *Journal of English and Germanic Philology,* 52:63-70, January 1958.

Gwynn, Frederick L. and Joseph L. Blotner, eds. *Faulkner in the University*. Charlottesville, 1959. Class conferences with Faulkner at the University of Virginia, 1957-1958.

Hoar, Jere R. "William Faulkner of Oxford, Mississippi," *Writer's Digest,* July 1961, pp. 15-16, 77-78.

Hoffman, Frederick J. *William Faulkner.* New York, 1961.

Hoffman, Frederick J. and Olga W. Vickery. *William Faulkner: Three Decades of Criticism.* Michigan State University, 1960.

Hopper, Vincent F. "Faulkner's Paradise Lost," *Virginia Quarterly Review,* 23:405-420, Summer 1947.

Howarth, Herbert. *Notes on Some Figures Behind T. S. Eliot.* London, 1965, p. 107.

Howe, Irving. *Sherwood Anderson.* [New York], 1951.

————. *William Faulkner: A Critical Study.* New York, 1952.

Howell, Elmo. "Faulkner's 'Sartoris,' " *Explicator,* 17:item 33, February 1959.

Hudson, Bill. "Faulkner before 'Sanctuary,' " *The Carolina Magazine,* 69:11-14, April 1935.

J. "The 'Mushroom' Poet," (article concerning Faulkner), *The Mississippian,* March 24, 1920, p. 3.

————. "Whotouches," (a parody of Faulkner's "Fantouches" [*sic*]), *The Mississippian,* March 3, 1920, p. 6.

Jack, Peter Monro. (Review of *A Green Bough*), *New York Times Book Review,* May 14, 1933, p. 2.

Jackson, Holbrook. *The Eighteen Nineties.* New York, 1925.

Jiggitts & Lester Inc. "A Pastoral Poem," (parody), *The Mississippian,* February 25, 1920, p. 3.

"Jiggit[t]s Plans Extended Tour," (unsigned article), *The Mississippian,* March 17, 1922, p. 4.

Jung, C[arl]. G[ustav]. *Modern Man in Search of a Soul,* trans. W. S. Dell and Cary F. Baynes. New York, n.d. Originally pub. 1933.

Kazin, Alfred. *On Native Grounds.* New York, 1956.

Keats, John. "Ode on a Grecian Urn," in *The Golden Treasury of the Best Songs and Lyrical Poems,* ed. F. T. Palgrave, rev. Oscar Williams. New York, 1953.

Kennedy, John F. "Lucius Quintus Cincinnatus Lamar," *Profiles in Courage.* Cardinal ed. New York, 1959, pp. 129-150. Originally pub. New York, 1956.

Kielty, Bernardine. "William Faulkner," (biographical note), *A Treasury of Short Stories.* New York, 1948.

Longstreet, Augustus Baldwin. *Georgia Scenes.* Augusta, Ga., 1835.

Lordgreyson. "Une Ballade D'une Vache Perdue," (parody of Faulkner's "Une Balad Hedes [*sic*] Femmes Perdues"), *The Mississippian,* May 12, 1920, p. 3.

Lovejoy, Arthur O. "On the Discrimination of Romanticisms," *Essays in the History of Ideas.* New York, 1960, pp. 228-253.

Lowenfeld, Henry. "Psychic Trauma and Productive Experience in the Artist," *Art and Psychoanalysis,* ed. William Phillips. New York, 1957, pp. 292-305.

McClure, John. (Review of *The Marble Faun*), *New Orleans Times-Picayune,* Sunday magazine section, January 25, 1925, p. 6.

McHaney, Thomas L. "The Image of the Railroad in the Novels of William Faulkner, 1926-1942." Unpublished master's thesis. University of North Carolina, 1962.

Mallarmé, Stéphane. *Mallarmé: Poems,* trans. Roger Fry. Binghamton, New York, 1951.

Maurois, André. "Le Portrait de Dorian Gray," *Études Américaines.* New York, 1945, pp. 61-71.

Mauron, Charles. "Introduction," *Mallarmé: Poems,* trans. Roger Fry. Binghamton, New York, 1951.

Mayes, Martha. "Faulkner's Juvenilia," *New Campus Writing,* no. 2. New York, 1957, pp. 135-144.

Meriwether, James B. *The Literary Career of William Faulkner.* Princeton, 1961.

————. *William Faulkner: A Check List.* Princeton, 1957.

Millgate, Michael. *The Achievement of William Faulkner.* New York, 1966.

————. "William Faulkner, Cadet," *University of Toronto Quarterly,* 35:117-132, January 1966.

Miner, Ward L. *The World of William Faulkner.* Durham, 1952.

Mississippi: A Guide to the Magnolia State. New York, 1938. (Federal Writers' Project of the Works Progress Administration.)

Mississippi Verse, ed. Alice James. Chapel Hill, 1934. Contains seven reprinted poems of Faulkner, pp. 31-35.

Mumford, Lewis. *The Golden Day.* Boston, 1957.

O'Connor, William Van. "Faulkner's One-Sided 'Dialogue' with Hemingway," *College English,* 24:208, 213-215, December 1962.

_____. *The Tangled Fire of William Faulkner.* Minneapolis, 1954.

_____. *William Faulkner.* Minneapolis, 1960. (University of Minnesota Pamphlets on American Writers, No. 3.)

O'Donnell, George Marion. "Faulkner's Mythology," in *Faulkner: Three Decades of Criticism,* eds. Frederick J. Hoffman and Olga W. Vickery. Michigan State University, 1960, pp. 83-93. Originally pub. in *The Kenyon Review,* 1:285-299, Summer 1939.

Oldham, Dorothy Zollicoffer. Interview. Oxford, Mississippi, 9:00 A.M., July 26, 1962.

Phelps, William Lyon. "Henryk Sienkiewicz," *Essays on Modern Novelists.* New York, 1929, pp. 115-131.

Phillips, William, ed. *Art and Psychoanalysis.* New York, 1957.

Price-Stephens, Gordon. "Faulkner and the Royal Air Force," *Mississippi Quarterly,* 17:123-128, Summer 1964.

Ramsey, Warren. *Jules Laforgue and the Ironic Inheritance.* New York, 1953, p. 201.

Rascoe, Lavon. "An Interview with William Faulkner," *Western Review,* 15:300-304, Summer 1951.

Reed, William McNeil ("Mack"). Interview. Oxford, Mississippi, 10:00 A.M., July 27, 1962.

_____. "Mr. Mack remembers 'Bill'," *The Oxford Eagle,* July 12, 1962, Sec. 1, pp. 1, 7.

Richardson, H. Edward. "Anderson and Faulkner," *American Literature,* 36:298-314, November 1964.

_____. "Faulkner, Anderson, and Their Tall Tale," *American Literature*, 34:287-291, May 1962.

_____. "The 'Hemingwaves' in Faulkner's 'Wild Palms'," *Modern Fiction Studies*, 4:357-360, Winter 1958-1959.

_____. "The Ways That Faulkner Walked: A Pilgrimage," *Arizona Quarterly*, 21:133-144, Summer 1965.

Rideout, Walter B. and James B. Meriwether. "On the Collaboration of Faulkner and Anderson," *American Literature*, 35:85-87, March 1963.

Runyan, Harry. *A Faulkner Glossary*. New York, 1964.

_____. "Faulkner's Poetry," *Faulkner Studies*, 3, nos. 2-3:23-29, Summer-Autumn 1954.

Samstag, Nicholas. "Elite vs. Substandard Protoplasm," *Saturday Review*, March 10, 1962, pp. 27, 37.

Saville, Mahala. Letter to Lois McClure (Head Librarian of Fullerton Junior College, Fullerton, California), June 13, 1962.

Schappes, Morris U. "Faulkner as Poet," *Poetry*, 43:48-52, October 1933.

Schevill, James. *Sherwood Anderson*. Denver, 1951.

Schneider, Daniel E. *The Psychoanalyst and the Artist*. New York, 1950.

Shell, George. *The Shapers of American Fiction 1798-1947*. New York, 1947.

Sienkiewicz, Henryk. *Pan Michael*, trans. Samuel A. Binion. Philadelphia, 1898. Originally pub. 1893.

Slabey, Robert M. "William Faulkner: The 'Waste Land' Phase (1926-1936)." Unpublished doctoral dissertation. Notre Dame University, 1961.

Slatoff, Walter J. *Quest for Failure: A Study of William Faulkner*. Ithaca, New York, 1960.

S[mith]., H[arrison]. "William Faulkner vs. the Literary Conference," *Saturday Review*, July 7, 1956, p. 16.

Smith, Marshall J. "Faulkner of Mississippi," *Bookman,* 74:411-417, December 1931.

Stallings, Laurence. Interview with the Fullerton Junior College Literary Club, recorded by H. Edward Richardson. Fullerton, California, 8:00 P.M., January 22, 1960.

Stein, Jean. "William Faulkner," (interview with Faulkner, New York, 1956), in *Writers at Work: The Paris Review Interviews,* ed. Malcolm Cowley. New York, 1958.

Stone, Emily Whitehurst. "Some Arts of Self-Defense," *William Faulkner of Oxford,* eds. James W. Webb and A. Wigfall Green. Baton Rouge, 1965, pp. 95-100.

Stone, Phil. Interview No. 1. Oxford, Mississippi, 2:30 P.M., July 27, 1962.

_____. Interview No. 2. Oxford, Mississippi, 10:00 A.M., July 28, 1962.

_____. "Preface." William Faulkner, *The Marble Faun.* Boston, 1924, pp. 6-8.

_____. "William Faulkner: The Man and His Work," *Oxford Magazine* (Oxford, Mississippi), vol. 1 (1934), no. 1, pp. 13-14; no. 2, pp. 11-15; no. 3, pp. 3-10.

Swinburne, Algernon Charles. *Poems.* Philadelphia, n.d.

Sykes, Gerald. *The Hidden Remnant.* New York, 1962.

"Tour of Pre-Civil War Homes in Oxford, Mississippi," Oxford, Mississippi, 1962. (Pub. Oxford-Lafayette County Chamber of Commerce).

Trilling, Lionel. "Sherwood Anderson," *The Liberal Imagination.* New York, 1957, pp. 20-31.

Verlaine, Paul. *Selected Poems,* trans. C. F. MacIntyre. Berkeley and Los Angeles, 1948.

Vickery, Olga W. "The Making of a Myth: 'Sartoris'," *Western Review,* 22:209-219, Spring 1958.

Waggoner, Hyatt H. *William Faulkner from Jefferson to the World.* Lexington, Kentucky, 1959.

Walton, Eda Lou. (Review of *A Green Bough*), *New York Herald-Tribune Books,* April 30, 1933, p. 2.

Webb, James W. and A[dwin]. Wigfall Green, eds. *William Faulkner of Oxford.* Baton Rouge, 1965.

Webb, James W. "William Faulkner Comes Home," *William Faulkner of Oxford,* eds. James W. Webb and A. Wigfall Green. Baton Rouge, 1965, pp. 198-211.

Wellek, René and Austin Warren. "Literature and Psychology," *Theory of Literature.* New York, 1956, pp. 69-81.

"William Faulkner Takes Last Ride Through The City He Loved Most," (memorial ed.), *The Oxford Eagle* (Oxford, Mississippi), July 12, 1962, p. 1.

Williamson, George. *A Reader's Guide to T. S. Eliot.* New York, 1955, pp. 80-82.

Wilson, Edmund. *Axel's Castle.* New York, 1954.

Woodworth, Stanley D. *William Faulkner en France.* Paris, 1959.

Young, Stark. "New Year's Craw," *New Republic,* 93:283-284. January 12, 1938.

Index

The works listed by title only in this Index are by William Faulkner.